Jens Kaeu

NEVER
BORING

Love & Fashion

Memoirs of a Creative Heart
in an Artistic Design World

To my children Betty, Stanley, and Lucy.

May your life be filled with love and wonder.

To my parents, Marc, Anja, and all my family, friends, and the ones I've loved'

The world would mean nothing without you.

"Being different was never
a choice;
it's who I am."

The story is based on true events.

This is the story of Jens Kaum.

BSL Publishing

As e- book, soft cover and hard cover was published by BSL Publishing.

Never Boring is a trademark by BSL Publishing.

Never Boring, Love & Fashion, Memoirs of a Creative Heart in an Artistic Design World.

ISBNs:
Paperback: 978-1-962624-30-5

For information, address BSL Publishing, 517 E 40th St, 31401 Savannah, GA.

Never Boring may be purchased for educational, business, or sales promotional use. For information, please e-mail info@jenskaeumle.com

Cover photography by Platon

©Photography by Platon.

Cover design: Albert Barbu

Second cover design: Stanley Kaeumle

Table of Contents

The "Eulenspiegel" test:

You have a creative mind; if you see, by staring at the blank page, a red dot materializing before your inner eye.

1. PROLOGUE

FIRST CLASS

I was sitting in my first-class seat on my Cathay Pacific flight from Paris to Hong Kong. Richard the magician had convinced Cathay that I was worthy of first-class status, and they agreed. I was in heaven. Three hours had passed, and there were nine to go. I was well lounged in my huge chair with three drinks in front of me, and I just swallowed a "STILNOX" to knock me out to sleep. The first two films had elapsed, and I watched through my window as the world passed by below me. It was dark, and there was no light to be seen below. We were crossing a deserted part of the world. Tomorrow, I will arrive at 6:00 a.m. in Hong Kong. My favorite city. It was 2009, and I was contemplating the next collection. My team, consisting of 18 designers and product developers, were already there and had prepared all the fitting stations we would need to work through 500 prototypes. The stations were divided into product groups: outerwear, shirts, dresses, pants, cut and sew, knitwear, etc. We had nine stations all together. It was a huge collection that we prepared for every main season of a Tommy Hilfiger collection. My boss Hans and I would have to work hard to get it all done in six days, but we were used to it and worked quickly and concentrated. We had a great team to support us, and we were taking good care of them. I would arrive Saturday morning in Hong Kong, and we would have the weekend to settle in and fight the horrendous jet lag that wouldn't allow us to sleep. Therefore, we organized a night out for our team. We lived by the mantra, "work hard, play hard." It was the best way to let off steam and get everybody ready for Monday and the long hours of creation. We had reservations at Dragonfly for drinks and dinner. We had a table surrounded by shark tanks on all the walls. Hong Kong was always good for the unexpected and exotic. After that, we would basically have fun. I hoped that Peter and Rolf would keep their hands to themselves and not take it to the next level, "a wild night out." A wild night was like throwing the films "Hangover 1, 2, and 3,"

"Harlequin" and "Project X" in a blender and pressing the button. The result is that you wake up the next morning with amnesia and a big smile on your face. It is the best team-building exercise ever, but not tonight, as I'd hoped. A good team works well when they are able to play together, but we still had a lot to achieve in the coming week, and we did not need to invite drama into our schedule.

Looking down at our small planet below, I started drifting off; the STILNOX was kicking in. How did I get here? It was a long journey and not a bed of roses. Hamburg, Ohio, design, fashion, desperation, failures, successes, smiles, Moschino, "J," our children, New York, Royal College of Art, Levi's, L.A., small town boy, art, Louis Vuitton, Milan, Amsterdam, Tommy Hilfiger…

Life had thrown quite a few curve balls, but I had come through so far. I became a fashion designer and had a wonderful partner and family. Life was good; I had found my passion and overcame all obstacles to live a creative career. "J" and I had created a life of love, fashion, creative curiosity, and wonder. How did it all begin? How did I get here? As my mother always said, "If you want to tell a story right, you have to start at the beginning," so let's begin.

Looking out, I wondered to myself, "Where do all the angels live?"

2. SMALL TOWN BOY

The journey had begun, like all journeys, at the beginning. It started as a candidate ready to travel life. I was born in a small town called Eltingen in the south of Germany. As a kid, it was an ordinary southern town situated in the rolling hills between the Black Forest and the "Bodensee," Lake Constance. The village was a beautiful spot, close to Stuttgart—sleepy, undisturbed by progress, where everybody knew everybody. The houses were built in the customary local style: wooden beams visible on the outside, small windows, and pointy roofs. It looked like a fairytale village from one of Brother Grimm's books: charming cottages, trees, and small gardens. It was a peaceful place. The residents had lived there for generations and knew each other well. Life was simple. The main sources of income were farming, traditional crafts, woodwork, spirits, and food production. Further to the east, textiles were produced in small quantities. Today, cars are manufactured by famous brands like Porsche and Daimler. When the car industry arrived, it was sure to change everything. But that was still to come.

When I was young, it was a time of recovery. Both world wars left their scars. Many young men and family fathers did not return or were prisoners of war. It was a time of sorrow and hurt. The old world had been proven obsolete and flawed; the new was not yet defined. A stoic pragmatism mixed with ancient tales was the fabric of this time in my hometown, a time when numerous family members lived together or nearby. Houses were busy places, and privacy was rare. Each house brimmed with strong characters, filled with emotions due to the stubborn, thickheaded nature of our community. The ups and downs of life played out daily, with drama and laughter side-by-side. Personalities were formed mostly through life experience, with little education. Good and bad were defined by the Bible, family, and occasionally by the local police, but in general, people were free to live their lives. Tradition and self-determination were the norm. People decided for themselves what was good for them. No health doctrines yet existed or were required to be adhered to. The local diet was hearty and high in calories, but nobody thought twice about it.

The local doctors often suggested better behavior and moderation, especially concerning smoking and drinking, but their advice was mostly ignored. People believed in the medicinal qualities of fermented spirits. Many families distilled their fruit harvests into Schnapps; it was "moonshine" days. The product was famous throughout the South, and many stories were linked to its production. Each family had its own recipes and secret ingredients.

One of those stories was my father's miraculous recovery from polio. At the age of six, my father's uncles were told to take him with them to the local distillery. They were to fill small wooden casks with the latest batch of Schnapps, which had been freshly distilled the day before for a client. When they arrived, his uncles soon began sampling the Schnapps. They didn't think anything was wrong with it and included my father in the party. When it was time to go home, my father had lost his ability to walk. My uncles, afraid of my grandmother's wrath, carried him home and declared they had no idea why he was unable to walk. My father, too intoxicated to speak anyway, was already sound asleep. In a great panic, the local doctor was summoned. He unpacked his instruments and checked my father's knee reflexes, which were nonexistent. The doctor confidently declared that my father had contracted polio and would never walk again. Hearing this news, the family's pain and sorrow were great. The curtains were drawn, and everyone went into mourning. The Vicar was called, and he sat and prayed with my family the whole night. The following day, my father awoke without any memory of the previous day and walked into the living room. The Vicar was delighted and declared my father a miracle of God. My father did not feel like a miracle; he felt hungover. As he began to faintly recall and recount what memories he could recover from the distillery, the joyous reactions quickly abated. The truth was out now, and my uncles caught holy hell from my grandma, his mother. Frieda Kaum. Our "Oma" was born in February 1915. To this day, we always refer to a hangover as a "miraculous polio recovery" and thank God for our good fortune.

At the time, travel was a rare luxury, and television was still rarer. Radio and books were available, but the habitual entertainment were stories told at the bakers, the butchers, and on the streets, but mainly at each family's dining table. The dining table was the place where news and lore were exchanged in abundance. Dinner and Saturday lunches were the times when the whole family, living under one roof, came together. Uncles, Aunts, Grandparents, parents, children, cousins, and often friends gathered around the big table in the living room. In fact, the big table was "mother's table." Stories were told there, and those stories were our fabric of life, and we children loved to hear them. Some were magical and funny, while others made us crawl with fear. They taught us about a life not taught in school.

The south of Germany was poor compared to the north, with its rich harbors and trade, but in the sixties, the south slowly lifted its head to a prosperous future: cars and computers. It was in this time of change—between long-lasting tradition and the promises of the new—that I was born.

Eltingen had a marketplace, town hall, castle, and horse market. My parents and grandparents were born there. My father was born on a May Day in 1941. It was still wartime. My father, named "Friedrich" but called Fritz," came from a family of barrel makers and carpenters, while my mother, Doris, born July 1943, was the only daughter of the local innkeeper and butcher. The inn was called "Zum Bären" (the bear), and my grandfather was known as the "Bärenwirt." We called him "Bären Opa." He was born in March 1911. In those days, when food was scarce, my mother and her older brother Rolf were considered royalty, and my grandfather was a wealthy man. My parents grew up together, meeting at the local school. Both were large families that were well respected.

My grandfathers had both been to the Second World War, and they had carried home deep traumas—physical and psychological. My paternal grandfather, whom we called "Opa," was born in December 1914 and suffered a serious bullet wound in his stomach during the war. Towards the end, he became a prisoner of war in a Russian war camp. He did recover from the bullet wound, but once home, he was a changed man. He died from stomach cancer before I was born.

My maternal grandfather, "Bären Opa," was a cook and butcher by trade. When he was a little boy, he was struck in the head by a swing, cracking open the left side of his skull. He carried a big scar on his left forehead for the rest of his life. As a result, his left frontal lobe was badly damaged, negatively affecting his personality—including an explosive temper that was not to be trifled with. He was a strong, unforgiving man driven by ambition who managed to build a small empire by the time he died. It wasn't easy for his children—my mother Doris and her brother Rolf—to be raised by him. Nothing was ever good enough. The word compassion was not in his vocabulary, let alone the ability to express it. But for some reason, he liked me and doted on me. My brother Marc, however, was not so lucky.

During the war, my grandfather, "Bären Opa," was stationed in France. He adored France. I guess the adventure and the culinary wonders of French cuisine gave him a somewhat warped idea about the war. He always told stories about him adventuring into the French countryside, meeting people, and enjoying the food—ironically, making his wartime experience and memories quite positive. His wife, "Bären Oma," alone at home, managed the inn "Zum Bären" with my mother Doris and her brother Rolf. My grandmother, "Bären Oma," was famous for her generosity. Daily, she gave away food to families in need. For generations, the people of Eltingen respected her for the aid she had given during those hard war times. This respect extended to my family, us children, and my cousins, who were treated kindly by our neighbors throughout our childhoods. The inn was a lifeline for many. It was the basis of income and food, so its survival ranked higher than anything else. It was hard physical labor, and the children were needed to help, so education came second.

Children needed to work to support families in general. My parents left school early—my mother, Doris, at 14, and my father, Fritz, at 16. My mother had to help at her father's "Bären Opa" Inn. My father became an apprentice at a metal tooling company. By the time he turned 18, he had progressed well enough in his work to be hired by Porsche at the small development center in Weissach. It was the beginning of his lifelong career there. Back then, Porsche was still small, more like an oversized garage. Over the years, my father became an engineer and metal specialist, heading the metal development department and succeeding inside the company as he found his passion—especially his expertise in casting magnesium. Porsche was always part of my family's lives, and I grew up watching its growth and success. I was also lucky to drive quite a few of them. As children, my father often took my brother Marc and me to the Porsche car-testing circuit, which was built in the backfields of the Weissach facility. Test drivers would take us for spins in the latest prototypes. The word "safety" did not exist for them, only "faster." When I was finally old enough to drive, you can imagine how this affected my driving style. Since then, I have adored everything with fast engines.

My mother worked at the inn and butcher shop until my grandpa died, and my uncle Rolf, her brother, inherited the business. She was fortunate to travel when she was young and experience different cultures, which shaped her tastes. My mother adored traveling. She was open-minded, curious, and never afraid to try something new. It was her doing that narrowmindedness and prejudice never existed in our family. Her eye for beauty and style were incredible. We were always impeccably dressed, which often led to some mockery from our friends. Especially when she dressed my brother and me in matching outfits. Her passion for fashion did not exclude my father's wardrobe. He was also always dressed in the latest fashion because my mother would not tolerate an imperfection in style. As the best-dressed and handsome man, he supported my mother in all her efforts. Deep down, he always dreamed of being an architect. He was a skilled draftsman and drew often. We all admired his drawings. His dream was not to be, but it did drive him to make sure we finished school and university. Since he never finished school, later in his career, he saw the value of education and a university degree. He made sure we learned how to formulate a plan for our dreams so they could come true. In their different ways, my parents were visionaries who gave us the gifts of critical thinking and independent minds. We were brought up to respectfully craft our own futures, visions, and dreams and to break free from common rules and expectations.

3. BIRTHDAY

I was born in May 1967 in a small hospital in Stuttgart, Germany. It was an uncomplicated delivery (or so I was told). After a few days in the hospital, my mother and I returned to our small flat on the second floor of my Bären Opa's house. The family was overjoyed over the arrival of the first-born *male* grandchild, the first heir to the Kaum name. My cousin, Claudia, the daughter of my Uncle Rolf, had been born a year before 1966. By all accounts, I had blond hair and a killer smile.

Soon, more cousins arrived—including my cousin, Anja (born three months later, in July 1967), and two years after me, my brother, Marc arrived in February 1969. The same year the first man stepped onto the surface of the moon, We three shared the Kaum name, so people began to think of us as siblings. Especially since we all grew up in our Oma's house. Our parents worked during the week. Work defined us, and being idle was frowned upon. My father had two siblings: Wolf Dieter, born March 1940, the eldest, and Christel, born February 1946, the youngest. So, like them, we were three, with me being the eldest, my brother the youngest, and Cousin Anja in the middle. We were compared to the three siblings of my father's generation. Then my cousin Georg (Claudia's brother) was born in 1969, the same year as Marc. He was the heir to the "Bären empire" accumulated by my grandfather. And then there were five in our generation: Claudia, Jens, Anja, Marc, and Georg. You might imagine our small elementary school with the five of us all together! Before we moved in with Oma, we lived above the butcher shop in my Bären Opa's house. It was a busy house, and there was always work to be done.

My parents, newly married at 23 and 21, did not have much money. My mother's father, our Bären Opa, who owned the Bären, offered them a small apartment on top of the Inn to live and start their family. It was cozy and full of life. The Inn was a busy place 24/7, with maids, butchers, and apprentices everywhere where drama mixed with laughter. I only know this time from photos. Our stay in my

8

grandfather's house was short-lived, though. The new in-laws had expectations about my father's presence in their business. They assumed he would now be part of the family business and would be committed to doing his daily part—especially on weekends. There was no free time or privacy. My Bären Opa considered my father's job at Porsche a "holiday job." To toughen him up, he scheduled the worst jobs for my father. There was no escape and no excuse for not participating; our Bären Opa ruled supreme under his roof. His "toughening" up of my father lasted about a year. Then, one Saturday morning, my father came down the stairs with his skis. Opa saw him and asked him where he thought he was going. My father said, "Skiing." Unamused, my Bären Opa said that he would not be going skiing so long as there was work to be done. The fight that followed was epic—shouting and screaming were heard throughout the village—and, by the end, knives were drawn. There were, after all, many knives in a butcher shop. For his grand finale, my father threw his skis in the big communal kitchen and stormed out, swearing he'd never come back. Fuming, sitting in his car with nowhere to go, he had an idea. He drove to his mother's house, Oma's, and asked her if he could build a small extension into the backyard. She agreed on the condition that it was OK with his brother Wolf Dieter and sister Christel. After a 10-minute drive and two stops, Christel and Wolf Dieter had both said "Yes." An hour later, construction plans were being drafted on napkins. My father called his architect pal, and by 3 p.m. that same day, our new little house was ready for the builders. That night, he called my mother to explain what he had done. She was distraught over what had happened with her father and took some time to be convinced—especially since they did not have much money. But he was determined for them to make it on their own. She knew they had to break away to evolve their marriage, and she trusted him. After a few days, the fight had calmed down, but my grandparents remained upset for years. I believe, though, that my grandfather respected my father for standing up to him that day.

Six months later, we moved my mother, my father, and myself into our small, unfinished house next to my Oma's house. Hers was an old house originally built for a big family. In the kitchen was a huge cast iron stove, fired with wood and coal, with rings you could lift with a hook. The toilet had a water jug you needed to use to flush. Below the house was a high, vaulted cellar with bad lighting, loads of spider webs, and many ancient, forgotten things. During the day, behind the house, the backyard was not fenced, so we could wander into our neighbor's orchards and steal apples and pears as we pleased. True freedom, nobody was burdened with the fear of constant danger.

Once a year, there were big wooden barrels to be refilled with cider. Cider being the common beverage for all ages in our stretch of the world. A very special occasion and event on our calendar. All our fathers and uncles were out for days during the preparation and cleaning of the barrels. An epic event for us all. To clean us all up, we were thrown into the bathtub. The bathroom was our favorite place. There was only one bathroom right next to the kitchen, and it had a simple tin bathtub. It was movable, so every Saturday, it was brought into the kitchen to bathe us kids. Anja, Marc, and I were all sitting in the bathtub, happy and content. The water was heated on the stove, and all three of us jumped into the tub at the same time. It was a riot. After, we were wrapped in towels, and the kitchen floor was flooded from our spill as we played.

Christel, my father's sister, and her husband, Yogi, lived there too. They had no children and were spoiling us rotten. Being rebels and hippies at heart, they were full of unconventional ideas and traveled a lot. On their journeys, they brought back many gifts. I will never forget the tribal drums they brought back from Kenya, Africa, or the football jersey from California. Although I hoped for a spear to kill non-existent lions with.

The house was always filled with life and laughter. Oma was a kind woman who helped everybody. She was the glue that held everyone together. After the loss of her husband, she was alone as a widow and never married again. With not much of an income, her children helped her keep the house together and the bills paid. Those were hard times, but we children never felt any of it. Nothing was too much for Oma. She was always helping and working, especially for her children and grandchildren.

After we moved into our new house, our parents worked long hours to make ends meet. So, it was quickly established that Anja, Marc, and I would spend our days with Oma. It was heaven. Also living with Oma was my great-grandmother, Ahne, born in 1887. She was 80 years old. All I remember is that she was very old. Legend has it that Ahne would drive a four-horse-drawn cart, standing upright on the seat, through the village. She was known to smoke, drink, and win many arm-wrestling matches against the men in the village. She was once strong and independent; she was also known to beat up her husband, but when I knew her, she was an ancient lady dressed in black. We never heard Ahne speak, though she was with us all the time. She barely moved unless Anja rubbed her furry teddy bear into her face. She could not stand the fur and would start screaming. We kids thought it was funny and never missed rubbing Anja's teddy bear into Ahne's face as we passed. I guess it helped Ahne's blood circulation because she lived for many more years, mostly sitting in her chair at the end of the dining table, being greeted by all guests with great respect.

Oma lavished us with good food and many scary and funny tales about family members, dead and living. People had good or bad characters in those, mostly both, which led to crazy stories and events. Those stories were shared at her table by guests and friends. The house had a revolving door, with friends and family constantly coming and going.

Our parents, along with Christel, were well-liked sports legends in our county. Only Yogi, her husband, wasn't very sporty. He was heavy-built and always late. Yogi was not from our village. He was born in Dresden, in East Germany. He and his father escaped from the Eastern Bloc, the DDR, through the "Todesstreifen" before the wall was finished. At the time, Yogi was only a boy when his father carried him over the heavily guarded eastern Russian-German border. His mother was left behind; she did not make it. It's incredible to think of politicians believing it is viable to separate a country with a wall. Many friends and family, old and young, sat at our Oma's big dining table, which we dubbed "Mother's table." This was our universe for the next 13 years. Everything happened around that table—all the stories and characters that passed by as we listened and watched. They were all so free. Success was not measured in money but in your deeds. Nobody told them what to do, what to drink, or what to eat. No government nor the internet gave them advice. They lived life and lived the consequences of their decisions too, good and bad. Around that table, we had christenings, confirmations, Easter, birthdays, and, most importantly, Christmases. On most occasions, the adults enjoyed getting us kids into trouble. It wasn't an easy task for them because our Oma watched us like a hawk. They knew if she caught them, they would pay with a thorough scolding.

On television, "Sisi, the Empress of Austria" was our favorite film. All of us watched it on an old black-and-white TV. Sisi was my first love, and Oma had to promise me over and over that I could marry whomever I liked and do whatever I liked, unlike Sisi, who married someone she loved but who strangled her freedom with his career. The Eurovision Song Contest was another highlight and was adored by all of us, but mostly by Anja. When we stayed overnight, all three of us slept together in Oma's king-size bed. Oma always put old metal hot water bottles under the covers to keep us warm because there was no heat in the bedroom. Oma would sleep on the sofa in the living room, snoring like a Russian coal miner. When we mentioned this to her, she denied it adamantly, insisting she never snored.

4. GIOVANNI

As was customary in those days, we entered kindergarten at age four. Most of the children we knew from our neighborhood, it was a small kindergarten. The church ran it, and two nuns were our teachers. This was not school, though. It was all about play and being together with other kids. They mostly taught us songs and basic melodies.

By age six, we had started elementary school. The idea of school and discipline was difficult for a free spirit like me. I was used to running and playing freely. To sit down for what felt like hours without end was an alien idea to me. I just could not sit still, much to the dismay of my teacher. But when I was caught running and jumping over school tables, my parents were summoned. My father was not amused, and I still remember the beating I received. We were not beaten often. They were rare occasions, but I deserved it every time! After the incident with jumping over tables, my behavior changed. I settled down enough for my education to start in earnest. I was lazy but quick on the uptake and had no problems in school—except for spelling. I could not spell. The teacher insisted that, with practice, I would get better, but I didn't. It took many years of torturous exercises and despair by my parents until someone determined that I was, and still am, dyslexic. I could recall poems and texts very quickly, but I could not spell them. I could recall and learn visual images instantly, but my mind would not comprehend the rules of organizing letters in order. My school tests were always marked red and full of spelling errors. Eventually, I found a way to simplify my writing into short sentences. Thank God we have spell check today. Otherwise, my school career was easy. I never became the best academically, but I soon understood how to get away with the smallest amount of effort.

In second grade, Giovanni arrived in our town and enrolled in our small elementary school. He was a big boy, two years older than the rest of us. He was put in our class because he did not yet speak German well enough. In second grade, a two-year difference in age is like two light years. After a while, Giovanni started waiting for me after school with the intention of pushing and harassing me as I walked home. He did this regularly and, in the process, made my life a misery that grew worse over time. What made it hell was not knowing how to make him stop. In the beginning, I fought back. I was strong and wiry and accustomed to scraps and fights, but not like this. One time, my fist hit him in the face and broke part of his front tooth, but that didn't change anything. Then, my best friend, Andreas, helped me and fought him. But Giovanni did not care and came for me again and again. Later, my Russian friend, Alexander, helped me beat up Giovanni. Again, nothing changed. After a week, Giovanni was back. Then Marco beat Giovanni up. But after a short while, he was back again. I tried to bribe him with food and sweets, but it seemed Giovanni was unstoppable, put on this earth to make me miserable. The beating was never the worst part; it was the unchanging certainty of not being able to win. After a year, I finally broke down and told everything to my parents. My father sat with me for a long time without saying a word. He just looked at me and then took my hand. We stood, he led me to his car, and we drove off—to Giovanni's house. When I realized what was happening, I was horrified. As boys, we had a code of honor: you did not snitch on your peers. Even worse, I imagined what Giovanni would do to me in the months to come. I imagined what Giovanni's father would do to my father. I believed this was the law of nature: the strong torturing the weak, and I assumed Giovanni's father to be twice the size of my dad. As we arrived at the house, my father calmed me down and took me firmly by the hand. We walked up to Giovanni's door and rang the bell. The door opened, and there was Giovanni's father. To my surprise, he was a small man, much smaller than my father. I did not understand how that could be.

My father explained, briefly and calmly, why we were there. Giovanni's father never spoke; he just listened. When my father finished, Giovanni's father called Giovanni, and he came to the door. There we were, face-to-face. His father asked him if all of this was true. Giovanni did not answer, but in his eyes, his hatred for me was palpable. His father asked again and again, but there was no answer— only a cold stare. Giovanni's father assured my father in very few words that Giovanni would never bother me again. The door closed, and we went back to our car. I was in shock. I did not comprehend what had just happened. My terror and fears were stronger than ever. I thought I was going to get killed!

At home, my father told everything to my mother. Both were very kind and assured me that it was over. I did not believe them.

The next day, I walked the short distance to school in absolute horror—the longest *short* distance of my life. Giovanni was not in class that day. Or the next. On the third day, he was back. I expected the worst, but nothing happened. He just sat in class and ignored me. After school, no Giovanni. Giovanni was no more.

5. DINA AND THE ENCHANTED FOREST

The first year after we moved out of my Bären Opa's house, things calmed down, and a rhythm developed. We usually had Sunday lunch at my grandparents' house at the Bären with all my mother's family. Those Sundays were special. My grandpa would "wind up" my father about his non-worthy "holiday" job while we children played in the slaughterhouse. It was a wonderland of machines, knives, and dead animals. We played hide-and-seek between dead carcasses. It was normal for us. We did not think anything wrong about it, nor did our parents. We understood where food came from. This part of my upbringing taught me to accept that death is part of life. By accepting it as part of every minute of every day, it becomes as normal as the food we eat and the air we breathe. We cannot escape death, but its presence reminds us to live life to its full potential, to cherish every moment, to be humble, and to live every day fully until our last.

There was not always time for us, and on those occasions, we were sent to Aunt Dina, who was not really our aunt. Aunt Dina lived with Frau Razel, a rich, eccentric woman from Stuttgart. Frau Razel had moved away from her family. I am not sure what happened, but I believe her husband and son were killed in World War One.

Both lived together at the border of our forest in a little witch's house. It was a small wooden house with a big garden, orchards, and a wonderful view of the valley. Toward the back of the garden, the dark borders of our forest began. The story goes that Aunt Dina was sold into service to Frau Razel during the war. Dina's father took her to Frau Razel when she was 15 years old because he did not have enough money or food to look after her. After which, Aunt Dina took care of Frau Razel. When we arrived, Aunt Dina had never married, had a boyfriend, or been in any relationship. Dina was like my Oma— a selfless woman with nothing but love in her heart. She always longed for children, which life never granted her, but she had us. The first time I spent time with them, I was about four years old. There was nothing around for miles but dark forest, Frau Razel's house, and the game warden's keep. The whole time, on our visits, I rarely saw Frau

Razel. She was there but never came out of her room. Sometimes, she rang a bell, but that was it. I do not know what the arrangements were, but Aunt Dina was allowed to invite us over as she pleased. None of that mattered to us. All we knew was that it was a wonderful house and Aunt Dina was the kindest person. The house really did look like a witch house from the fairy tale "Hänsel und Gretel"—without the gingerbread," of course. The house was filled with antiques, art, mystical objects, and loads of beautiful clothes: smoking jackets, top hats, wedding dresses, party dresses from the 20s, jewelry, gloves, and much more. They were relics from a rich, privileged life unknown to us. A life of tradition, etiquette, and a wider world beyond our comprehension.

We were allowed to touch everything except a toy display of "cowboys and Indians," which was a shrine to Frau Razel's son. The display on the top of the stairs had been set up by her son before he went to war, and it was beautiful. All the figures were hand-painted. I spent a lot of time observing it from afar. We religiously obeyed the rule not to touch it. But everything else was free for us to take.

Aunt Dina was a master of inventing special occasions and games for us to play in disguise. She would say, "Children, we are going to have a wedding or a dinner party," and we would go dress up. Afterward, there was always a big parade in the garden in our top hats, makeup, and shoes, which were much too big. Aunt Dina's German shepherd, Wicky, barked like mad, running after us, trying to figure out what was happening.

Apart from the disguises and games, we were allowed to roam free in the forest. It was normal at the time. Children were meant to explore and learn their limits on their own. We never got really hurt, aside from some bloody knees or scratches. Sometimes, Aunt Dina would take us for a walk and explain flowers, herbs, and bird songs. Next to Frau Razel's house was the game warden's keep, Förster Stapf, a small hut on a large stretch of land where he kept wounded animals. It was glorious to visit him there. Better than any zoo. He had "Bambi's" small baby deer that were abandoned by their mothers; wild boars with their babies; rabbits; hares; and anything else that lived in the forest. He would wander the woods and collect injured or abandoned animals to nurture them back to life. We were allowed to help feed them. Those were our times. On the one hand, we were used to death with animals used for food, but there we were, bringing life back to wounded animals. The most special was the warden's talking raven. I desperately wanted one, but my mother very firmly said, "No." The warden also maintained a small stable with four ponies. Ponies! At our ages, we all wanted to be "Cowboys and Indians" like in the Western films we watched on TV, and owning a pony would be the ultimate. I begged my grandfather to buy me one, but he refused. I did not give up, though, stubborn as I was, and I started drawing horses. Hundreds of pages filled with horse drawings. They were always in the same position. I drew them day and night, encouraged by my mother, who recognized my passion and bought me art supplies as needed. When it was time for our annual horse market, which is still a big event today, the mayor announced a big art competition. The competition's subject was to draw or paint horses. A lot of local artists participated—including me, at only seven years old. I did not win, but I was recognized as the youngest artist to have ever entered the competition and received a medal. My first artistic achievement! My parents understood then that even though their son could not spell or write properly, he had artistic talent.

Aunt Dina, who is as wise and inventive a soul as there ever was, started and carefully instigated all those events. She and Frau Razel provided us kids with a magical experience, and without their generosity, I would not be who I am today. They offered me a glimpse into a fading world that no longer exists.

6. LACHMANN AND GETTING DRESSED

When I was seven and still running home from Giovanni, I often hid in Lachmann's Toy Shop, an old store full of wooden toys as well as all the latest gadgets a child dreamed of. The shop was owned and run by Mr. Muschner, an older gentleman, and his young associate, Toni. They knew us children from my Bären Opa's inn since everybody shopped at my grandfather's place. In return, my mother bought all the children's gifts and toys from Lachmann's. This was common practice in our village. People supported each other and made sure business was good. When I escaped from Giovanni into Lachmann's, it usually didn't do much good. Giovanni was cunning and waited patiently, knowing I had to come out at some point.

Toni noticed that I came in often without buying anything but that I was in no hurry to leave—observing me as I frequently checked the front window to see if Giovanni was still outside. After a few weeks, Toni stood behind me to see what had me so paranoid and what I was looking out for. He saw Giovanni but said nothing. Then, one day, he took me by the hand, looked me in the eyes, and said, "I know a quick way out." The shop's back door connected to the side playground of our school and was hidden from sight. It took a few moments to realize that he understood perfectly well that I was never going to buy any toys and that I only needed an escape route. This trick helped me for about two weeks until Giovanni figured it out. Luckily, my father's intervention happened shortly after that. Once I was free from the threat of a Giovanni attack, I had a deep curiosity to go back and see what Lachmann's store had to offer. The shop was a special place with a wonderful selection of toys. It was like being in a Christmas movie. There were incredible displays curated with great taste. Before then, I had never had the opportunity to experience the enchantment of the shop.

Mr. Muschner was a gentleman, more reserved than Toni, but he appreciated my company in the store. So, as I concentrated more on the shop than on who was waiting outside, we slowly started talking. It took about two weeks until we had a friendly conversation, enjoying each other's company and banter. One day, Mr. Muschner and Toni asked me if I could lend them a hand in the shop. I thought to myself, wondering, how can I be of help to two grownups?" They explained that they needed help watching the store. On their way home from school, many school kids stopped in and stole small toys and games. They needed me to wander the store and keep an eye out for those delinquents. It was a great job offer. I loved the idea of being with them and earning some money. Walking home, I thought the job was too good to be true. I felt very proud to be asked to work in such a distinguished place—a toy store, no less! The next day, I went back and said, "Yes." It was the beginning of a wonderful friendship and education. Lachmann's store contained not only toys but also books, photographs of exotic places, and, most importantly, a record player and records. Mr. Muschner and Toni had a deep passion for classical music and opera. During quiet times in the day, they played those records. It was the first time I heard "Lacme" and "Bolero." Beautiful music. I had no idea what I was listening to, but that music touched me. We had no classical records at home. My mother went to the Stuttgart Opera or Ballet regularly, but she never brought home any recordings.

It was a strange new world to discover. As they played their records, they laughed at my innocent comments. They were the kindest people in the world, well-educated, and open-minded. My parents were happy for me; they enjoyed the stories about my discoveries, and they instructed me to always behave well. I enjoyed my time at Lachmann's very much. They opened my young eyes and ears to many new experiences. It wasn't until later in life that it dawned on me that they were a gay couple.

Years later, I ran into Toni at a gay bar in Stuttgart. We were so happy to see each other. After much laughter and catching up, he told me that Mr. Muschner had died and that he had moved away from Leonberg. I still think a lot about both. They were different in a deeper, more cultural, and modern way than most people in our village. I cherished their universe and sense of beauty. They were rare, and they hold a special place in my heart.

The episode with Giovanni took me to a dark place, and soon, the whole family knew all about it. To make a change and cheer us up, my Bären Oma decided it was time to get us out of our village and into the city more often. So, we began taking day trips to Stuttgart once a month. My Bären Oma took my grandfather's Mercedes with my mother (who drove), my brother Marc, and me. It was only 20 kilometers away, but for us, it was a different world. Stuttgart was a big city with loads of buildings and people we did not know, situated like Rome in a valley surrounded by seven hills. My mother and Grandmother knew it well and enjoyed their shopping trips immensely.

Once there, our first stop was the children's hairdresser, which had wooden animals for us to sit on and get our hair trimmed. While the children were safely stowed away, the two ladies went shopping. When we were properly groomed, they picked us up, and we all went shopping to get clothes for Marc and me. Much to our dismay, our mother loved the latest fashion and chose to dress both of us in the same outfits. We looked like circus attractions ready for a photo shoot. The one outfit that still haunts us today was a shiny, bright red pleather overall with white turtlenecks and a red balloon hat. We looked like the "Dukes" from Brooklyn.

In hindsight, it was hilarious, but in school, it invited lots of ridicule. At the end of the day, we went for tea and cake, and everyone was content. My Bären Oma was a shrewd businesswoman but very generous; no money was spared to buy only the best for us.

7. OMA DIES

While Bären Oma introduced us to the finer things in life, the center of our universe was Oma Kaum's house. That's where everything happened, and that's where Anja, Marc, and I felt loved and safe. It was our island, where we were allowed to dream and be who we wanted. She was the only person I ever met who truly gave to everyone without expecting anything in return. Every night, she collapsed into her bed, knowing she had given all she could to make others feel whole. Our house and village were full of people who needed fixing, but under Oma's watch, we were all loved and looked after.

It was a happy house—dysfunctional at times but happy.

I was twelve when Oma died. I do not remember much leading up to her death. We children were kept aside as the grownups talked amongst themselves in hushed tones. The mood was somber. No more laughter, only whispering and sad faces. Her illness passed quickly, and Oma died in her bed. It was a dark day. I remember the Coffin leaving the house. The flame that kept everything and everyone illuminated had been snuffed out. Everybody cried, but I couldn't. I still felt her with me. I talked to her every night, and I could hear her speaking back. At twelve, I had no knowledge of or even words to describe my pain. Only raw emotions, but still, I could not cry. In the days following Oma's death, the house was like a beehive. There was a lot of laughter as well as many tears while all the old stories were retold. The heart and soul of the house had died, and we knew that Mother's Table was no more.

The funeral was held in our small local cemetery. Everyone walked there. We children were lined up in our suits and dresses and made to shake hands with the mourners. It was a closed-coffin service, so I never saw Oma for one last time. They carried the coffin to her final resting place, a priest spoke, and music was played. Then, Anja, Marc, and I were pushed in front of a hole in the ground with Oma's coffin in it, and we had to throw a flower into her grave. Still, I could not cry.

For a long time after, Marc accused me of not having loved Oma because I did not cry at her funeral.

The reception after, at the "Leichenschmauss," was a blur—too many people, too much drink, and then it was over.

A few weeks later, Marc and I were moved under my Bären Oma's supervision. Our lives had irrevocably changed. Marc could not easily adapt, and he suffered. Anja was sent away to her grandparents. For the first time, we were separated from each other.

8. PUNK

Though my father continued to advance in his career at Porsche, the more the company grew from a small tractor manufacturer to a world-renowned sports car company, the more he felt his lack of education. Having left school at 16, he had only a basic education and studied hard in the evenings to keep up with the latest engineering. The thing he missed most was a knowledge of the English language. More and more meetings were being held in English. Engineering texts, books, and journals were available only in English. He took night classes and listened to language tapes on his way to work every morning. In the car, Marc and I were listening along and repeating the words while my father drove. It became my father's obsession that his sons would have a proper education and speak English fluently as adults.

When I was 13, it was decided that I would go to England on an exchange program during summer break. I would stay with an English family for three weeks and immerse myself in the English language. I was never asked if I wanted to go; I was told, packed up, and was driven to the airport. After the two-hour flight, a friendly man picked me up and delivered me to a family. I had only studied English for one year in school and had listened to those tapes in my father's car. I didn't know any English. It was kind of hilarious because I basically understood nothing. England was completely different from everything I knew. The houses, the buses, the food, and, of course, the language!

We arrived at a small house in Sidmouth, and the man who drove me there carried my suitcase up a narrow path that led through a small orchard of Cox Orange trees. We arrived at a run-down, cramped cottage house, and he knocked on the door. It opened to reveal a small man with enormous ears. This was my host father.

"Full of charm" would be a polite way to describe the interior. Everything looked ready to collapse. At home in Germany, we would have torn down the house and burned the remains. The lady of the house gave me a big hug and pulled me deeper inside. My driver was happily assured that I would be well, and the door was promptly slammed shut in his face.

All alone now, I felt like I had been abducted by crazy serial killers from outer space. They looked so different! I was introduced to their three children: George, Ann, and "Mouse." They all had the same big ears, so I wondered why all of them weren't called "Mouse." Probably, that would be too confusing. Thankfully, my English was not yet good enough to comment on anything, so I didn't utter a word. I just fixed a frozen grin of horror on my face and politely shook everybody's hand.

Dinner was fish and chips, wrapped in a newspaper and paired with some green mush (later revealed as mashed peas). The most bizarre thing was that they all poured vinegar on their chips. Vinegar! But it was all very friendly, and the expression on my face was of great amusement to the whole family. I did not know what I was eating, nor did I know how to converse with them, but what was most amusing was that I did not understand their jokes about me, flying back and forth across the dinner table. After the first awkward hour, we found a way to communicate by pointing at things. (Full disclosure: since then, I have very much enjoyed chips with vinegar and mushed peas.) During dinner, they explained that they had owls— plural. It took me a long time to understand. In Germany, nobody owns an owl. I thought I misunderstood. I assumed they had owls in the nearby forest, but no—they kept two owls in an outside extension. I was excited and wanted to see them. After dinner, the children took me to the owls, located in a big extension with a small door you entered through. There they were: two big, beautiful owls. I was dumbstruck. Who ever heard of keeping owls as pets? Even though it was England, this was long before Harry Potter.

From the owls, I was led to my room, which I shared with Mouse. While I was unpacking, Mouse watched me and explained that he and his siblings were "punks." I had no idea what he was talking about. I had never heard of a punk, and now I was sharing a room with one of them. *Was this something to worry about?* Mouse played me some records, mostly "Sex Pistols" and "The Clash." I've never heard anything like it. Punk was cool. I loved the cover photos and the wild look of the musicians. Their safety pins and rawness struck a deep chord in me. I loved it and instantly connected with it.

The next day, my exchange program unfolded with the precision of a summer school. Every morning, after breakfast, I strolled through the apple orchard, where I picked one delicious Cox Orange apple and ate it on my way to the bus. School started each day with language and history courses, then lunch, and in the afternoon, activities like tennis or other games. It was fun. Then I made my way home to my "mouse" family. I loved playing with the owls and enjoyed the cozy friendliness of my punk pseudo-siblings.

One Friday, Mouse informed me we would be attending a punk concert on Saturday. They all started preparing, cutting up their clothes while listening to "Sex Pistols." Safety pins were the main ingredient. Since I had no punk clothes, I mastered transforming my jeans and T-shirt. I enjoyed the process and found that I loved customizing my clothes. On Saturday, George, Ann, Mouse, and I had transformed. Ann was running around the house half-naked, wearing a super-sexy bra. She completed her outfit with fishnet stockings, a mini-skirt, and a short, cropped leather jacket. George spiked his hair, and they both had enormous fun applying makeup to my face. Mouse corrected my clothing while his siblings spiked my hair too. By 6 p.m., we were ready and off to the local pub. We were too young to drink, but everybody else in the punk scene was there and met before the concert. It was incredible. Everyone looked special and outrageously different. The half-naked outfits and rough, raw mannerisms of the girls were intoxicating. By 8 p.m., we had moved to a local club, which looked more like an abandoned garage. Skinheads and Psycho Billy's joined in too. They were different breeds. Their dress codes were similar, but they were very different in style. But in the end, everyone loved the same raw music. In Germany, Eltingen was still stuck in the 1970s. I was used to the long hair and flared jeans of the hippy generation and music like "Uriah Heep," "Deep Purple," and "Led Zeppelin." Punk was from another planet. Planet Punk!

The concert started, and everybody went crazy. Drink cups were flying, and everybody was pushing and being pushed around in what was called "pogo dancing." I instantly fell in love with a girl who wore a ripped-up wedding dress. She was more naked than dressed; what a beauty! Meanwhile, Mouse enjoyed being bounced around like a rubber ball.

After the concert, Mouse dragged me home while George and Ann went on to another club. As we walked home, two rival gangs started a fight. It was a cruel fight, and the brutality displayed was like nothing I had ever witnessed before. One guy picked up a steel rod and slashed open his opponent's head. Blood was everywhere. Chains, which were belts to hold up trousers, quickly turned into lethal weapons and were used without mercy. The fights we had in Germany were harmless compared to this open violence. There was an animalistic hatred, which was frightening. Girls were fighting as viciously as boys; there was no difference. Mouse dragged me home quickly through back alleys, and he made sure nothing happened to us. We made it home safely, and we laughed after the first shock abated. Despite the violence we just witnessed, we felt alive like never before.

We sat up all night telling and re-telling the witnessed events to Ann and George as they came home. It was crazy, and I was in shock as much as I was in heaven. I was transformed by clarity in understanding human nature, and for the first time, I understood the role fashion played in transforming people and behavior. A uniform makes a soldier, as certain clothes transform teenagers into punks. Punks who were ready to do unheard-of violence, just as I, the next day, had to transform back for an afternoon school tea party with all the exchange students. I wanted to show my new "punk" friends to the other students, so I asked Ann if she would join me at the party.

Ann came with me, wearing not much more than she did Saturday night. She looked outrageous, and I was so proud. All the older boys could not believe their eyes! Her lace bra under her leather jacket was just too much for them. She was an alien from Planet Punk, but with such charm and perfect manners, no one could resist her. I will never forget that day.

That Monday, I went from an awkward, thirteen-year-old German exchange student to the coolest kid in town. Everybody in the exchange program wanted to know more about punk and the cool family I was staying with. I didn't know much about Punk, but I was happy to tell them all about the concert, the Skinheads, and the Psycho Billy's—how wild they were when they danced, staring at the ceiling, flailing their arms. I did not mention the fight, though. The local police were still looking for the people involved since three were severely injured.

The next weekend, there was another punk concert, and everybody wanted to go. We all met again in the local pub, and what a sight! All those usually properly dressed Europeans transformed into punks. Mouse was in his element, the perfect tour guide into the wonders of punk, and he was happy to introduce everyone to the local punk aristocracy. The concert was a riot—most notably because I kissed a girl for the first time. A great success, and no more fights.

The summer holiday was over far too quickly, and we all had to pack our things and fly home. At the airport, when we arrived home, I still recall the faces of all the nice German parents waiting for their children, shocked to see an army of punks spilling into the terminal. I had a new haircut too: the first "hedgehog" in the history of Eltingen.

My confirmation was two weeks later; the vicar nearly refused to accept me with my haircut, and it took a lot of convincing from my mother. There was only one small accident. In England, they spiked their hair with what they called "wax." Obviously, this was a special hair wax. I misunderstood the concept and melted down two candles, working the results into my hair. What a mess. Luckily, I was able to get it all out before anyone realized and managed to look the part in church. The first in church confirmed punk. My Bären grandparents vehemently disapproved, but I would not budge. As a sign of solidarity, I wore a safety pin stabbed through my cravat. Mouse would have been proud.

9. PRISONER OF FEAR

As I returned from England in my punk glory, my father had transformed the attic space. It was now going to be a room for me and Marc. In this space, beneath the crossbeams of the roof, Marc and I slowly came to know and understand ourselves better. We found our callings. More and more, Marc turned to computers and electronics. He had just received a Commodore 64 computer and was quickly turning into a nerd. His talent for understanding the machine amazed me. I had no interest, not even in playing the simple games it offered. Marc also developed the habit of dragging home any old television he found and dissecting it. In those days, people piled up furniture and electronic equipment on the streets for the garbage collector to collect. My half of the room was filled with chemistry sets. I loved the idea of being a modern alchemist, creating secret potions and tinctures. In school, I was very good at biology and loved everything to do with nature and science. I loved old books about alchemists and wizards. I turned the attic into a chemical bomb hazard without realizing it. With my good friend Carolus, also called "Lolo," we built pipe bombs, blew up tree trunks, and went dynamite fishing until one day he ended up in the hospital, and his mom put an end to our explosive period. Years later, my father was deeply worried about finding all the chemical substances I managed to amass and mix without supervision. There were enough explosive compounds in the house to blow it to smithereens.

During those days, we roamed the nearby woodlands unsupervised and rode our bikes everywhere without anybody worrying about where we went. Responsible parenting was considered to allow us to roam free. Nobody worried about accidents. We learned by trial and error. If we hurt ourselves, we would be more careful next time. We learned to assess risk. We taught ourselves how to build fires and climb trees. We learned that fire can be controlled. We learned to be alive.

Often, we met in a little valley called "Täle" where there were rock faces and caves. We would build forts and treehouses there. Different gangs formed and attacked each other, fighting battles and conquering each other's lairs. To make it worth our while, we needed treasures to rob. Luckily, there was a shooting range close by. Fenced in, but the fences were easy to climb. They had barrels filled with empty brass bullet casings—golden gems.

We were all good climbers. One day, we needed more brass to establish the treasure for our new cave. As we got closer, I saw movement in the corner of my eye. We stopped, waited, and listened for anybody in the shooting range. After five minutes, nothing had moved, and I gave the signal to climb in. Jumping in first, I was ten yards ahead of the others when a big man came running up behind me and cut me off. Terrified, I tried to escape, but he was faster, and he grabbed me by my shirt. I was caught kicking, fighting, and screaming like a wild animal. My friends were all around and were thinking of attacking the man, but the man controlled them with his threats about what he would do to me if they came closer. They were good friends, but there was nothing they could do. The man shoved me into his car and started driving. I was scared to death while he was screaming that I was a little thief and that he would bring me to the police. He told me that I would end up in jail and never get out. I begged him to let me go but to no avail. He dragged me into the police station, and after explaining my crime, they showed us into an office and told us to sit and wait. It was absolute silence that seemed to last an eternity. I was in an absolute panic. In my mind, the police station was only for murderers and other *real* criminals. Prison would be the end of me; my life would be ruined.

The door opened, and a middle-aged, slightly overweight police officer entered and sat behind his desk. He asked the man to explain again why we were in his office. The man told the police officer that I had broken into the shooting range and destroyed the target mechanism. I immediately contradicted him: We never broke anything; we only wanted the empty brass casings to play with. They did not believe me and told me to shut up. The police officer took a piece of paper from his desk and started rolling it into his typewriter. "Name," he demanded. I told him my name. He stopped, looked up, and asked me if I belonged to the "Bärenwirt." I was in disbelief. He knew where I belonged. He asked again, and I gave a slight nod. Both stared at me, then the police officer said, "The questioning will stop here." He said they would let me go with no charges pressed—for now—but if they found out I lied, they would come to my grandfather's house to arrest me. He stood up, took me by my arm, led me to the exit, opened the door, and pushed me out of the building.

After a moment, I heard a faint whistle. It was my best friend, Andreas, hiding behind a bush with my bike. He asked if everything was OK. I honestly didn't know. I grabbed my bike and pedaled home. Inside my front door, I told my parents I had to go to bed and disappeared upstairs. I was deeply traumatized. In the coming weeks and months, I fully expected a police car to stop in front of our house with a warrant for my arrest. Whenever I heard a siren, I thought they were coming for me. To make matters worse, the local police bought their food and lunches at my grandfather's. Every time they entered, I thought they were coming to get me. I never told anyone about this. The "monster" of this terror lived inside me all the time. It was a cruel and lonely time. I was living in such constant fear, withdrawing from everything and everyone.

10. LIBRARY, MY SANCTUARY

As I lost myself in fear and loneliness, the world around me was changing. It was the beginning of the eighties, and industry was transforming our region into a wealthy part of Germany. The old poor South had turned into the rich South. The car industry exploded. And as Porsche did well, so did we. My father advanced higher in the company, and his career blossomed. For our family, the world blossomed too—first with summer holidays to Italy and Spain, then we bought a small apartment in Saalbach, Austria, that became our second home. I always loved the mountains and alpine nature for their raw beauty and awe-inducing sense of power.

But another consequence of our region's success was that supermarkets arrived and nearly destroyed my grandfather's business. Fortunately, he was able to adapt and evolve. And a time of change it was for the village and the people. Everything was different.

When I was 14, a library was constructed in our town—a modern-style building with a big, open space and floor-to-ceiling windows. It had a functional, Scandinavian design with a clean, minimalist interior and, of course, lots of bookshelves. For everyone in our community, this was something new and fresh. For me, in my loneliness and fear, the library became my home. I stopped hanging with my friends, terrified that the man, or the police, would find me again and throw me in prison. But I could not stay home either; my mother would wonder what was wrong. I had to go somewhere. So, as a young, scared, lonely punk, I found the library and its magazine section. They had all international publications: music and fashion magazines, with articles about the punk movement and all the wonderful things happening in the youth culture. The library was my refuge, my sanctuary; in there, I hid myself for more than two years. Every day after school, in Germany, school finishes at 1:00 p.m., I would cycle there and leave the world behind. I borrowed books and sat at the long tables by the tall windows, reading. I moved from magazines to comic books, science books, novels, and art. I read everything without prejudice. I had discovered a real treasure. Not the fake gold of discarded brass bullet casings but the real riches in books and stories. The stuff of life, and I was hungry to learn it all.

I learned about all the different myths, gods, and religions. To me, they all appeared the same, just presented in different settings, and all centered upon the concept of a higher, universal power. I still can't understand how humans can kill each other over their religious beliefs. The God I read about was good—all the gods were essentially good. Their stories and systems were about birth, a good life with purpose, and accepting the reality of death. All around me, I felt a godly, universal energy; I was part of it, and it was a part of all things. The library brought order to my feelings of chaos. I read about evolution and the animal kingdom, dinosaurs and their time, galaxies and planets, and Greek classics like *The Iliad* and *The Odyssey*. I loved reading philosophers like Nietzsche, with his aphorisms and clear-eyed observations on human nature. I did not understand why no one else could see what he saw. It was all logical to me. I began to understand why so many people misinterpret ancient teachings and how they struggle to connect the dots in more empathetic and productive ways. I learned how leaders throughout history have abused knowledge and the lessons of philosophy to their own advantage. Being German, Hitler was the closest of all history's monsters. It was impossible for me to comprehend how a whole world of people allowed something as grotesque as him and his movement to grow and gain power until it consumed the entire planet in destruction, misery, and death. Today, older and a bit wiser, I better understand how this is possible, having witnessed so many horrific events in my time. Humans never seem to learn. What a better world we would all live in if our leaders were more like Oma, if our natural inclination was more toward charity and kindness rather than fear, greed, and violence. Because I was young and read so many books without guidance or any system of approach, I formed my own worldview by learning to read between the lines. No one explained things or offered context. I just read what I wanted and thought about what I wanted. I moved from biology to history, chemistry, rockets, music, art, comics, soft porn, science, war, fairy tales, science fiction, and authors like Hemingway, Hermann Hesse, Kafka, Ibsen, Orwell, Golding, Siegfried, Machiavelli, and Huxley, just to name a few. So much foresight and wisdom, something so fundamental that feels so lacking today.

I loved books of art because pictures spoke to me better than words. I could sense and interpret their symbolic truths. Art offered me a form of storytelling and a unique insight into a universal knowledge that, for so many others, was hidden in plain sight. Maybe being dyslexic helped me understand and react to art in this way. It opened doors for me to many new worlds. The books became my family, my friends, and my universe. Whoever chose all the books in my library was wise and enlightened enough to not censor uncomfortable truths. I never again found a library with such an eclectic mix of books and such a variety of controversial content. It was my temple, my secret university, where I formed what would be, throughout my life, my core principles, philosophies, and beliefs.

At school, one of the immediate results of all this time in the library was that my religion teacher called my mother, informing her that I needed to transfer from the religion class into the ethics class. "Ethics" was the class for those free spirits not bound to traditional religious beliefs, not willing to sit through long lessons about bearded men living on mountains or clouds, a God, his son, and golden calves. He further explained to my mother that my understanding of the world and the many questions I kept asking were disrupting his teaching.

11. ROCKY HORROR PICTURE SHOW THE TRANSEXUAL

As the years passed and my exile in the library progressed, my body was changing. And with that change, I suddenly discovered girls! It started slowly in the schoolyard, at the bike racks. I guess in every school, you have a corner where the cool kids hang out—and especially the cool girls. In our school, it was the bike rack. As I approached the age of 15, my interest in the other sex was awakened by desire. In the library, it was amazing how much soft porn material was available at the end of the seventies. Although I was not much of a porn connoisseur, I was interested in the real thing. I was still too young for the bike rack cool kids, who were mostly 16 to 18 years old. Those two years were like light years of experience. They had small motorcycles, girlfriends, and even mustaches! I wanted it all. Luckily, some of the older girls thought I was cute and dragged me along. Bit by bit, I became part of their gang, and so, to become as cool as they were, I started smoking. All the older kids smoked back then. My parents were absolutely against it. We were a sporting family, and nobody smoked but my Uncle Yogi, who was definitely not sporty.

One day, up in the attic, my mother caught me smoking out the window and was very upset. When my father arrived home from work, he was immediately informed, and I had to discuss matters with him at the dinner table. Discussing matters with my father at the dinner table was never fun. He was very upset, and it was one of those rare occasions where I got a serious talking to. My punishment was to stay home after school for four weeks. No going out, no seeing friends. This was a harsh punishment. I had just been accepted into the cool group and wanted to be part of all that was going on—especially since I was secretly in love with a girl and couldn't stand the thought of not seeing her for four weeks.

In week three of my punishment, big news arrived. Our local cinema was showing "Rocky Horror Picture Show." I had no idea what that film was about but was eager to find out because the newspapers were condemning it as the biggest piece of sexual trash ever perpetrated on the general public. Naturally, this was the most magnetic publicity a film could hope for. Everybody in school wanted to go; it was the event of the century. Family arguments were raging in every house in town. Parents forbade their children to go, and the kids were fighting back. As for me, I was still grounded, and my parents had no intention of letting me go see this piece of cinematic filth.

When the day of the screening arrived, we had two camps in school: one allowed to go and one not. It was a unique moviegoing event because you had to go in drag. The film was about Dr. Frank N. Furter from Transsexual Transylvania. It was not easy to acquire the costumes. Our village was not overflowing with sexy underwear or sex shops, and the internet was not yet invented. So, for two days before the event, girls were swapping underwear with us boys in school. Every bit of black, sexy lace was in high demand. At home, I was fighting every night to be allowed to go, but my father and mother would not budge.

Finally, the big day arrived, and the screening was at 8:00 p.m. I was devastated that I was not allowed to participate in the biggest social event of my young life. That evening, Sigi, who was a famous Garden architect and a close friend of our family, arrived for a visit. He was a real character with strong points of view and two very beautiful daughters a couple years older than me. He had three daughters, but the oldest had died in a tragic motorcycle accident. At the dinner table, Sigi wondered what I was still doing at home since his daughters were going to see "Rocky Horror Picture Show." I told him my predicament of having been grounded for smoking and, on top of that, not even being old enough to attend the film. Sigi declared that I *had* to go. He explained to my parents that I needed to see this milestone in film history and that his girls were going to come pick me up. Of course, the question of punishment had to be negotiated first, and he resolved, with my parents, that my sentence would be prolonged for one more week but that I could go and see the film. Fifteen minutes later, Sigi's daughters arrived wearing crazy makeup, and my parents immediately regretted their decision.

Inside the car, it was a mad, moving sex shop. Everybody ripped off their clothes, down to their fishnet stockings, garters, and corsets. Since I was a late addition, there was not much left for me. I had to go as "Brad," so they gave me some thick black eyeglasses and a beige blouson jacket. I had no idea who Brad was, but the costumes were not the end of all the preparations. We also had to bring newspapers, water pistols, umbrellas, and plain white rice. I asked why, and they laughed and assured me I would find out soon enough.

It's hard to put into context how controversial this all was at the time. I believe I was the youngest audience member. Our village had transformed into Planet Transsexual Transylvania! What a sight: over two hundred kids in drag and makeup. It was insane and very different from Carnival. For my teenage self, the message was extremely powerful: clothes make you free. Clothing can be a disguise, a power uniform, or simply the carrier of a message. Clothes can unite people and overcome boundaries and preconceptions.

There was kissing and touching, and everyone was drinking and smoking. The atmosphere was welcoming and highly sexual. I enjoyed the hell out of it. It's no understatement to say that this was the most transformative moment of my life. Everything fell into place. My fantasies, my desires, my hopes, and my dreams seemed to fit the creative energy that evening. I saw a world beyond my world, a world that felt right. My creative journey as an artist and designer had officially begun, and I was ready for the adventure.

Just before the crowd devolved into a crazy orgy, the cinema doors were flung open. The cinema was an old cinema with a few hundred red velvet-covered seats and red velvet curtains drawn closed in front of the screen. After a brief period of frenzied chaos, we all settled in for the show. The cinema owner appeared on the small stage to welcome us to the greatest spectacle ever and beg us to go easy on the rice and water pistols. To that end, everyone booed loudly and whipped rice at the owner until he exited the stage. As the curtain slowly drew open, the magic began. Onscreen, red lips appeared, singing the most beautiful song ever. Then, the narrative part of the film started, and I understood what the rice and water pistols were for. During the wedding scene, the audience threw rice at each other.

When the car broke down, and it started to rain, everybody fired water pistols into the air while we covered our heads with newspapers (some even opened real umbrellas). When the song "Time Warp" arrived, we all got up and danced to it.

By the end of the film, we all felt we belonged through the magic of being different, being proud of our differences, and feeling a sense of community with our fellow weirdos. None of us was truly alone, and there was strength in numbers. We felt powerful. Like we would be the ones to change the world rather than the world forcing us to change. I realized that being different was never a choice; it's who I am. And I understood that clothing has the power to change the world. The goal of clothing was not beauty but change, transformation, and power. I wanted to announce to the world that I am alive, and only I control my destiny!

12. NEW WAVE AND THE NEW ROMANTIC, ANDROGYNY

After the premiere of "Rocky Horror," the newspapers were filled with photos and articles about the decadent, perverted youth of our region. During our Sunday lunches, my Bären Opa would repeatedly state that he wanted to send us all into the army to learn discipline or worse. But his world and the attitudes and ideas of his generation were in the past. Whether they liked it or not (and they didn't), the "New Wave" and the "New Romantic" movement had arrived.

Sure, punk had been around for a while, but it never really caught on. It was too rough and violent, too radical; the music was everywhere, but the real punk lifestyle was less so. Also, as a practical matter, it was difficult to sleep with spikey hair. In big cities, though, especially Berlin (which was still like some island in the east), the punk scene was exploding but quickly transformed into the New Wave and the New Romantic scene. They were movements where a growing number of young people felt they identified more strongly, offering them an alternative way to adapt and transform. It was also a time for "androgyny." Sexual orientation did not matter. Gender fluidity was key, but "fluidity" did not mean we were not attracted to each other. Gender fluidity would mean that boys would become birds of paradise and girls even more so. Sexual orientation and gender identity were gone. It was a playful "anything goes." It was a highly sexual time! Today, it is common for people to think that the clothes of this era were all newly designed and purchased, but that is far from the truth. The styles of the early 1980s were largely based on the 1950s suit styles, with their high-waisted baggy trousers, pointy shoes, and repurposed military uniforms—especially old jodhpurs from World War II. It was one massive art project—an effort to adapt the past into a contemporary style that best projected the vibe of our generation. Military uniforms, oversized 50s suit styles, lots of make-up, bleached hair, and Pirate-style patterns prevailed. It was very colorful.

The Music landscape developed and changed, too. The "Neue Deutsche Welle" exploded into a musical wonderland. Nightclubs popped up like mushrooms, and, of course, we all went. The biggest challenge was getting into the clubs. Get past the bouncers at the doors, who were cruel Gods, deciding about the success of our evenings by allowing us in or not. Therefore, everyone dressed up, wore makeup, and created new clothes. Every weekend was one big fashion show, and we created it for the event of being seen in the clubs. It was all about making, repurposing, and altering—not buying. Although Kenzo scarves were everywhere—big, beautifully colored, and expensive— But this wasn't just playing dress-up, far from it. Again, it was about transformation. We really believed we could change the world and that we were in the process of doing just that. Gender and sexuality explored the concept of androgyny (that was the term the media gave it; we never thought of it in that way). We just felt free to explore and were not interested in being labeled. How can you label a generation and define that they are all following the same doctrine? This is absolute nonsense. We were all different: open-minded and non-judgmental, respectful, and horny. Before the ubiquity of mobile phones and social media, we were allowed to make mistakes and misbehave without the whole world watching and judging. That said, many parties were only available to those "in the know," and their locations were shared carefully and discreetly. We spent many hours in parking lots, styling our hair and painting our faces. Girls taught the boys, and soon, many boys were better at applying mascara than the girls. Sex was everywhere. Awareness of a mysterious, deadly disease that would soon be identified as AIDS was just arriving on the scene. As awareness grew and more research and articles entered the mainstream, we grew frightened. There's no question that it had a sobering effect on the way we viewed our sexual freedoms.

In school, my days were spent ignoring class and designing outfits for the weekends. For me, drawing and making clothes was pure heaven. I had not been trained to pattern cut or sew, so my friends and I just made it up as we went along, admiring those who clearly had real talent. Getting it right was difficult. I will admit that quite often, I looked like a complete disaster. But creativity and effort were appreciated, and nobody judged—at least not too harshly.

The biggest challenge at the clubs and exclusive parties was just getting past the highly selective bouncers at the door. They were the key to a fun night, and only they knew who was worthy of being admitted. They were not those muscle guys of today; they were super stylish and in the know. They knew who was "in" and they knew how to create the right atmosphere of cool. They could read clothes as a language, one that defines us and is understood on a deep, ancient, emotional level. I continue to be amazed that it is still not common to teach this very important language in school! The oldest language on Earth for millions of years. We have communicated through our exterior selves for thousands of years, whether it be fur, scales, feathers, skins, crowns, colors, military symbols, tattoos, piercings, breasts, cocks, makeup, or anything else you can name. Anything we wear, we are born to read and understand as a form of emotional language. We speak with the clothes we wear. Clothes! From the Garden of Paradise, caves, royal courts, and night clubs to Givenchy and beyond. From our mother dressing us when we are born to our grown-up individual selves. We communicate all our lives with our clothes daily.

But anyway, back to getting past those bouncers. This was good training for us—better than any fashion school—because the bouncers were paid to make our lives hell. I would love to pay a bouncer to check fashion students' outfits at the university door every day and allow only those to enter the building if they paid attention to what they were wearing. You can only get to class if you've made an effort. Back then, you had to know the trends and have fierce originality; otherwise, you would soon find yourself driving back home alone, looking stupid. The trends were not in the magazines. The fashion press did not know shit; they only reported the same boring stuff from Paris and Milan. You had to look for what worked, hunt it down, observe the right people, and develop a feel for your personal style— then pray the bouncer was sufficiently impressed. To make it more difficult, the hot crowd never stayed in just one club. They migrated, sometimes overnight. Once a club started filling up with the "unworthy" and the bouncers had given in to satisfy the masses, the fashion royalty moved on. It was heaven to watch how a place was happening from midnight to 2 a.m., then emptied out as the crowd progressed to the next club. But once there, the problem began again: Will I get past the bouncer?

Since I was only sixteen, I was not allowed to go out for too long, which was a problem because all my friends were older and had cars. Since the clubs were in Stuttgart, there was no way to get home other than waiting for somebody with a car getting tired and wanting to go. If you were lucky, they drove you home. I always arrived home after my curfew. This situation found me in constant trouble. My parents were not amused. To their credit, my parents softened over time and didn't give me too much hassle.

Over the years, we grew into one big group, and when we gathered, we all dressed up and drove in a convoy to the clubs. It was outrageous, wild fun. We loved fast cars, and there were very few cops around at the time.

Not only making clothes but also art, designing, and sketching interested me. I needed to keep my creativity flowing, so I started taking art classes in factory-style settings in the "Glaskasten." It was once a week that they offered life drawing classes. I signed up and explored my talent. I found out fast that I had to practice a lot and that sketching a human body was not easy—thanks to Bernd Mack, I did not give up. He helped me through those times and encouraged me to explore further (although I mostly made him laugh with my nude drawings). This was the point when I decided to become a fashion designer—to walk into the world with my eyes wide open and make my mark. During this time, I learned to sew some basic stuff and create my own looks. Some were spectacular, and, piece by piece, I created a massive wardrobe of madness.

In eleventh grade, we took a school trip to Berlin, as was the custom in our school. Berlin was a magical unicorn on our planet. A city like no other. Berlin was in the eastern bloc of the DDR, and West Berlin was still surrounded by a wall. Forgotten by the industry, it had evolved into a place of creative anarchy. At the time, Berlin was the only place in Germany that did not require compulsory military service for its citizens. Everywhere else in West Germany, you were drafted at age 18. This made Berlin the perfect hiding place for free spirits and artists. There was no industry in Berlin. Therefore, it had an abundance of empty buildings abandoned after the war that were dead cheap to rent. Berlin was a fertile breeding ground full of runaway creatives. Anything and everything was happening in Berlin. There was no curfew, either—everything was open 24/7. It was the place to be, and we were traveling there for a whole week. One destination was the Holy Grail for all of us club kids: the Dschungel. Nina Hagen and David Bowie hung out there, along with all the coolest German bands and famous artists. We had to be sure to make the best outfits before we went. The preparations were crazy. From all our friends who had to stay behind, we were given shopping lists for clothes and records to buy.

We made the journey by bus, and just getting to the city was an adventure by itself. To get to Berlin, you had to drive through East Germany first. East Germany was separated from West Germany by a massive wall and was under Russian supremacy. To travel to Berlin, one had to pass through East German border control. This border control was not to be underestimated. They did not allow Western propaganda or "press," as they called it. Everything on our bus was checked for smuggled magazines and books—anything. They were especially looking for East German refugees that might be hidden somewhere within the bus. East Germany had been completely walled off. It looked like a prison as we arrived at the border: fences, dogs, and soldiers with guns (without a smile to be seen). It was the most intimidating thing we had seen in our young lives. No words can describe the horrors people inflict on each other. We had family in Dresden that we never saw again after the wall separated us. At the border, I saw for the first time what they were suffering through: we were free, but they were locked up in this hideous gray state. Hours later, we arrived at another wall surrounding West Berlin. Everything changed again as we entered the free part of Berlin; it was not glorious, but an abandoned capital still haunted by ghosts. It looked like the war had ended only yesterday. I could see bullet holes still in the buildings. Our once-proud capital looked like a distant planet. The light—or lack of it—was amazing. Everything was dark and gray. The photographer Helmut Newton once said he liked to shoot in Berlin for its "Schwarzes Licht," or "blackened light." People said it came from all the coal-burning stoves in the buildings. I think it was the historical residue of sadness. Berlin had the residue of a technocratic leviathan from another time—the carcass of a terrible monster left by history to rot. This was the apocalyptic setting we had come to explore. We arrived at our hotel in a somber mood.

The next day, we took a trip to the city. We had a full program of sites and museums, but the most impressive was our trip to East Berlin. We drove to Checkpoint Charlie, where we underwent body searches and then had to exchange 25 West German Marks for 25 East German Marks. Entering East Berlin by foot, it looked like an empty country. The shops were bare, with nothing to buy, but we had to spend all our money that day because we were not allowed to bring it back. We bought anything we could find, but, in the end, we just gave away the rest to our fellow countrymen. We felt saddened for them and how they had been cheated by history.

During the day, we were on our best behavior and paid attention to our cultural program and our teachers, but at midnight, we snuck out to join the vampires of Berlin. Berlin was a city of night creatures. All the lost children of Germany came out at night. Our Bible was the book *Wir Kinder vom Bahnhof Zoo*, the story of a young girl addicted to heroin in desolate Berlin. David Bowie was described in the book, and we were ready to explore all its locations. We didn't just want to meet David Bowie; we wanted to be him.

We quickly realized that we did not fit in. In Berlin, everyone dressed in black. Back home, we were used to a lot of color and patterns in our clothes, but Berlin was black clothes only.

We had our first drinks at a bar called The White Pony, then entered the Dschungel. After all, it was the Holy Grail. The entry hall was a long corridor covered in graffiti. The graffiti was not colorful like in New York; it was in black and white spray can tones. Sad, and even more so through the sterile neon tubes that were hanging from the ceiling and walls like a bomb attack had just shaken their foundations. The girl who was the magic key to paradise looked stunning in her haggard but cool, boyish frame. She wore a platinum blond wig and was covered in tattoos. Her white military tank top was literally transparent. She immediately understood that we were not from Berlin. Initially, she was not amused, but with the help of some charm, she allowed us in. Inside, it was incredible. The Strobe light turned the main room into a surreal zombie land. The level of clothing and style was far superior to our own—despite their coolness, it felt rougher and more joyless. In the end, the Dschungel was a disappointment. There was no fun to be had, and the music worked only if you were drugged up to the eyeballs. Too many youths had hollow, empty eyes. They were not a creative force; they were just a reminder of a happier time at the Dschungel. Still, it was impressive to see because I saw beauty in those self-destructive, lonely-looking gods and goddesses of the night. They had seen things I still had to learn. They were absolute in their choices, a purity we lacked in our innocent playfulness and the safety of our lives.

Sneaking back into our hotel, we slept only an hour before we were back in the daylight, continuing our cultural tour de force under the guidance of our teachers. Berlin retains a very special place in my heart. I feel lucky to have been there when history was being made and unmade. The wall came down in 1989, and Berlin is a different place today.

13. USA

As my father's career roared forward like a Porsche 356 and my Bären Opa's business continued to do well, my family prospered. An addition was added to our house, and Aunt Christel and Uncle Yogi moved back into Oma's house next door. They had moved to Frankfurt for two years. We were having a wonderful time. In the attic, I was painting, drawing, and designing while Marc tried to hack into the Pentagon with his computer. We played a lot of sports, and my intimate life was developing wonderfully.

Only one objective was left unfulfilled: learning fluent English. My father was still obsessed with his children learning to speak English. Every day at work, he realized the importance of doing business in English and knew that English would soon be the primary language for international communication. As it happened, a new exchange program was introduced in Germany: language schools offered a one-year study program abroad in the United States. When we were 16, my cousin Anja and I were informed that we would be sent to America to spend a year in high school and learn the language. We had both been on language trips to the UK before, but not for a whole year. The US was considered a wonderful country at the time. My aunt just returned from a trip to California, and the stories and pictures she showed us were incredible. America was the land of wonderful landscapes and freedom. Germany was very pro-US, and it was considered a great honor and privilege to attend school there. We were immediately enchanted by the idea and wanted to go. Her boyfriend and my girlfriend were much less enchanted. I was madly in love with Caroline. It was with her I made love for the first time. We both lost our innocence together. She was 17, and I was 16. It was on an afternoon when her parents were gone. It was an awkward first time. We both were too worried about accidentally creating a baby than enjoying the moment. We made up for it the following times. Caroline was the one and only for me. I was very much in love with her. We were together for a year and serious, but in 1984, it was decided that Anja and I would leave for a year abroad. The preparations, applications, and interviews began, and both Anja and I

46

made it to the selected candidates list. We were going to the USA. I promised Caroline the year would fly by and we would be together again. It was hard for us to accept my absence for a year. There was nothing we could do; the preparations continued, and my departure date to the USA arrived far too quickly.

But before that, there would be a three-day introduction seminar in Frankfurt before we could board the planes bound for our assigned destinations. The exchange program did not allow us to choose where we would go. Indeed, it was the American host family that chose you. As such, the wheel of destiny chose Ohio for me, and for Anja, it would be Upstate New York. We both had hoped for California and knew nothing about Ohio or Upstate New York (remember, this is all pre-internet). Basically, we were clueless about the places we were being sent. A month before our departure, I did receive a photo of my new host family and their dog, but that was it.

We were young and craving adventure, so we didn't really care. The idea of being independent away from home was intoxicating. Our fantasies filled the gaps in any lack of information.

After our parents loaded the cars with our suitcases and delivered us to Frankfurt, we realized we were far from alone. About 150 youths from all over Germany were dropped off at this huge hostel. In the lobby, through many tears, we said our goodbyes. Once we checked into our rooms, which we shared with others, we quickly got acquainted, and the party started. The goal for the next three days was to party and drink as much alcohol as humanly possible. We knew in the US, we would not be allowed to drink since we were underage, so it was our mission to imbibe as much as we could before that. What followed was an epic three days of sex, drugs, and rock n' roll. We never slept. When we were finally transported to the airport, the hostel's staff was very glad to see us leave.

Anja and I boarded a plane bound for New York City's JFK airport, where, upon arrival, we would be separated for the next year. Anja and I had been very close since we were born and had never been apart for that long. In our minds, we thought we would visit each other every month. The enormous distances between places in the United

States were not yet apparent to us. On the plane, the party continued—partially because we were excited but mostly to mask our anxiety and fear. When we landed at JFK, I was so exhausted that my nose started to bleed like crazy. We were waiting in line for immigration, and my nosebleed was so bad that someone called emergency services, and they put me on a stretcher. I panicked as they strapped me in and rolled me away to the emergency room. I could not even say goodbye to Anja. I did not understand a word they were saying. Their American accents, mixed with medical terminology, were incomprehensible to me. Thankfully, after a doctor examined me and my crazy nosebleed from hell had stopped, they released me for my flight to Ohio. I was in a sorry state, covered in blood. I looked like I had just come from a chainsaw massacre. The guy next to me on the plane kept one eye on me the whole flight.

In Ohio, my host family, Al, Lynn, Matt, and Cuda, were waiting at the airport with big hand-drawn welcome signs. My host mother, Lynn, was a nurse, so as I tried to explain my bloody shirt, she took it in stride and got me all sorted out.

14. OHIO, WEST PORTSMOUTH HIGHSCHOOL

After a short drive, we arrived in West Portsmouth, Ohio. My new home was in a rugged part of town with gravel roads pocked with potholes. Theirs was a bluish wooden house, which was already odd to me since homes back home were made of stone. It was a warm, charming place, and after a short introduction to the family pets, I collapsed into my new bed and slept for two days. Occasionally, I got up to eat but then went straight back to bed. It was still summer break, and school had not started yet. Slowly, my body recovered from the severe punishment I inflicted in Frankfurt. I called Anja and assured her I was fine. We discussed the strange places fate had dropped us into and promised to call again soon—though calling each other was complicated; it was very expensive, and I did not have enough pocket money to call Anja often. After Anja, I called my family and my girlfriend, Caroline. I missed Caroline very much; we wrote to each other weekly after my first phone bill had arrived, and I found out the hard way that calling was too expensive. With the expense of long-distance calls, I realized I would need to write letters to keep in touch with home. After that, I was all alone in Ohio.

After those first few days of recovery, I slowly explored the area around the house. The lawns and houses were big, and I began to comprehend the enormous dimensions of America. There is no way to get around on foot. The only possible way to explore was by car, but I did not have a driver's license or a car. People in the neighborhood looked funny at me as I wandered around. Nobody went anywhere on foot.

Since my language level was still quite basic, I started watching TV with my two younger host brothers, Matt (9) and Cuda (6). First, we watched "He-Man" followed by big-time wrestling. I had never seen anything so crazy in my life. This was unknown in Europe: huge, muscled guys in weird costumes pretending to beat each other up. It was hilarious, especially as my new younger "brothers" tried to explain the rules—or absence of rules—in this spectacle. Both enjoyed demonstrating their latest wrestling moves by jumping on top of me. Daisy, the family poodle, happily joined in with frenzied barking. This was my earliest introduction to American culture.

My host dad, Al, was an assistant coach for the high school football team. I always wanted to learn to play football. In Germany, we only knew this uniquely American game through films. We did not know the rules but were fascinated by the players and their uniforms. Football jerseys were sought-after and difficult to get at home. Before coming to the US, I wrote to Al that I would love to try out and play if I could make the team. It was a dream come true, sitting in Al's pickup truck on the way to the practice field. I was excited and nervous since I had yet to meet anyone my age. We pulled into the high school parking lot and parked behind the locker room for the players. All the coaches and players were dressed casually in their football sweats and tees, no pads yet. It was Day 1, and we needed to get into shape before playing any actual football. Many of the guys were bigger than me, but I adored the sight of the football field, the bleachers, and the joking mannerisms of what I hoped would be my future teammates. They gave me a warm welcome, probably because they were more scared of Al and his "training" methods if they gave me a hard time. The initial introduction was quick and to the point before we started warming up. Then came the running. We were expected to compete against each other. I was fast and could outrun almost everyone. Later, I learned that the head coach, Dick Tipton, would tell the established players that if they didn't practice harder, he would put "The German" on the field. By the end of my first practice, I had a nickname: Pineapple Head. That was thanks to my outrageous, punk, New Romantic haircut: long on top, shaved on the sides, and a back part with crisscrossing lines carved into my scalp. For unfashionable, uninitiated Ohioans, this apparently resembled a pineapple. I took it in good fun and knew I had earned their respect. It was a good start.

I made the team, and a week later, we received our uniforms. I loved playing football and being a part of the team; it was a sport made for me. I loved to run and hit people. Since I had never played before, it was difficult to learn all the plays in a few weeks, but my coaches and teammates were kind and forgave my mistakes. I was more the mascot of the team than a vital player, but during the season, I played kickoff and defensive end.

Two weeks later, the high school officially started. The American school system and scheduling were very different from what I was used to in Germany. In Germany, you started school at 7:45 a.m., finished at 1:00 p.m., and ate lunch at home. The rest of the afternoon, you worked on your homework and had time to meet with friends in cafes. Sports were up to everyone as they saw fit. It was not linked to the school or organized by school coaches.

In the US, high school starts at 9:00 a.m. You ate lunch in the cafeteria and then returned to classes until 4:00 p.m. During the day, you had study hours during which you finished your homework. Immediately after school hours, you played sports or engaged in extra-curricular activities like music, arts, or other. I enjoyed the American system very much. It suited my sporty side and my talents. The German system had 13 years until graduation, but since the American system used just 12, I was already in my senior year.

I was fitting right in, but my hairstyle and clothes? Not so much. Two worlds had collided, and I had to bear a lot of ridicule in those first weeks. It did not bother me, mainly because I didn't understand half the insults directed my way. It turned out that all the football players got their hair cut by the head coach's wife. Her son, Mike, was our quarterback, and I found myself beside him in his mom's hair salon. My lines needed to be re-shaved into my scalp. This undertaking needed to be performed with a straight razor and required real skill to get the lines straight. Mike was sitting there reading his magazine and making fun of me until, suddenly, his mom exploded, calling him a narrow-minded coward who should respect the courage it took for me to be different. She called him a chicken and ridiculed his non-existent manhood. We were both stunned into silence.

When I was finished, Mike sat in the chair and decided on his new style. We left with two fresh haircuts: me with my pineapple head and Mike with a mohawk and two parallel lines shaved into the side of his head. To say the least, his girlfriend was not too happy when she saw him.

The next day in school, everyone was stunned and tried to make fun of us, but Mike was the quarterback, and quarterbacks are not to be ridiculed. He was sending a clear signal, and as a result, the team wanted new haircuts. It was already a great team with talented athletes, but once we all got wild haircuts from Mike's mom, we were unbeatable. Unstoppable. Once again, fashion transformed people in front of my eyes. We were easy to spot on the street, and no one dared touch us. We were legends in those days. It was our time, and, best of all, the girls loved us too. Go Senators! (Although we called ourselves the Siders.) It was the best football season in decades for Westside High. A simple haircut had changed it all.

The Westside was a poor area of Portsmouth and much feared, as I found out later in the year. The teammates, as kind as they were to me, were also savagely violent when challenged by outsiders. After having seen blood and vicious fighting as a punk in the UK, the West Siders made them look like school kids. I witnessed fights with guns and baseball bats, and I am not sure if the beaten ever left the hospital again. It was an understanding that nobody would insult West Siders and live to tell the story. It was made certain that this was understood by all outsiders. They were fiercely loyal to each other, which I respected, but I tried to stay away from the worst. Now I understand where the musical "Westside Story" got its inspiration from.

15. ART AND THE PRATT NATIONAL TALENT SEARCH SCHOLARSHIP

Football season ended, and I was no good at baseball or basketball, so it was time again for me to concentrate on my art. The art teacher, Mrs. Rapp, was a kind, curious woman who allowed me to join her class and draw whenever I had free time. It was a special privilege, and I took advantage of it often. In her class, she introduced me to artists and illustrators. It was a wild mix of everything; it was not curated at all. I had to pick an image of my choosing and then paint or draw it in different mediums. This approach produced many different artworks using different techniques. We would discuss my point of view, my dreams, and my ambitions. She saw my curiosity and joy for art and showed genuine interest in my artistic talent. This was all very new to me. Back home in Germany, art or fashion design was a breadless endeavor, a career without income or a future. My parents and all our family friends were sending their children to university to study medicine, architecture, engineering, or the law—not art. I'd never spoken to my family about my hopes and dreams. In my head, my future was still an unformed concept, but my art teacher drew those thoughts out of me through discussion. She directed me and showed me books and examples of design in its historical context. Our conversations inspired me to research deeper and farther from town since the library at our school was a small one. One day, she handed me a page torn from an art magazine. It featured an advertisement for the Pratt Institute's Annual National Talent Search. I had never heard of Pratt, but my teacher explained that it was one of the leading art and design schools in the world and encouraged me to enter the competition. After some hesitation, I agreed since, after all, I had nothing to lose. I was required to send a deck of 10 slides of my work. The guidelines asked for work executed in various mediums, such as pencil sketches, gouache, and watercolor. And so, my first portfolio began to take shape.

I didn't have much time to make the end-of-February deadline, and we had to start from scratch since all my previous work was still in Germany. Every day, I would come to her classroom to paint and draw as, step-by-step, a collection of thirty pieces took shape. It was a wide variety of pictures and media, and not all of it was good, but they were my first artistic creations, and I was very proud. It gave me enormous pleasure to paint and sketch. It was a universe that spoke to me, and I understood. As the weeks passed, Mrs. Rapp and I assessed and discussed my work in progress. Finally, we selected the ten best pieces and photographed them to create the slides. Taking the pictures for the slides was an adventure, too, because I had never photographed artwork before, but I learned fast and figured out the proper lighting. My submission to the competition came together in a frenzy of excitement and a little bit of despair. When we sent off my portfolio slides, we knew it would take five weeks to complete the judging and announce the results.

It was a long five weeks. Every day on my way home from school, I checked the mailbox until, finally, I looked inside to find a beautiful, heavy manila envelope. It felt important and stylish. I was not used to such posh envelopes and stationery. It felt like I'd received a letter from God. But I didn't open it right away. I kept it next to me on my nightstand, then brought it to school the next day. I put it in front of Mrs. Rapp like it was the Holy Grail, and we stared at it for some time. Then she uttered the magic words, "Open it."

I took a deep breath and tore it open. I slid out the letter and began reading. I couldn't believe my eyes—I had won a trip to New York to meet them!

The letter explained that because I was not an American citizen, I had not been considered for a prize as advertised. Instead, they were planning a special scholarship offered only to me. I was invited to go to New York City in May for a final interview.

We screamed with joy, hugged, and laughed. It was unbelievable. I was offered a significant art prize from a prestigious American art institution. It meant that other artists—professional artists and academics—thought I was good; they thought I was ready. They thought there was a place for me in a world that was closed to me back home in Germany.

16. NEW YORK, KEITH HARING, AND JOHNNY SEX

Before I knew it, I was packing my bag for New York and organizing the original artwork in my portfolio case, which was large, bulging, and difficult to carry. I had been to New York City before, but only long enough to have a massive nosebleed at JFK International Airport. I was nervous and excited when Al drove me to our local airport in Ohio.

On the ground in New York JFK, I hopped on a bus that brought me to Manhattan first; once there, I had to grab a cab headed to Brooklyn, where I had a room reserved in one of the Pratt dormitories. Since this was all pre-mobile phones and GPS, I had to find my way with an actual, impossible-to-fold-and-unfold map. I had no idea how far Brooklyn was from Manhattan or Manhattan from JFK. The bus ride, the first leg of the trip to Manhattan, brought me from the suburbs close to the airport to the skyline and the heart of New York. I was glued to the window, taking it all in.

The skyscrapers in Manhattan made London, Paris, and Berlin look like quaint country villages. It was incomprehensible to me how those buildings stood so straight with so much stone and steel. After about 30 minutes of staring straight up in awe, my shoulder reminded me how heavy my bag and portfolio were. My first impulse was to skip the cab and walk to Brooklyn. It was a nice day, and I needed to be at Pratt by 4 p.m., so I started walking, map in hand. I soon realized it was too far to walk, and I finally hailed a cab. Once the driver told me what the fare would be, I jumped back out and decided to take the subway instead.

The subway system did not strike me as complicated, but it still took some time to figure out how to get to Brooklyn. With the help of a friendly member of the NYPD, I was directed onto the correct train. I must have been quite a sight: dressed in my best fashion, an orange geometric print shirt matched with a red double pleated 50s suit trousers and pointy shoes, wielding a massive bag and a giant black rectangle containing my portfolio, after all, I was headed to a fashion school. I needed to dress to impress in my most outrageous clothes— making me appear less like a tourist from Ohio and more like an alien from the outer rim of the galaxy. It was liberating to break free and dress how I desired in New York. In New York, nobody cared.

Emerging onto the street from my Brooklyn station, I was disappointed by the drastic change in the cityscape. Brooklyn was not Manhattan. To me, it looked like a dirty, nearly abandoned suburb peppered with sad little shops. As I awkwardly unfolded my map, some shady-looking characters appeared from the shadows of a nearby newspaper stand, asking me if I needed some help. Instinctively, I knew they were sizing me up as potential prey. As we locked eyes, they realized I was too smart and football-strong to mess with. Plus, in my strange clothes and with my portfolio case that looked like a ship's sail, I looked like a lunatic. New York in 1985 was a dangerous, violent place. When I arrived, all five boroughs were on high alert due to a policeman being shot in the subway a week before. I felt confident, though. I was used to rough neighborhoods from my many nightlife exploits. And I soon learned that Pratt's local street thugs were kind to art students roaming their turf. Students were granted safe passage since they were fun and good "customers." So, as the alley thugs and I made fast friends, they pointed me in the right direction, and I once again started walking—once again forgetting the vast distances between places in America.

After an hour filled with detours and fully formed blisters inside my pointy shoes, I arrived at the Pratt Institute on Willoughby Ave. in Brooklyn. The main building was an impressive edifice that, for me, served as my gateway to paradise. *My* art school—a new universe filled with artists, designers, and other like-minded souls. The friendly guy at the entrance quickly found my name and explained how to get to my dorm room, which I would share with a roommate for the next three nights. Dorm living was all new to me. In Germany, we had no concept of dorms, and from my travels in England, I never encountered a dorm either. In Germany, going to university meant finding an apartment by yourself or staying in a youth hostel, but Dorms only exist on military bases. The Dorm at Pratt was glorious;

the building itself was hideous, but it was a building filled with art students! And parties!

My roommate, Jeff, was a boy from Texas who was hoping to study graphic design. We hit it right off and chatted happily as we unpacked and settled into our new environment. At 6 p.m., we made our way to the library for a meet-and-greet for all new students. The orientation started with a speech and slideshow about art and the history of fashion. It was boring, so I started checking out the crowd. There were some folks dressed like me, fashion being the universal language, so during the break, I sought them out, and we got on like a house on fire. Not everyone was there to study fashion, but as artists, we all shared similar interests and tastes. During dinner, the group bonded even more. There was a girl from California called "Cat" whom I immediately took a liking to. She had some friends who were undergrads at Pratt, so we went to a dorm party on campus where the coolest NYC nightclubs and must-see shops were discussed. The older students took us under their wing and explained how things worked at Pratt and where to go in NY. After midnight, I found my way back to my bed and fell asleep with a big smile on my face.

The next morning, we were split into groups relevant to our fields of study. The fashion crowd—flamboyant as Birds of Paradise—was ready to conquer the world. A senior led us to the fashion department, where we were allowed to join in on classes and sit for lectures.

In 1985, everything felt more relaxed than today. In the classroom, there was a free exchange of ideas and a lot of intellectual discussion about the power of clothes, the freedom of dressing, and the liberation of mankind through style and fashion. The faculty and students were open-minded and tended not to care about things like sexual orientation or people's moral and political agendas. Indeed, we were ready to break every taboo possible. As far as we were concerned, it was an era of "anything goes."

That afternoon we went on a shopping trip to Soho in Manhattan—the hippest, coolest neighborhood on Earth—even though, at the time, it was still a forgotten district of shitty warehouses where artists had loft studios, some fashion boutiques, and art galleries for the young, talented, and crazy. We split up into groups and explored the area. Cat, my Californian girlfriend, was with me when we stumbled upon a fashion boutique called Parachute, the ideal shop for fashion-hungry kids like us. We made it our mission to become immediate friends with the owners and staff, they were soooo cool. After many questions from us and much laughter, they invited us to an art opening that evening, so we promised to meet them back at the shop and attend together.

As it happened, the opening featured a then-little-known graffiti-style artist named Keith Haring. It was held in a small gallery packed wall-to-wall with fashion people, musicians, and artists. As we milled about, we noticed a cool-looking guy in the corner. It was the artist himself! We started talking. Since it was the Parachute Gang who knew him and monopolized the conversation, I drifted away to check out Keith's art. Prior to that night, I had no awareness of his work. I was amazed and fascinated by the walls and canvases filled with his now-iconic figures, forms, and scribbles. Staring at them, I thought they had the power of church windows. The powerful symbolism spoke to me. Keith's pictures told stories about fighting the system and sexual liberation. It was a fresh, graphic take on humanity's oldest story: the struggle between good and evil. The pictures were simultaneously simple—almost childish—and deeply complex. Even as a young man and a beginner artist, I knew I was in the presence of masterpieces created by a rare genius. I didn't know it at the time, but I was experiencing art in its original, ephemeral form. As the evening came to an end, it was time to head back to Brooklyn and my dorm pillow at Pratt.

When I woke on Saturday, I had two things on my mind. I knew that night I would go with the Parachute Gang to the infamous nightclub Danceteria, owned by the band Visage. But more importantly, that morning, I had my scholarship interview for the National Talent Search Prize. The reason I was in New York in the first place!

I was nervous about the interview and wondered about who might sit on my committee. I knew it would be made up of four members:

three faculty and one student. It was the first committee for me to meet ever, and I had no idea what to expect.

After a quick breakfast, I dressed and then obsessively shuffled and reshuffled my portfolio pieces. I arrived five minutes early to the fashion department and was told to wait in a lobby. Sitting there, alone, in anticipation of the biggest moment of my fledgling career as an artist and designer, a strange thing happened. My body and all my senses were swept away by a wonderful calmness. Some force, something pure and untroubled, took hold of me, and all my nervousness just evaporated. My mind was completely clear. Then, the door opened, and I was invited to enter with my portfolio.

Behind a large table stood four people unknown to me. The group consisted of a stylish woman in her mid-forties dressed in Gaultier, a man dressed in very stylish "Japanese" black clothes, probably by Yamamoto, a frumpy-looking character in grey who turned out to be the HR representative, and an older gentleman in a tweed jacket, oxford shirt, and bowtie, the Dean of Students. They asked me to come forward and lay my portfolio on the table. They began with a friendly conversation. I was expecting an FBI-style interrogation, so I was pleasantly surprised. They asked where I was from and how I came to be standing in front of them. All my cautiousness disappeared, and the words flowed out of me with ease: my upbringing in Germany, my art teacher, Mrs. Rapp, in Ohio, my passion for art and design, and my dreams for the future. They interjected now and again with questions, and then, before I knew it, my interview was over. I packed up my portfolio and exited the room. In the lobby, I was informed that I would be notified of the results by mail. My interview was over, and I was now free to do as I pleased for my remaining time in New York.

Outside the building, I sat on a park bench, looked up, and watched the clouds pass by, still feeling that sense of serenity. I can't recall how long I stayed there, but at some point, I felt hungry and made my way to the student union for something to eat.

That night, we prepared to celebrate our time at Pratt at a farewell party some students had arranged for us. At midnight, though, I still had plans to accompany the Parachute Gang to the Danceteria.

The farewell party was packed with fashion students enjoying music, booze, drugs, and each other. As midnight approached, I found myself the only one sober enough to make the journey into Manhattan, so I decided to take the subway alone to meet up with the Parachute Gang. I had to go since this was a once-in-a-lifetime opportunity, I had no idea if I would ever return to New York. Passing my local gang member friends on the way to the subway platform, they warned me to be careful, but, as always, my ignorance was bliss, and I ignored them. On the subway, I was alone in my filthy, graffiti-covered train car with an NYPD cop. He stared at me in disbelief. Just a week before, a cop was shot in a subway station. Now, there were police everywhere on the platforms and on the trains to make sure no more violence would occur. I had read about it but never felt there was real danger concerning my midnight train to Manhattan. I finally made it unharmed.

At the door at Danceteria, there was a small crowd gathered. It was still early. Dressed to kill in my high-waisted, mint green, suede leather, pleated suit trousers, a faded black "John Wayne" shirt, and pointed shoes, I presented myself to the "door." The look was inspired by my hero, David Bowie. There was nobody else dressed remotely close to as stylish as I was. As always, it was a gamble, especially since I did not know the NY scene. It worked out, fortunately, I knew what it took to enter the most exclusive nightclub and sufficiently impressed the bouncer. In fact, it was the main *girl* at the door who gave me a nod, lifted the velvet rope, and waved me in. She was a true "girl with the Dragon tattoo," all dressed in black leather. At the entrance, I paid and entered the main room on the ground floor. The club was sort of empty, with its wide dance floor abandoned and the DJ playing standard, boring music. The Danceteria had four floors, so I bought a drink and started to explore. The second floor featured a large bar area, blaring punk rock, and television screens broadcasting hardcore gay porn in black and white. Wanting to ascend the stairs once more, the bartender informed me that floors three and four were closed until later that night. The bartender was topless, and nobody else was in the "hardcore area" and we started a friendly, teasing conversation. It was quite common to flirt and get to know people that way. He liked my outfit and asked what brought me to NY. I told him about fashion, Pratt, and the Parachute gang. It turned out he knew them well. He was friendly, the bartender, so I chatted with him until the Parachute Gang arrived. We stood there drinking and talking, cock-sucking and ass-fucking flashing on screens all around us as the room filled with people. We decided to try downstairs again, and it was awful: horrible, non-fashion people dancing to stupid hetero pop. By that time, the third floor had opened, so we made our way up there, briefly delayed by another bouncer who controlled access to the third-floor VIP area, a smaller, exclusive dance floor. We had no problem getting in since the Parachute Gang was well-connected in the New York nightlife scene. What a difference! Exclusivity has its benefits! The third-floor DJ was fantastic, as was the curated third-floor crowd. The clothes and style of those New York creatures of the night were far more outrageous than anything in Berlin. Berlin was rough and dark, but New York was glamorous. The boys and the girls (you were never certain who was which) were beautiful and exotic. AIDS was not yet fully a factor that stopped strangers from making out, and the toilets were a crazy place where the only existing rule was "anything goes." The only downside was that this caused the bathrooms to always be fully occupied. I was in heaven but had to pee, so I made my way back downstairs.

By then, the second floor was mostly empty. I guess the loud punk music and hardcore porn were not for everybody. After relieving myself, I felt like chatting some more, so I returned to my new friend, the bartender. Into my second drink, he informed me he had a "surprise" and told me to wait at the bar for two minutes. This gave me just enough time to start to worry about what he had in mind. Just about ready to leave, he returned and told me to follow him—so I did, back up the stairs. At the top, I was presented to yet another bouncer—this one being the coolest, sexiest trans I had ever seen. She winked, opened the door, and welcomed me to the fourth floor.

No words can properly describe what I laid my eyes on. "The Rocky Horror Picture Show" was kindergarten compared to this.

There was a birthday party in progress for Johnny Sex. I had never heard of Johnny Sex, but his friends immediately impressed me. There were women leading boys on a leash, dressed in leather and fur. There

61

was a group with rhinestones glued to their shaved heads, wearing exquisitely tailored suits, ball gowns, glitter, space suits, and uncanny versions of Ziggy Stardust. Indeed, David Bowie would have looked like a farm boy next to those New York gods and goddesses. As I moved among them in a fugue state, I steered clear of all their sexual advances. And then, the elevator slid open to reveal His Lordship himself: Johnny Sex.

He wore a knee-length white fur coat over his bare torso. His trousers were low-cut, skin-tight, black leather, and laced at the sides. His foot-long, peroxide-bleached white hair stood straight up, defying gravity—a cheeky wave curled at the top. The sides of his head were shorn clean, and his eyelids were crystal-encrusted, sparkling like mirrored balls wherever he set his gaze. On either side of Mr. Sex stood a girl dressed in a way that would make Dita Von Teese blush. He bathed in our cheers, the king and queens of a new world order had arrived, free and equal to make a dream—any dream—come true and live it, even if it was for just one night.

Although it was his birthday, Johnny was the main musical act. He strode onstage and started singing "Hustle with Your Muscle" and everyone in the room absolutely lost their minds.

The next day, I woke up in a sun-drenched loft in Manhattan. The kind girl who offered me shelter for the night was an adorable textile designer. We ate breakfast, and then, to my surprise, she drove me back to Brooklyn on the back of her Harley. No description can quite capture the visceral feeling of sitting astride a motorcycle, arms wrapped around a gorgeous textile designer, the wind in your hair (when you still have it), driving down Broadway in New York City, then over the Brooklyn Bridge. At the Pratt gate, we kissed goodbye. I packed my bags and left for Ohio.

Watching the city skyline recede below the clouds as my plane climbed from JFK, I vowed to return one day.

17. OHIO IS NOT NEW YORK, PROMISES AND A DREAM HAS TO WAIT

Stepping off the plane in Ohio, I wandered through the small terminal toward the exit, where Al was waiting to drive me back to Portsmouth. It was good to be back, and everyone in my host family was so kind, curious, and supportive. They wanted to hear all about my adventures in the Big Apple. In school the next day, everyone wanted to hear my stories. My art teacher, Mrs. Rapp, wanted to know every detail. I tried to explain about the Danceteria and John Sex, but I realized there was no way they could truly understand. They did not want to understand. The gay androgynous side of fashion upset them and their way of life. For the first time, it was apparent to me that not everyone wants to hear the truth. For many, the concept of total creative and personal freedom and transformation is scary. So, I kept my stories about Pratt and the magnificent sights of New York, leaving out those strange, beautiful creatures of the night I wanted so badly to become a part of.

High school and daily routines soon set in until, about two weeks later, I arrived home to find everyone sitting around the table, waiting for me to see that my letter from Pratt had arrived. I was nervous again. What news would the letter hold this time? This time I did not wait and tore open the envelope. It was a wonderful letter. They wanted me! Prior to this Pratt had informed me that I was not eligible to participate in the National Talent Search because it was only for US citizens, but that they had finally decided to create a special scholarship for me and offered me a full ride. Everything would be paid for. It was finally real.

Loud cheers erupted around the table! I would go to Pratt! I called my art teacher, Mrs. Rapp, and promised to show her the letter the next day in class. Graduation was fast approaching, so right there and then, I decided my fashion career would start in New York and I would not go back to Germany.

Just before my eighteenth birthday, I got a call from my father inviting me to meet him in Chicago. He was invited to an automotive convention to speak on behalf of Porsche about a new magnesium casting technique he was specializing in. It was a great birthday gift. I hadn't seen anyone from my family for a year, having only exchanged phone calls and letters. I was excited to travel to another big American city to see my father. We stayed downtown in a fancy hotel and spent that first night chatting and getting caught up. I helped him practice his presentation for the next day and accompanied him to the convention, where I met many of his colleagues for the first time. His speech went well, and that night, we were invited to a fancy dinner at a famous steakhouse restaurant. We dressed up and were picked up by a limousine in front of our hotel. The restaurant turned out to be a private members-only club, which presented a small problem. Members and guests were required to wear a jacket and tie, both of which I did not have. The maître d' helped and provided me with a complimentary blazer and clip-on tie. The steak that night was the best I'd ever had, and I was even allowed to drink wine.

The next day was Saturday, and we had the whole day to ourselves. This gave me the perfect opportunity to explain to my father everything that had happened in New York and the Pratt Institute, the details of my scholarship opportunity, and my decision to become a fashion designer. My father listened patiently and was open-minded. He always only wanted the best for me, but he was concerned that a career in fashion design was a challenging way to make a living. He didn't take it seriously. There's no doubt he thought this was only a phase I was going through, one I would eventually grow out of. He was proud of my achievement through this first art competition but cautioned that it was too early to decide on such an important matter as my college education. An American high school diploma would not be recognized in Europe (since school lasted just 12 years in the U.S. versus 13 years in Europe at the time), so my options to study in Germany would be limited if things didn't work out. After a long, passionate discussion with my father, he proposed the following: I would return to Germany, finish my high school education, and graduate there. After that, I would complete my mandatory military service, and then I would decide on my college studies. My father advised that if, at that point, I still wished to pursue fashion design, I could enroll in Germany, where the university was tuition-free. And finally, if I earned my undergraduate degree and wanted to pursue post-grad studies, he would finance my master's degree at any university in the world.

This plan was not what I had in mind. Frankly, I didn't like it at all. The best I could do was promise Dad that I'd consider his proposal. The next morning, we hugged our goodbyes, and once again, I was on a plane back to Ohio.

With only four weeks left in the school year, I would soon find myself back home in Germany. Every day, I pondered my dad's big plan for my academic future. Also, I was still in love with Caroline, and, in the end, it was she who convinced me to come home and accept my father's proposal.

My time in West Portsmouth came to a close. We took our senior class trip to Myrtle Beach (which is a whole book in itself), then walked for graduation. Days later, I was standing in the terminal at JFK, reuniting with Anja as we boarded our flight home to Germany. It had been a year since we'd seen each other. Unfortunately, Anja's time in Rochester had not been nearly as fun, eventful, and positive as my experience in Ohio. I'd been incredibly lucky with the host family I drew and the teachers, coaches, and mentors that entered my life at such a critical and formative time. I was leaving America with a deep sense of gratitude and the confidence I would need for all the adventures that lay ahead.

18. COMING HOME; MAKING PLANS, ANATOLE LAPIN AND PERSEVERANCE

Anja and I talked the whole flight back to Germany. It was so good to have her back in my life! In Frankfurt, our parents were there to pick us up. We were home, and we were both different in many ways. We had matured. The extremes of living in a different culture and the challenges we had to navigate daily had given us a broader horizon. It had given us perspective. Our year abroad had changed us in ways our family and friends would never fully understand.

Anja seemed to have an easier time settling in than I did. New York, England, and Ohio, and my years haunting libraries had formed me into a restless wanderer, hungry for new challenges and opportunities for growth. Germany had become too small for me. I wanted to explore the world. Now that I knew this, the hardest part would be surviving the years at home until I could move towards an international fashion world once more. I would have to be patient, I realized. It would take time to leave home again.

Our families and friends were wonderful in welcoming us back. But it wasn't all good vibes. Caroline dropped a bomb: she had fallen in love with my best friend Klaus, breaking my heart for years to come. I loved her deeply and was hurt beyond measure. Maybe it was for the best. After she broke it off, I disappeared into my attic studio and drowned myself into working and sketching. As far as school went, it was a rocky start. The problem was that I was lazy, to be honest, I was bored. The curriculum and teachers did not interest me nor motivate me to learn. It was too easy, but at the same time, I could not be bothered to engage. In response to my lack of ambition, my father offered yet another proposition: if I kept my grades up, he would not interfere with my nightlife escapades. This motivated me, freedom in exchange for some schoolwork was a good offer. I accepted it readily, and this concept of "work hard, play hard" has stayed with me as a core philosophy ever since.

Another important figure entered my life in that period, Bernd Mack, who was based in Leonberg. He was an artist and in his early thirties. He had created an "evening class" art school. He had his studio in the local Gallery complex called the Glaskasten," and in this complex, he held evening classes in figure drawing or nude drawing. I took several nude drawing classes with him before and started again. He was a good listener, and we talked a lot about my dream to become a fashion designer. He was a formative figure and supported me through this period. Later, Bernd relocated to Stuttgart and created the art school "P.ART."

This was a productive time for me. I learned to draw and sketch the human body. My training was purely artistic, though. With Bernd, I did not practice any fashion-related studies. Being back in the small town of Leonberg, I became increasingly restless. Starting to research into German fashion Universities, it quickly became apparent that in Germany, fashion was not an important part of our value system. We dressed because we had to, not because we embraced it as part of life. In German culture, we Germans thought of fashion as an unnecessary distraction. This made German design schools inferior to schools in other fashion-relevant countries like France, Italy, and the U.K. Therefore, I started researching fashion programs at universities in Paris, London, and Milan. The European fashion capitals. But sticking to the agreement with my father, I also had to first find a German school for my undergraduate degree, then set my sights on an international school for my MFA. All the while, my father remained confident that I would grow out of fashion and want to become an engineer. He had no idea that I was meticulously planning my next ten fashion years instead. I had graduated in Ohio, but my German school did not recognize the year abroad and my US diploma and I had to repeat the 12th grade. This put me into a new school year with peers I did not know. Now, to finish and graduate, I had two more years until I would finally receive my "Abitur" and leave school once more.

In the two years leading up to my graduation in Germany, I visited many fashion schools.

At the end of the eighties, there wasn't exactly a clear concept of how to make fashion design a career. The job of "Fashion Designer" did not really exist in the educational system. Fashion design was a finishing school for girls before they got married. Many of the educational and industry opportunities we take for granted today were still evolving, so, for me, this meant I had to be more imaginative, proactive, and inventive about the path I would take to achieve my dreams. For example, just finding the addresses of fashion schools was an arduous job at the time. I had to write to international fashion magazines, like Vogue, asking them for school addresses. Handwritten letters to magazine editors, sent by snail mail! I'd wait for weeks or longer in anticipation of a response. One thing to my advantage was that it was very rare for a young person in Germany to be researching international university fashion programs, so there was a decent response rate to my queries. It was an exciting game to reach out to people and build up a network. It was even more exciting when they returned letters and answered mine.

The one thing I knew for certain was that Germany was suffocating me. I'd had a taste of seeing the world, and I wanted more. Other countries had so much to teach me, each with its own language, culture, and aesthetics. I wanted so badly to travel, discover, learn, and deepen my understanding of the world and my place in it. After a great deal of time and effort, I compiled a definitive list of addresses and contact details for the most famous art and design schools in the Western world: Pratt, which I already knew; Parsons (New York); Studio Berçot (Paris); School of Chambre Syndical de la Couture (Paris); Marangoni (Milan); Central Saint Martins (London); Kingston (UK) and the Royal College of Art (also London). It was an impressive list for an eighteen-year-old with no money in his pockets but ample dreams and endless energy. How they would come alive was now the challenge.

My father had no intention of financing any reconnaissance missions to these colleges since he never wavered from his hope that I would drop the idea of fashion school altogether. Therefore, the solution to my money woes was summer jobs, of which I had many.

Whenever I saved up enough, I'd take off in my car or plane for a long weekend to visit another school on my list.

Paris was first. I'd never been there before and was awed by its overwhelming beauty. With my portfolio tucked under my arm, I made my way to all the schools on my list, meeting with faculty and students. People were always helpful and enthusiastic, and each school was impressive in its own way. I began to recognize and compare the differences in curriculum and teaching approaches when it came to fashion design. In France, my lack of language skills was a big roadblock. My communication with people at Studio Berçot and Chambre Syndicale de la Couture was more through smiles and gestures than words. But what quickly became apparent was that the language of great design was universal. We communicated through our work. I showed my portfolio, and, in turn, the students showed me their work. Berçot was the most creative—very cutting-edge, very French. I couldn't see myself there, though. I thought I would have felt too much like an outsider. Chambre Syndical de la Couture was a technical school based on "making" skills and traditional tailoring techniques. It was not focused on the new, evolving world of fashion but rooted in old-school craftsmanship of the highest level. Parsons, in Paris, was the school that resonated most with me—probably because its primary language was English. It was a small school that still needed to establish itself. Also, to study in Paris, you had to first be enrolled in its New York fashion program.

In Milan, Marangoni was a wonderful experience. The people there were warm and welcoming, and I immediately felt at home. The students were younger than usual due to a difference in the school system. They were more like high school students—with incredible style and craft—but lacking the excitement and sophistication characteristic of the fashion happening in Berlin, Paris, London, and New York.

Next came Central Saint Martins and the Royal College of Art in London. This required more planning because I couldn't just drive there in my car. Central Saint Martins was the newer of the two and the coolest school on the planet. As a result, the faculty couldn't make much time for me, and even the students were not very forthcoming.

It was a fiercely competitive environment. Everyone was very protective of their designs, and I only caught glimpses of the students' work. It was a cutthroat environment, which I did not believe in. At the time, they did not have a graduate program either.

On the contrary, the Royal College of Art was very welcoming. The folks there took the time to show me around and explain everything. The student work was outstanding—the best I'd seen at any of the colleges. They had such clarity of vision when it came to what design is. The RCA was also the only graduate MFA program for fashion design in Europe. They were very selective in their student admissions.

The RCA building itself was a crude high-rise concrete block; situated right next to the Royal Albert Hall, it had a spectacular view overlooking the park. I had many questions, and I still didn't quite understand what qualifications were needed for graduate school. A very kind professor patiently explained that I first needed to finish my BFA degree to be eligible to apply to the Royal College's MFA program. The professor was kind and showed me some incredible student work—better than anything I'd seen so far. I fell in love with the idea of attending and began forming a plan in my mind to attend there after finishing undergraduate college, which meant that I still had to find an undergraduate college in Germany with a decent fashion program. The thing is, Germany is good when it comes to logic and manufacturing fine-tuned automobiles, but the emotional, instinctive realm of beauty and clothing is not our forte. After months of research, only two German schools were up to the standard I was looking for. Pforzheim Hochschule für Design and the Fachhochschule für Gestaltung in Hamburg (which everyone simply called "Armgartstrasse"). As far as Berlin went as a potential college destination, those fashion schools were not yet fully functional due to Berlin's location in the Eastern Block on the other side of the Wall.

The Pforzheim school was only thirty minutes by car from my home, and I had friends there. It was a good school, well organized, but too small for my ambitions. I wanted to be in a large, cosmopolitan, international city, which left me with only one choice:

Armgartstrasse in Hamburg and afterward the Royal College in London.

My research and visits to those other European Universities allowed me to observe the different approaches to fashion and teaching styles in each country and the unique atmospheres and aesthetics at each school. I came to understand that each establishment had its own chemistry—a mix of campus, faculty, and student body—and, later, that was the deciding factor for my choices: "Chemistry." Most schools, in their own ways, are good, but the peer quality around you is a major factor in your development. You want to play with the best to become the best. It is the level of competition you seek out for yourself that will ultimately make you succeed. Not only the best faculty but also the best students around you will shape and form you. That said, the Royal College clearly had the most talented faculty and students of all the schools I visited. Its acceptance rate was notoriously low. The Royal College received applications from the best artists and designers from around the world.

So, I knew what I wanted, and I knew the odds. The plan was made. The only thing left to do was get to work and make it happen.

As I started to work on my fashion design career, I also needed to make money. On one of those jobs, I ended up at Porsche Weissach in the technical design center. My father had helped me get a four-week holiday job there. I was helping to update technical drawings, which were still drawn by hand in those days. The studio was huge, with big vertical drawing tables. Next to our office was the Porsche design studio, headed by the famous and notorious Anatole Lapine. Mr. Lapine was a race driver in his youth, now a car designer at Porsche, he had just developed the legendary 928 model. Since my father wanted to know if my work was any good, he arranged for us to meet. The day of our meeting approached, and I prepared a portfolio to show to Mr. Lapine. In his office, Mr. Lapine just looked at me in a grumpy mood. He had no time and did not want to deal with me. He immediately started a monologue about young designers and their inability to design. He stated that none of the new generation had any style or the necessary work ethic. I let him talk for twenty minutes, and then he focused on me and wanted to know what I was doing in his office. I told him about my plan to study fashion design and that I had received a scholarship from Pratt University in New York. Mr. Lapine laughed and told me that this was no reason to waste his time. I suggested I show him some work and would be happy to hear his opinion if I was any good. He finally agreed to look at them, and I walked him through my designs. Finally, he was quiet for 15 minutes. At the end of my presentation, he started to advise me that schools would only add another 10% to my God-given talent. He explained that we all have a skill set and talents that we could not enhance further with training. He explained that, like a basketball player, we would never succeed if we were not tall enough from the start. Looking at my work, he stated that I had talent, but if it would be enough, he could not tell. Then, he sent me back to my technical drawing studio. I was upset about his rough and unpolite manner and told my father later that this man was impossible and rude. My father laughed and stated that this was a well-known fact. Thirty years later, looking back, I must admit that Mr. Lapine was right and that his assessment of a maximum 10% growth through schooling is correct, but I also must add to his point of view that experience is a factor he did not consider. Experience, persistence, and determination are what makes a designer successful. Talent is only part of the equation.

19. ART MAJOR

Back from my year in Ohio, I had to declare my two major study subjects concerning my final two years towards my Abitur. I was still in German high school, and I declared my two majors to be Art and English Literature. It was a no-brainer since, during my year in America, my English had improved to an expert level, and I did not have to do much work in class. On the other hand, German schools took art and art history very seriously, so I had to work hard in my art major. Art was an art class, and no design was taught, especially no fashion design. Fashion design was considered a superficial pastime. They didn't see it as a medium worthy of artistic expression, which, by the way, offended me to the core. Fashion was the oldest language we spoke as a species. It was a form of communication that was historically relevant—from the lower classes to the military to the clergy, the aristocracy, and all the way up to royalty, clothes defined who you were for thousands of years. Everything in life is connected to our clothes, a visual language that most of us have forgotten or never learned to speak. Over the millennia, animals have evolved their fashion language through mating rituals. Male birds, for example, seduce potential mates with their exquisite plumage as they dance in swirls of color—just as our contemporary titans of industry, politicians, and even modern royalty strut and sashay in bespoke garments of the finest thread and craftsmanship to exude power, sensuality, and grace.

Nevertheless, my classmates disagreed. They were offended by the very idea that a person's outfit is a form of sculpture and that a fashion designer is an artist on equal par with a sculptor, painter, playwright, or novelist. It made for some heated discussions, and I would often grow angry in class, quoting references from fashion history and trying to convince them of the importance of fashion in every generation's movement. But my efforts fell on deaf ears. My German art education was destined to be a traditional one. It's a good thing I was a talented draftsman and painter. Portraits were my first endeavor.

My subjects were my beloved creatures of the night: punks, gays, lesbians, musicians, thinkers, drinkers, artists, searchers, and lost souls. My painting professor, Frau Kresslein, was intrigued and supported my choice of subject matter and point of view. We connected, and she took me under her wing.

German art instruction was very thorough, presenting lessons in all traditional forms and media—including ceramics and sculpture, from clay to wood to stone. After my initial resistance and role as "class pain-in-the-ass"—arguing passionately for the proper respect of fashion designers and their place in history—I began to settle into the curriculum, realizing the depth of knowledge and pure pleasure I received from my art training. The history of art was a long, evolving story that I was now a part of—to which I could now contribute my chapter. So many once-fuzzy concepts and theories began to dial into focus as I accepted that I had much to learn from my instructors and allowed Frau Kresslein to become my mentor. She was not like my art teacher in Ohio, from whom I learned certain techniques. Frau Kresslein taught me the meaning of art and its deep revelations—and trust me, Germans can go deep. She made me discover and understand how art spoke. A symbolic language without words. The ancients spoke to me. I learned to paint and draw master copies, which then evolved into my own art. Art became fashion, and fashion became art. As beautiful as the dance of that Bird-of-paradise, I swirled shapes and color into my fashion paintings, slowly learning how to merge the two forms into a harmonious "one."

At the end of my two-year studies, the finals approached, I was required to pass a two-part exam in my art major: a written and then a practical part. For the written exam, I was asked to compose an essay— for the review, we had to choose between a sculpture by Ernst Barlach and a landscape painting by Paul Cézanne. I chose Barlach because I liked his crude handling of tools and his delicate balance of beauty and suffering. We had to write a three-hour analysis of the artwork. For the practical second part of the exam, I was required to complete a winter landscape in the Grisaille technique. We could use any material we liked, from graphite, charcoal, pencil, to acrylic or oil paint. A painting all in gray tones. Lucky for me, I was the master of gray shades. Bernd Mack, my evening class mentor from the Glaskasten, had taught me a special way to mix different mediums with graphite dust. Once the dust was mixed into the painting dissolvent, it produced the most incredible gray shades. My graphite shading and blending technique were fast and furious, and I was ready to go. We had five hours to paint, draw, and complete our one piece of artwork, our "Grisaille Winter Landscape."

My artwork was finished in an hour, and it looked fabulous, but what to do for the remaining four hours? I decided to start a second piece. Our final exams were a serious matter, and an official from the state, some boring bureaucrat, sat in our classroom to make sure we didn't cheat. Frau Kresslein was also in the room with us. She knew me and knew how fast I worked. When she realized what I was about to do, she slowly made her way over to me. Realizing that I was prepared to drown that guy in a tsunami of paintings, she whispered over my shoulder, "Only two." I turned, wanting to protest, but when I saw the concern in her eyes, I understood she was only trying to help. For once, I kept my mouth shut and did what I was told.

With much time on my hands, I finished the two landscapes—then got bored and started messing with them. I still have those paintings, and it hurts to look at them. They were perfect before I spent three hours messing them up. Thank God for the bourgeois taste of bureaucrats, because he loved them, and I received a good grade. It taught me an important lesson: There are talentless hacks and imbeciles in this world who have no taste and no clue, but that will never stop them from evaluating and grading you.

When I asked Frau Kresslein afterward why she had stopped me at two paintings, her answer was simple yet disturbing. She said, "Jens, the world does not want outstanding; it wants what it expects— and nothing more." She basically said that if I had "shown off" by displaying my full potential, I would have been punished with a bad grade. This shocked me to my core. I have always tried to work my hardest and achieve the most. It had never occurred to me that such effort and display of talent could be viewed as negative or that I could be punished for them. I realized that day that an artist exists in two worlds: the world of bureaucratic mediocrity and the world of the few

who see the truth in excellence. Striking a balance between them will
be a lifelong challenge.

20. WAR AND HAMBURG

Finally, I graduated for good. To graduate in Germany is a simple affair: you get your degree by mail, go to a few parties, and say goodbye. It was uneventful—no ceremony, gowns, or hats. The summer break was planned to be a road trip with my brother in the USA. We started in California, where he had stayed with his host family during his exchange year, and we set off with a rental car to Ohio. It was a glorious trip. This side of the United States was new to me. The vast distances and changing landscapes were breathtaking. Our destination was Ohio, where we visited my old friends and family, and then we flew to New York for some great parties. My friends from the Parachute boutique were still there, and we saw new clubs like Nell's and the Tunnel, which was a big eye-opener for my brother. He had to dress up to get into the clubs. He was not used to the preparations since the club scene back home was not of interest to him. Danceteria was no more and had closed its doors for good. As our trip came to an end, I had to face another necessary evil before starting my fashion education.

At home, the military waited for me, something I was not looking forward to, but it was mandatory, and we had to do it. A fashion designer was not well placed in the military. Uniforms and boot camp drills were not my thing. They placed me in a tank division in the middle of nowhere. It was dreadful. I hated it; you were not allowed to leave in the evenings, only on the weekends.

In good old Jens' style, I quickly converted the uniforms into a fashion project, much to the dismay of my superiors. Since I was bored, I looked at all the ill-fitting garments and decided to refresh my company's look. The cargo pants were adjusted and made slimmer for all my friends. Shirts were made smaller, and small styling details were added. We were the best-looking unit there.

After three months of boot camp, probably because I was having trouble, I was transferred to the medical team. The company doctor needed a new assistant, and it was decided I was the man for the job.

I became the company doctor's assistant. This was a very influential and powerful position. Most importantly, I could shed the dreadful "olive." I was allowed to wear white, and nobody bothered me once I started restyling this uniform. Since I was the person you had to get past to get a doctor's appointment, everybody was nice to me. General or private equally! I had enormous power. The whole base had to make appointments through me when they needed medical treatment, which was often. Not only was I scheduling all appointments, but I was also vaccinating everybody. If our medical staff didn't like you, we used blunt needles, crude but effective, and they all knew it. Those measures were necessary to maintain our status in the pecking order.

The military was a rough place, a melting pot where everybody was mixed, rich or poor; it didn't matter. Another perk of the medical unit was the ambulance cars. We had to take a certain number of emergency driving lessons. Driving with sirens at high speed was a skill vital to our jobs. My favorite was on weekend duty when we took the ambulance car and drove with sirens through the villages to get pizza. There were no rules you had to follow. During my daily duties, I sat in on every examination the doctor conducted, and I learned a lot about medicine. Biology was one of my secret passions in school, and I learned quickly. My mother was hopeful I would become a doctor, and I thought about it, but it was just too boring. Life is too short, and I wanted the excitement of fashion and art, not a stable life.

As the year passed, the application date to my chosen fashion university in Hamburg, Armgartstrasse, came closer. I had to get into that fashion school to make my dreams come true. Pratt was gone, and the new door to fashion design was not open yet. To get in, you had to send in your portfolio. Once your portfolio was accepted, you had to go to Hamburg to pass a two-day test. To get accepted was difficult; it was a very selective process. Getting into Armgartstrasse was crucial to being able to apply to the Royal College later. While in the military, I converted an unused storage room into my design studio and worked hard to get the mandatory portfolio done. Bernd Mack and my friend Boris helped me. They reviewed my work and were crucial in getting me ready. Finally, the portfolio was sent to Hamburg, and I waited. It was nerve-wracking since it was the only application I had sent out. If I failed, I would have to wait another year since Armgartstrasse only accepts new students once a year. So, I waited, and finally, the letter arrived. The letter came in an official envelope, no Manila paper this time. As I opened it, I started smiling. I had passed! The first step to Hamburg was accomplished; my portfolio was accepted, and they invited me for the test. The test was a mystery; nobody knew what it was about. All my friends were of little use; they were not trying to become fashion design students. The letter only stated the materials we had to bring. It sounds funny that nobody knew more since we all made and designed clothes, but fashion design and entry exams were still unknown territory. I asked everybody, and the best I received was, "don't worry, it will be fine."

The day arrived to drive to Hamburg. I packed my car with the necessary items and looked forward to staying with my friend Robert. He was so kind to receive me and take me in for the long weekend; the dreaded test was scheduled for Thursday and Friday. I arrived in Hamburg on a Wednesday night. Robert was waiting, and we had a quick meal. I was nervous and anxious about what the next day would bring.

The next morning, after a restless night in a new city, Robert drove me to the Armgartstrasse and dropped me off. There I was, standing in front of those doors that would decide my faith, and I entered. After a short check-in ceremony, I was ushered into a school room and seated at a table. The first part was a drawing test. I had to draw my "hand holding an object of my choice" in pencil. We had three hours to complete the test. This was easy; I was used to sketching and managed well. The second part, after a short break for lunch, was "color and form." We had to paint a landscape in gouache or watercolors out of our imagination. This part was more challenging to me: what technique should I choose? Which colors? Since I was used to copying Cezanne in my art major in school, I started painting a landscape in his style. I improvised by adding chalk to the painting. After another grueling three hours (and this time, I needed the three hours), the first day was done. One more to go! At the end of day one, we were informed we had finished the first part and to return the next day at the same time.

Robert was waiting outside when I was exiting the school. I was exhausted but happy. He inquired how it went, and I confidently told him it went well. We had food, and Robert casually told me that we must go out that night to a new club. I was apprehensive but ready to see the town's nightlife. He promised me we wouldn't be late and I would see something new. After dinner and a bottle of wine, we dressed up. Robert told me to dress lightly and be comfortable because we would dance. I just looked at him and thought, "What is he talking about?" He was driving, and we went to the "Opera House" on the Reeperbahn, the Hamburg red light district. It was one of the first clubs in Germany, next to the "Front" club, where they played Acid House. I had heard of Acid House before but did not really know what to expect. Robert knew the door guys, and we entered without any problems. The room was huge, with massive loudspeaker towers in each corner, and the space was empty. Only a few people were milling in the open space. A new era had begun; this was the beginning of something new, and very few people knew about it, and then Robert introduced me to "Eva." Once I met her, the music amplified, and I started dancing by myself and with the music. The experience was out-of-this-world. I could feel every beat, and every note of the songs played. We danced all night. At five in the morning, we made it home and went to bed.

In the morning the next day, I had to wake up at seven to get ready for the second part of my test. Robert laughed as he woke me up; he hadn't slept all night. He made strong coffee and then drove me back to school. I was still dancing in my head when I entered the school for the second time.

The test in the morning was a free piece where we could choose to paint whatever we wanted. Since I was used to painting portraits, I painted a fashion portrait for the test. It was easygoing, and I painted while I was humming to the music from the night before. The piece came along nicely, and I was happy. The second part of the day was an interview with the faculty. This was more challenging, but in the afternoon, after lunch, I was sufficiently sober to engage in a normal conversation. The interviews were held in separate rooms, and we had to explain our portfolios to the professors and then answer questions.

This presented no challenge because I had done many interviews during my visits to all the other art schools over the last two years. Then it was over. Again, time flew by, and everything went smoothly.

Exiting once more, Robert waited for me, grinning mischievously as he asked how it went. I just replied that it went well with an even bigger grin. There and then I understood that "fashion is fun" and "fun is fashion" coexisted side by side. Coming home, we had dinner and an early night. We were both exhausted and knackered.

Waking up, I felt great; it was my leaving day, and I had to drive back to my military base that day. As a farewell present for the road, Robert gave me a self-made mixed tape with house music, which I happily accepted. After my introduction to house music at the Opera House, I was an instant fan. Driving home was like flying with the stars. The exam had gone well, and I was confident it would work out.

Two weeks later, I received a letter in which the "Fachhochshule für Gestaltung, Armgartstrasse" officially offered me a place to study. I had done it! The first step was done; I was in and on my way. My plan was starting to take shape. The military ended as uneventfully as it had started. All the generals were happy about not getting vaccinated with blunt needles anymore, and most importantly, I left the service knowing that I did put some sexy-fitting uniforms in military circulation, and our pizza place was glad that we did not visit with loud sirens anymore.

I was ready!

21. HAMBURG HERE I COME, COLLEGE TIME

Not quite yet!

To be allowed to start in Hamburg, the requirement was a six-month sewing apprenticeship. In the past, I had taught myself how to sew basic things, but I had never tried pockets or complicated details before. Luckily, Anette, the wife of my best friend Dr. Hans Georg Grossmann, was a master tailor and had a sewing studio at their house. Annette agreed to teach me if I would babysit their daughter Amelie from time to time. It was an easy bargain, and I started my apprenticeship right away. We started with shirts and different pocket types. It was hard to get my head around the different sewing techniques, and much went wrong, but after a month of practicing, I was getting better, and I produced and sold quite a few shirts to my friends. They were very colorful and had many different buttons on their front button placket.

It was great to learn a craft that I had never known before. In school, everything was theoretical; the practical application and realization of my ideas only happened by designing on paper. I loved the three-dimensional space and the creation of real garments. Annette had a lot of patience, and since I was her only apprentice, she lavished all her attention on me. It was the best sewing education I could have wished for. Six months flew by; I had learned a lot and was ready for Hamburg.

In those years, 1988–89, the flamboyant time of punk and the New Romantics came to an end, and a new era began. House parties, Acid house, and House music arrived in Germany from London, and the U.S. Fashion changed; it was no longer about gender-neutral androgyny; the new look was boring in comparison; it was all about comfort, loose-fitting t-shirts, and wide pants. Once you started dancing with Eva, there was no stopping, and everybody was sweating like crazy on the dance floor. You needed clothes that you could take off easily and use as towels, hence the t-shirt. Fashion moved from fantasy to practicality. Everybody was shifting to easy, relaxed clothes like loose-fitting jeans and T-shirts. The loose jeans were also introduced through the hip-hop rapper style from the States and Chicago House. Nobody cared anymore how you looked; the only concern was how you would be able to dance for hours, take your t-shirt off, and not worry if you never found it again. Eva arrived on the club scene, and touching skin, body contact, and dancing were more important than looking special and posing. This simpler look was a massive fashion change. The rave-house scene exploded next to the grunge style during the early 90s. Both dress codes developed parallel in the 1990s.

1988: Hamburg was the center of House Acid music and a vibrant gay scene. In 1989, it all shifted, the club and gay scene moved rapidly to Berlin as the "Wall" came down and Germany was reunited.

Stuttgart had become boring in comparison, and I happily packed my bags and set off for Hamburg. I did not have much to pack, and all fitted in my red VW Golf as I left. My most precious possessions were a sewing machine and a serger, both used but solid. Arriving in Hamburg, I would stay with Robert and then hope to find my own apartment soon. This turned out to be more difficult than anticipated. Back home, I was used to using my attic space to work, paint, and design. In Hamburg, square meters were expensive, and I did not have much money to spend on rent. I found my first apartment under a roof in an ugly building with a massive garage steel door. Robert made fun of me for moving into this place. It was more like a camping caravan than a flat. The kitchen and the bathroom were combined, and I had one small room to live in with a mattress on the floor. My first flat away from home was small, but it was mine, and I was happy to settle in. School would start soon, and the first day approached quickly. At long last, I would be in a fashion school with like-minded designers.

On the first day, all the students congregated in an empty classroom, and the program was explained to us. The BFA program was built to be completed in four years, but you could choose the number of classes you took each semester as it suited your needs. Therefore, it was possible to study for ten years, and nobody minded. You could stay a student for all your life if you wished to do so. Students could adapt their work and study time as needed. I had no intention to do so. The plan was to get to London quickly. I signed up for the maximum number of classes in the first semester and the following semesters. Quickly I came to realize the German teaching approach was very different from what I knew from the other schools I had visited. The initial foundation courses as a fashion designer were considered a sculptor's education. In Germany, fashion was considered art, not applied art, and the education in the first two years was based on an art education and not a fashion design program. We had painting, nude drawing, art history, color and form—anything and everything—but no fashion design. The only fashion-related courses were textile chemistry and pattern cutting. Everything else was art. The fashion design courses were to start after two years of study.

After the first week, I loved it. I was used to art from my art major and excelled in all the classes. I quickly became the best, especially in pattern cutting. I was the darling student; I had a knack for constructing garments. We were taught by Herr Lichtenstein, an old diva queen and a genius pattern cutter, with whom I got on like a house on fire. We were taught the Müller & Sohn system of flat pattern cutting. One of his special quirks was a game in which he tested our abilities in class. He would give us a catwalk picture of a difficult garment, a historic couture garment from Balenciaga, Dior, or anybody else relevant, and we had to reconstruct the pattern. I loved the exercise, especially when he picked Issey Miyake. Issey's garments were exquisitely complicated, and his cutting techniques were out of this world. Balenciaga was special, too, but nothing compared to Miyake's skills. All the students in the class were up and ready to win the race to recreate the pattern, but no chance; I always won the crown and the attention from Herr Lichtenstein. I became his favorite.

In year two, I dyed my hair bright blue, and Herr Lichtenstein loved it. He believed fashion designers had to be outrageous and laughed when I told him I earned the nickname "Blaupunkt" from my fellow students.

Textile chemistry was my Achilles heel. Our teacher was a chemistry professor and did not understand that we were fashion students. His tests were legendary and difficult, and I only passed by the hair of my teeth. His persistence in teaching us the deeper meaning of textile construction and its chemistry ingrained such deep textile knowledge, which later in my fashion career became very helpful because most fashion designers had no idea whatsoever about textiles.

The art classes were wonderful. As a new platform after my art major, I enjoyed painting and all its techniques very much. My professors were magicians. The door to art was initially opened during my exile at the library and later through my art teachers at high school. Now, in College, they taught me to fly. It was the best education I could have hoped for! I became an artist through and through in those years, and I cherished all the positive attention I received. Coming from a German family in Leonberg, art was not considered an important part of education, but now in Hamburg, the attention I received has kicked all doors wide open. My teachers were masters, dedicated to teaching. They fed me since I was hungry like a starving child; I sucked them dry, and they were happy to give readily.

My favorite class was painting with the "Schlumpers." Professor Laute was part of the art initiative "Die Schlumper," and he liked to bring his group to class. It was an art group entirely composed of young adults born with Down syndrome or other genetic conditions. They came to our class and were meant to participate in the same way as us. The first two weeks were challenging until we were all used to each other, but their creativity was unmatched. They saw things invisible to us. Although they were different from us, my friend Rene and I enjoyed working with them and challenging them in friendly banter. Until today, I admired their clear and free view of life. They did not have to follow or were burdened by morals and rules; they were born free. Every day, though, in their regular lives, they had to pay with pain and suffering for being different, but during our art classes, they were free, and they became our genius teachers. They were respected and taught us many precious lessons about humility, kindness, and passion.

Those art classes made time fly, and the first two years passed quickly. The "2-year" midterm exam I passed with an "A+" and was well-loved and respected by all my faculty.

Life was good.

22. PARTY TIME AND STYLING

After the first few months, I moved out of my attic flat with the steel door and moved into an apartment with friends. It was a much nicer place in an old regal merchant house close to the Alster, a big lake within the city of Hamburg. It had high ceilings, plaster ornaments, and tall windows. It was a beautiful house and apartment. We shared with two other friends, Manosh and Nordin. All of us were into fashion and serious about our work and studies, but going out was the highlight every week. Manosh was a make-up artist, and Nordine was a male model. We all liked to party, but Nordin took it to new heights. Our rhythm was to party from Thursday until Sunday, but the rest of the week was reserved for work. Nordin was on the roll 24/7. He never stopped, and his favorite habit was to bring the after-party home to us. People would flood our flat at seven in the morning, dancing and drinking. Life in the flat was wild, and soon, I could not handle my studies and the nightlife routine anymore. I had to move out and find a quieter place more suitable for a balanced life of work and play. I found this place with Holger, a fellow student. It was a smaller apartment situated in a quiet part of Hamburg called Barmbek. Once I settled into the apartment with Holger, I managed to bring order to my previously chaotic life. I worked hard on my studies and found a job with a fashion photographer called Frank Wartenberg. Frank was a local photographer and did interesting photo shoots for German fashion magazines. He had a beautiful photo studio where I started to hang out, and I was welcome to watch, observe, and learn. While I spent many hours there, he introduced me to some of the stylists he worked with, and I was allowed to assist them with their styling. This was an important learning curve for me to understand the complexity of a photo shoot, the planning of an idea, the story telling with clothes and photography, and the collaboration of camera, stylist, and model. There I found the lost world of beauty I was looking for. What the Hamburg "House" club scene had lost from the flamboyant eighties party scene, "the dressing up," I had found back in Frank's photo studio.

Since I was working hard and gaining experience, Frank gradually gave me my own styling jobs, and I earned good money with them. I will never forget the special Christmas story Frank wanted to shoot in July. We needed a Christmas tree, but where to find one in July? This was 1991, and the internet was not yet in existence. Everything had to be organized with phonebooks and garden centers. There was no Google to check out all the available trees in the vicinity. The planning took ages; first, you had to call the garden center and then drive past the garden center to check out the trees. 90% of them were useless. We had two days to prepare, and on the last evening before the actual shoot, I had not found a tree yet. It was seven in the evening, and everything was closing. Devastated, I passed by my soulmate, Jörg, and shared with him my dilemma and that I did not know what to do. Would I have to cancel the shoot the next day? No Christmas tree, no photo shoot? All was set up—the studio, the models, everything lined up and ready to go. The cost of canceling the shoot would be high. I would also lose Frank's trust and my well-paid job. Jörg and I had dinner, and after a bottle of wine, we had an idea. There are more than enough Christmas trees in the gardens of Hamburg's suburbs. We rang our neighbor's doorbell, borrowed a hacksaw, and fetched my red VW Golf. We were going to find a tree, and we were not giving up. After a thirty-minute drive, we landed in a nice neighborhood with plenty of Christmas trees in their front gardens. Now, we had to find a place where nobody was home. After another hour, it was close to midnight, and we had found our tree. We picked up the hacksaw, and I climbed the tree to cut off its beautiful three-meter-high tip. Climbing (we were tipsy from the wine, and it was pitch black), I scratched my whole face and arms. Finally, it was done; the top of the tree fell. Jörg stuck it in my car, and we drove off with our stolen Christmas tree sticking out from the back. Luckily, no police saw us. It would have been difficult to explain why my face was totally scratched and a Christmas tree sticking out of the back of my car in the middle of July. At home, we put the tree in the garage. That night, I slept very well, knowing that I had found a solution and the photo shoot was saved. The next day, I was the hero. I had to admit the story because I looked like I had been kissed by a hedgehog. My face and arms were all scratched from climbing the tree. In the end, the shoot was a success, and I continued working with Frank.

My life slowly started to revolve around three things: studying fashion, styling photo shoots, and going out. With my styling job, I earned enough money to finance my lavish nightlife. It started Wednesday night at the "Front," a famous gay club, and on Thursday moved to the "Opera House" on the Reeperbahn. The Reeperbahn was still untouched by tourists. It was the most famous red-light district in the world, next to Amsterdam. The "Underworld" was a dangerous place full of left-wing extremists, artists, the Hells Angels, ladies of the night, and lots of pimps protecting their interests on the streets.

In the middle of this criminal underworld, there were all of us, a young, creative crowd hungry for life. Wolfgang Tillman was there with a big star bleached into his hair on the back of his head. Hanging out with him were Julia Jentsch and Lutz Huelle. Many of Wolfgang's early photographs were about those days and their lives. Klaus Stockhausen was the best DJ in town and, at the time, already a fashion icon in Germany. Klaus was the musical heart of the Front, where he DJ'd Wednesdays and Saturdays. Adriano Sack was still studying architecture and worked with Jürgen van Wackeren at the "Front Bar." Jörg was my best friend, and I spent most of my time with him, Rene, or Robert. Robert lived with Sandra, Christopher, and Minou. Hamburg and its nightlife were very different from Stuttgart or New York. It was raw and rough. In the morning, at the Reeperbahn bars, the girls came in from their night shift. They were exhausted, and their brutal reality of life was visible. It was a very different kind of beauty, cruel but honest, something I had never seen before. When the sun came up, it was a friendly moment for all of us to laugh together. For a couple of hours, we could forget the past and the future as the night changed into day.

In Hamburg, part of this nightlife was a flamboyant gay scene. The loyalty, support, and complexity of the gay scene were new to me. I felt at home there. They were my family; they looked after me; I was part of it, and I felt safe. It was a free environment, but a lot of friends did not make it, either because of drugs or AIDS. In those days, Aids had hit the German gay scene big time. When I was in New York, you heard about it, and it was kind of in the air, but nobody knew what exactly it was. In Hamburg, all of it was crystal clear—all the brutal, horrific details and the fatal outcome. There was no cure, and nobody cared. Nobody outside the gay world cared; everybody thought of it as the "gay" plague. They thought it would only afflict those who lived in the gay world. It was the second time that I was truly ashamed of the human race and its two-faced morals. The first time was me being German after World War II. It was a tragedy of epic proportions, and everybody ignored it. Everywhere, there were articles on how to avoid contracting HIV and how to use a rubber, but no help or research for a cure was funded. Only years later, as some big rock stars had died, the pharma industry slowly reacted and started investing. Small amounts of money, though, since there was not enough profit to be made. Our friends Eva, Claudia, and Lucy did not help either. (Eva = ecstasy, Claudia = cocaine, and Lucy = LSD.) The scene was full of it, and everybody was happy to meet those three whenever they could. These friends made it very hard to maintain a safe lifestyle. Before in Stuttgart, I came home at four or five in the morning; in Hamburg, I was out for two days or more in one go. There was always a place open to hide and avoid daylight. We all became vampires. It was a look we all shared after a while; it was the look of the lost children of the night. The night marked us. We all changed, but this time not by our own design. Our lifestyle created and formed us; the toxins in our bodies shaped our looks. In those years, I had my first AIDS scare. With Eva and Claudia on the party scene, everything was more tactile. Everything was about touching or kissing, but actual intercourse became a rare incident unless in a solid relationship. From time to time though, things progressed and got out of hand; sex became unprotected, a wild moment in a nightclub or bar. After one of those incidents, it became apparent that one of my partners was infected with HIV. I was shocked when I was told. Until then, I knew death well from my Oma's departure and the butcher shop, but now it was personal; death was knocking at my door. It changed everything—my outlook on life, the intensity of my breathing, and my acute awareness of everything around me. It was like somebody took away the blindfold from my eyes; at first, you are blinded by the light, but gradually, you see life from a new perspective. You are grateful for every minute given and see beauty in the smallest of things. In those days, an AIDS test took a week. Friends gave me the address of a gay doctor who was experienced with the mental strain that comes with the infection. Hetero doctors were a nightmare to consult. They treated you like shit because they thought that you deserved the virus due to your irresponsible lifestyle and choices. This doctor was nice, and calmed me down somewhat, but we had to wait. I will never forget that week of waiting and not knowing. I did not want to talk to anybody; the fear was within me, within me, and I did not want to share anything. Death was with me, and it was a very enlightening moment to ponder its absolute finality at this young age. After a week, which today I consider a gift of reflection, the test came back negative. I was fine, not infected, and would live. The experience had changed me, though, and it was time to move on. If I had stayed in Hamburg, I would not have survived.

Many did not!

23. PREPARING SURVIVAL; NEVER GIVE UP I

After the first "two years" and midterm exams, many things changed. In the third year, we finally started our fashion design classes, and I was not happy. In Germany, the university system and art studies are completely different from the rest of the world. There is no pressure to graduate. As a student, you did not have to pay for your studies; you had all the equipment, space, ateliers, and a solid tax break at your disposal. For a German student, there is no pressure to finish your studies after four years; you could study for ten years or forever if you wanted. The eternal student was a reality, and some artists lived that way. Nobody was in a hurry to graduate but me. Therefore, I decided to give it a shot and applied to the RCA after my midterms.

Here I was, with my plan to graduate early and join the Royal College of Art. The southern youngster with the abhorrent notion of finishing his diploma within three and a half years to then move on to the RCA. In Hamburg, fashion design was all about wearable sculptures and art. My Professors in Germany only accepted "fashion art," a form of fashion which did not at all coexist with the fashion realities of London, Paris, or Milan. My solution to the challenge was easy: after six months, I stopped going to fashion classes. At this point in my university career, we did not have to attend class; everything was project-based. We were autonomous, and a professor was a mentor to guide us and give us feedback. The requested assignments were easy to create, hand them in, and get a grade. To me, it did not matter anymore what grade I received for my assignments; I just wanted to get the hell out of there and go to London. One of our sketching professors did graduate from the Royal College of Art; I signed up for his class and started preparing my work for my application portfolio. This time, I had no support with my portfolio. The sketching Professor was no fashion person and had only limited experience with fashion design. He was a pure artist and frowned somewhat on my design ambitions, but he respected me and supported me where he could. To get more feedback, I flew once more to London and arranged another meeting with a fashion faculty. This time, the meeting was not helpful, and I prepared the best I could by myself.

The application deadline came quickly, and I sent my portfolio to the RCA by mail and waited. Mail was the official postal service; you could register your packages, but there was no tracking service. You received a postal note once the recipient received the delivery and accepted it. It took time to find out if a delivery had arrived at its destination. I waited and waited, but no reception slip arrived. Finally, I called the RCA, and they confirmed that they had never received my portfolio; it had never arrived. I started the search process with the local postal office, but they did not find it either. Finally, time had passed, and the application process had come and gone. The window was closed, and the year was gone. The RCA only accepts new students once a year. I was not accepted into the RCA. What now?

Two months later, I received a phone call from the RCA fashion department saying that a package, beaten and torn, had arrived and contained my missing portfolio. They asked if they should send it back to me. I told them to hold on to it and that I would come and pick it up personally. To get accepted into the Royal College, you had to beat roughly four hundred competing students. They had many applications for the eighteen open places each year. They only picked the best, and the head of the department was John Miles. I had met John before, and since I was coming to London to pick up my portfolio, I hoped to get a chance to show him my work and get feedback. Since so much time had been invested in that book, it was important to me to find out if it would have been good enough. After many phone calls, John Miles agreed to see me to look over my designs. Back in Kensington Grove, I was sitting opposite John Miles. He was an impressive character, all dressed in black. The clothes were by a Japanese designer; I assumed it was Yohji. He had my portfolio in front of him on a small table. He was very kind; we started chatting for a while. I told him all about my dream of coming to the Royal College and my trouble with the German College, with its way of confusing teaching, all technical and art, but no fashion understanding at all. He listened and looked at my work patiently. He asked further questions and commented on certain technicalities. As we finished my work, he asked me what I wanted to do if I did not get accepted to the school. He wondered if I was inclined to study fashion illustration, and I replied that I was not but that I wanted to study fashion womenswear design. He nodded, called in his assistant Margaret, and told her to get some portfolios from graduating students. The portfolios arrived promptly, and he then showed me their work, the coin dropped in my head. There it was, easy to see and absorb what needed to be done. I immediately understood what a professional fashion portfolio had to look like. The next time I had to be successful, and those books were the key. What John presented was clear and structured professional work. Mood boards, the muse, fabrics, sketchbooks, designs, sketches, embellishments for textiles, draping, and finished looks all beautifully packaged, as opposed to the separate artwork and illustration pieces I had sent. My portfolio, which was lost in the mail, was wrong and off the mark; I had to rethink and rework everything. John Miles, the head of the program, then explained to me in detail the difference between "art" and the "applied arts" called design. In Germany, art and design were still considered to be the same. Hence, my art-based education in Germany. Fashion was considered a form of "sculpting." John explained that art has the responsibility to always question and challenge the general understanding of the world. It examines the social structures we live in. It is philosophical and spiritual. Art was at its foundation, looking for the original visual language of a universal truth. It had no need to create profit or be liked by humanity. On the other hand, "design," better called "applied art," had the responsibility to translate art into desirable objects. To make art accessible to the public. Designers, with their designs, were opening a door for art to be understood and consumed by a broader audience. Designers make art beautiful and desirable. Design was a product reproduced in quantity for everybody, while "art" was unique and not to be shared but in museums, galleries, and print reproductions. Most important of all, he stated, "Design is a business." He opened my mind, and I absorbed every word of it. After I had seen the portfolios of the graduating students and listened to John, I understood, and John made sure I had digested everything. He told me to apply next year .So, I packed up my book and left. Determined I would make it next time.

24. DETERMINATION

Back home in Hamburg, I started to work on my next portfolio. Now I knew what to do. For a short while, I tried to share my excitement and what I had seen in London with my fashion design class, my fellow students, and my fashion professors, but they did not want to hear any of it. They thought I was on the wrong path and did not want to help me with my application to the Royal College. We were at the beginning of my third year, and I wanted to get my diploma and leave. After two weeks back in Hamburg, I was downstairs with the registrar and discussed all possibilities to finish and graduate after three and a half years. In theory, it was possible, but it had never been done before. Without a BFA degree, I would not have been accepted to the Royal. I needed that degree, and I knew I would have to fight for it because they did not want to support me in my endeavor. As time moved on, I was working hard and creating a lot of work. I did not get any feedback in Hamburg; therefore, I flew to London every two months and showed my progress to John. He was surprised to see me so frequently. I enjoyed his attention, and I kept coming back for more and more and could not get enough. The new application date finally approached, and I bought another plane ticket to get to London. This time, I would hand in my portfolio personally. The risk of my portfolio getting lost again was not an option. Back home, all the courses had been scheduled so that I was ready to graduate no matter what. I was confident I would make it. Dropping off the portfolio in person was another challenge because nobody had ever dropped one off personally before. The postmark was important to register the book officially as "received." It took two hours until they accepted it with a signature from the registrar, and I was in the race. It would take another three weeks to find out if I would get invited to an interview before the final acceptance. Waiting anxiously, the letter arrived, and opening it, I read the magic words: I was invited for the interview. The best letter ever, and I was happy and ready to go. In Hamburg, back in class, I was too cocky, of course, to keep my mouth shut, and I taunted the faculty. The swift retaliation was that they took me off my graduation date. They stipulated that I did not have enough experience to be successful in London, and they wanted to save me from failure. I was furious and started the holy war with them, which was not the best idea in hindsight, but there was no stopping me. Within two weeks, I was off my graduation course and back in deep trouble. How would I ever get accepted without my diploma? Devastated, I boarded the plane for my interview in London, knowing full well I would not be able to meet the requirements. At the RCA, all went according to plan. I was ushered in front of the acceptance committee and started talking; it all spilled out of me. I forgot everything else around me; I had no fear, I was calm, and I was in my element. My portfolio was good and sound; I presented like never before; it was like a breeze, and it was done. Everybody stared at me, and the crucial question arrived: "When would I graduate?" My heart sank, and I told them that I would not be able to graduate in time to start at the Royal College with a BFA degree under my belt. The registrar was not amused at not having mentioned that crucial fact before. I tried to explain but to no avail. Then John Miles stepped in, sent me outside, and told me to wait in the corridor. After an hour, they called me back in. Another hour of my life was spent in absolute agony, worrying about what to do to solve this dilemma. As John called me back in, he winked at me, and I sat down still wondering what was going on. The registrar had a stony face, and John explained that I had been accepted, but I had to finish my studies within six months my degree in Hamburg. I couldn't believe my ears. I was accepted and could start at the RCA. There was a God—a fashion design God—and I could not believe it. Leaving Kensington Gore, I was elated and happy beyond belief. John called me later that day and explained the ramifications if I failed. I acknowledged the rules, accepted the challenge, and flew back to Hamburg. The joy was short-lived, as I knew the Hamburg registrar would be as unamused as the London one was. Once back, I immediately started scheming and pulled all the legal strings at my disposal. In the end, they gave in, and a professor agreed to follow my thesis progress and final diploma project. The graduation date was set. I called John, confirmed my BFA graduation schedule, and then the RCA officially offered me a place in the coming year's class.

My Hamburg diploma topic was "Artificial Intelligence" or "AI." In 1992, Artificial Intelligence was defined as the creation of an artificial human machine that was capable of independent thought and behavior. AI was basically an independent robot. My research was about the role of a "thinking machine" in our modern society and what the society would look like. The thesis started with Greek mythology and took a tour de force through art history, religious mythology, and modern machine engineering. Back in 1992, "artificial intelligence" was a robotic entity with a computer brain and a conscience, a living mechanical being with a digital brain. My friend Andreas introduced me to this topic and helped me with some of his research to get started. I loved the research and its possibilities. The research came easily. I loved to connect my findings and theories with all my art history knowledge. After all, I was still an educated artist since my fashion education had not yet begun. There was not much time, and I tried to get as much done as possible before I moved to London, but it was too tight, and I fell behind in my diploma schedule. Again, I was in peril of losing it all. My professor, the only and last one willing to give me a chance, was not happy with my progress. She threatened to fail me if I would not honor my promise to the Hamburg BFA commitment. I assured her I would deliver all required materials and looks on time. There was no other choice; I had to leave to start my next chapter in London, and I went.

25. LONDON

The first week in London, I stayed in a bed and breakfast. I arrived with one suitcase and the essentials. It was still three weeks until the semester started in September. The Royal College had a housing service; in Germany, nothing similar existed, and back home, every student had to find their own accommodation and struggle with safety deposits and grumpy landlords. Climbing the stairs to the housing office, I was marveling at the student work exhibited in the hallways. As I arrived at the office, there were about 10 more students waiting patiently outside with their folders and excited faces. We all started chatting and introduced ourselves to each other. A group from all corners of the world with different majors, we were all happy to start and exchanged excitedly about London and where we hoped to find an apartment. After about 15 minutes, I was called into the office, and a friendly Jamaican lady received me. She explained to me the first steps, and the most important one was that I had to open an account and put a deposit of 200 pounds sterling in there to guarantee the first rent. She handed me all the necessary school documentation for the bank to accept me. Then she progressed to inquire what type of apartment I had in mind and how much rent I could afford. Everything was fine until I told her the rent I was paying in Hamburg. She informed me without further ado that the London rent prices were at least double. I was shocked and wondered how I would be able to afford London's housing prices. I figured that I would have to work during summer breaks and that I would have to work harder in the next two years. I had some money from my father; he had kept his word and had given me a generous lump sum so I would be able to concentrate on my studies instead of waiting tables at night. Still, I had not thought of such elevated living expenses. As my smile slowly came back after the initial shock, she told me about two apartments that were currently available and called the landlord. She arranged appointments for the next day, and off I went to set up my bank account. The next morning, I had a hearty breakfast and looked at the two flats. They were horrible. To be honest, they were dumps, and I had no intention to repaint and redo the apartment for only one year.

I returned, slightly demotivated, to my housing officer and hoped for a lucky break in the London apartment search. In those days, you had to go and see apartments; there was no other way. There were no virtual tours; you had to travel around London and visit the places described in a few words in an announcement. The biggest surprise was the fact that all bathrooms were carpeted. How to clean a carpeted bathroom was a mystery to me, but it was the expected standard in those days in the UK. After three more flats, the lady asked me if I would mind sharing with a girl. I happily confirmed that there was no problem, and I was sent to Stockwell, close to Brixton, a notoriously dangerous part of South London. The area did not matter to me, and I was on my way to meet Vicky, my new roommate. The apartment was on a quiet street. The area was somewhat rundown but not too bad. The house was lovely, and so was Vicky. There was a smallish kitchen but a big living space with a big table and a big television. My room was not big but quiet, with a view onto a small back yard, a nice big window, and ample sunlight streaming in that day. Vicky was a ceramic and glass major in her first year. We did get along well, and once back in the housing office, the friendly lady informed me that Vicky was also agreeing to live with me. The housing worry was solved, and I had found a house. It all happened quicker than I had anticipated, and I had two more days in London to visit museums and galleries before going back.

In Hamburg, everything happened quickly. I packed, sold my car, said goodbye, and returned to London within a week.

26. ROYAL COLLEGE OF ART

In the first week at the Royal, there was much paperwork to be filled out. John Miles had a big surprise, too. He had a tuition scholarship for me! I did not have to pay the school fees! I was very grateful and even more determined to succeed in my endeavors. The biggest excitement was seeing all my new fellow students. The fashion department had three "schools": womenswear, menswear, and millinery. The departments were not big; womenswear had about 18 students, menswear had 8, and millinery had one. Philipp Tracey, the Irish hat maker and latest fashion genius, had just left college and was the hottest big star in the fashion circus. The Royal College was the only school in Europe with a master's program, and nobody else was offering a graduate degree in those years. Most UK students worth their salt had applied to the Royal. Especially since there were new government grants for scholarships, and everybody had a chance to get one if they were talented enough, passed the portfolio reviews, and did get accepted. Most of our classmates were British and Irish; they all knew each other from their previous BFA studies at fashion colleges and Universities around the country.

As we all sat for the first time around a table in the canteen downstairs, we happily introduced ourselves. The selected students at the table were the elite from all UK fashion schools—the best and most talented. Intimidating it was. As I tried to make friends and break the ice during our first lunch, I was quickly informed that Germans were not considered to have much taste. I happily agreed and informed them all that this was the exact reason why I had come to London to change that fact. They all laughed. At the table was Christopher Bailey, the winner of a national competition between all English fashion schools; he was crowned #1 and the new golden boy. Brian of Britain (Brian Kirkby) just came back from drug rehab and was ready to rock and roll. Jane Whitfield was the star from New Castle, a beautiful girl with killer style; Aisling Ludden was the Irish fashion madness; Darren Davey was the most stylish man ever; Andrew Buckler was the businessman; and Sean Ryan had the most outrageous humor and sophistication. It was an amazing group, and forgive me for not naming everybody in our class; it would be too long a list! It was heaven; we were all there to make our mark, and we knew those young designers in the room were the best England had to offer, and England ruled fashion education!

Another new reality was the College bar. There was a bar in the college for students and faculty to meet and drink. This place was the most creative hotspot and party place in college. Students from all disciplines met up there and had a drink and a bag of crisps. It was a melting pot, and we quickly met everybody in college.

The first week flew by with paperwork and setting up our workspaces, introducing everybody, and then it started. The first project was a t-shirt design assignment. We had to design a t-shirt for the RCA college shop at the entrance. Darren Davey had the best design ever; it was a word play, and we all loved it: out of RCA, he made "arsey-ey." The College President was not as happy with the design as we were and changed it to an ordinary logo t-shirt. Anyway, it was fun, and we warmed up quickly to the massive workload and assignments we were given continuously. The first year was all project-based and only interrupted by visiting lecturers on Wednesdays. We had one main project in the first semester: a collection with three looks to make. This suited me well because it resembled the BFA collection I had to deliver in March in Hamburg, but now the stakes were even higher. John Miles had awarded me a scholarship, and of course, I intended to make him proud. He was the person who fully believed in me, and I did not want to disappoint him. Time moved slowly, with a lot of design projects being dropped on us daily. The others in the class were far more advanced in design than me. My technical skills in pattern cutting and sewing were better, though, and I learned fast. After three months, I had caught up and was on par with the others. Only Chris, Bryan, J., Grit, and Julia were better. They had this incredible instinct for getting things right. They had the magic touch, which you could not learn. I finally understood what the difference was between training and natural talent. Mr. Lapine at Porsche was right; now I understand what he meant when he stated that training added only 10% to our natural skills. We are born with a natural limit that only a few will manage to overcome during their lifetime, and I was determined to do just that. I was there to die trying. We were all driven, and the environment was friendly but highly competitive; we were there to make our mark in the world of fashion. Day by day, we grew into an incredible group of designers. We pushed ourselves and worked day and night. John had to establish a curfew at midnight so we would go home and sleep. The school opened again at seven, and we all waited at the door to get as much time as possible in the studio. The school was an open, creative atomic bomb. You could freely wander and see what all the other majors were doing. In Germany, this never existed; you came to school for class but then worked at home on your own. At the Royal, you could see and observe everything. Everything was accessible, and everybody was happy to share. Life was good, especially when we went for a pint in the college bar. My old party fever was still alive, and I frequently went to "Heaven" and "Trade," two famous clubs at the time. Vicky, my flat mate, usually joined me on those nights out. The "Fridge" in Brixton was another stamping ground for creative, restless souls.

The most important learning happened in class watching what all my peers were doing. To see what they came up with and try similar processes. We helped and pushed each other. It was an incredible group and team. I wish we all could have started a company together; it would have been a most successful powerhouse. We naturally also found time to go to the college bar for drinks and dance at Heaven, Trade, and the Fridge. We lived the mantra "work hard, play hard." It was at the college bar that J. and I finally connected. Darren and I were sitting at the top of the stairs, with J. and Aisling below us. While talking and fooling around, I knocked over my beer by accident, and it spilled down J.'s back. She jumped up, not amused at all, and started calling me names.

Her whole back was covered in beer. Darren and I laughed, and I offered her my shirt to change into. Later that evening, it was the first time we kissed. It was wonderful; I was in love!

She was an incredible girl, and I admired everything about her. She was from Newcastle, where I had never been, and there were many jokes about Geordies in class. She was my angel, and after many weeks of wooing, we became a couple. It was a slow process. We were very different characters. J. had the messiest table in college; it was a dump, and I was the most anal student concerning my color pencils, which she regularly borrowed and ruined. Apart from that, J. could have done anything, and I would have forgiven her. J. became not only my love, but she also opened the doors to a design level that I never thought possible. I learned from her daily, and we realized we needed each other and were, in a very odd way, meant for each other. I wanted to marry her and have children. It was all there in our studio.

Those were the days of happiness and the incredible satisfaction of unhindered creation.

As March approached, the situation in Hamburg gradually deteriorated. The school was offended by my blatant disrespect and bending of the rules. I only had one choice left: to blow them away with a killer presentation, and I intended to do just that. During my regular trips back, I had to present my work to my professor to be guided through the graduation and thesis processes. My artificial intelligence thesis was well-researched but lousily written. I loved to research but had no time to write; it all had to be typed out on a typewriter without spell check, and I was dyslexic, so many mistakes and rewrites occurred. Luckily, my father's assistant helped me type; otherwise, I would have never managed. Drawing and sketching were easy since I incorporated my Hamburg thesis workload into my RCA college projects. The graduation requirements were a thesis, the written part, two fashion collections with a minimum of 40 design sketches with technical drawings, and two finished looks each. One collection was for a futuristic city person, and the second was about a rural farm culture. The future I predicted in 1992 was a vision that, due to AI, our world would develop into two separate societies, a technocratic city culture and an agricultural counterpart with a sustainable and ecological value system, both equally balanced and in harmony. What a nice vision of mine, but not of much interest to anybody back then; they were looking for artistic concepts like the Bauhaus movement. Art as inspiration was paramount; I had enough of it and was ready to break that tradition. My concept was alien to my professors, to say the least. I spent hours explaining the context of "the godly dream of man to create life and the possibilities of AI creation" linked to our technological advances and their implications. Nobody wanted to hear it, and the more they fought, the bolder I became. The date of my thesis presentation arrived, and I set up my collection. There was no fashion show for students in Hamburg. You were given a classroom; you had two days to set it up, and then the jury committee would sit for two hours in your room, questioning you while you were presenting and defending your work. During the last five months, I had learned a lot about presentations at the Royal, and I didn't spare any expenses to frame and hang all my 80 illustrations. The room was beautifully lit with spotlights borrowed from Frank's photo studio, and I had my model friends wearing the clothes and performing a dance presentation in the room. Once my part of the presentation was finished, there was a deep silence in the room. The jury committee was furious at my disregard of protocol and tradition and stormed out of the room. There was a lot of shouting and uproar, and then the committee came back in and announced the result. I had failed, I would not receive my BFA diploma, and I was meant to represent in six months. It was a disaster; I would lose it all. I was the first graduating student in the history of Armgartstrasse who had failed their BFA exam. Through all the commotion in the hallway, the chair of fashion was alarmed and joined the upheaval. She calmly came in and questioned me about what I had presented. She asked me if I had delivered all the required quantities of designs, words, and outfits. I told her that I had done all that was required and more. She then stepped out and talked to the faculty present. After half an hour, she came back in; all the remaining faculty had been sent home. We were alone, and she explained to me that I would pass with a "D," the lowest possible grade. Furthermore, my thesis would not be held in the archives. I would graduate with a tombstone to my name, all my achievements would be erased, and nothing would ever hint at my existence in Hamburg. I would only receive a diploma in the form of a written letter, and she asked me never to come back. I agreed readily since I did not intend to come back. We shook hands, and she parted with the warning that I would fail and never make it in the world of fashion. I did not care what she thought. I had accomplished what I needed to do and packed up. Later that night, we partied hard, and I was ready to go back to London. Once in London, I went to John

Mile's office, put my diploma on his desk, and he looked at it and then at me and shook my hand. He did not say much; he just shook my hand.

27. FIRST YEAR

Now, I was a fully accepted student at the Royal College of Art in my first year of studies. The Royal was a two-year MFA program. It was intense. We worked simultaneously on various projects given to us by our faculty. The projects were part competitions, part industry-related, or relevant portfolio work created for us by our professors. Some projects only lasted two days, others for months. The workload quickly became too much, and we had the first student revolt. We all believed we were pushed too hard. We had no problem working, but we felt we could not deliver the best quality work with such an overload. John had to be called up to our studio. He was not amused to be called away from his duties and appointments. He was a feared man, and he could be very strict if he needed to be. After listening to all our complaints about having fewer projects to work on, he only looked at us and explained very quietly that we better get our asses back to work and stop whining. He then stated in cold but clear words:" In fashion design, there is never enough time. Find a way, find creative solutions!" We were dumbfounded but understood immediately that he was right; we had to find ways to make those requests and projects work. Some still complained, but we all were dumbfounded in that moment. He was right. It was simple. All we had to do was to find creative solutions, and we did.

At this point in the first year, we were working on our pre-collection. It was a big project, and we had to create two outfits and design an exhibition for the downstairs entry hall of the main building.

Sustainability was a big story in the fashion industry. Back then, sustainability was more about creating awareness and bold artistic statements than recycling and organically grown fibers.

Sustainability was my story, and I was obsessed with it. My collection concept was to grow grass on clothes and use animal bones for embroideries. I found and collected those bones on the banks of the river Thames during low tide. It was great fun. When the water was low, I went down to the riverbanks and collected those bones. The banks were full of them and other wonderful objects, from old vintage medicine bottles to glass shards to metal objects. I collected them in big black garbage bags, brought them back to our studio at the Royal College, then washed them in the sink downstairs in the textile department and after laid them out to dry under my table. My fellow students were not amused, the bones stank, and everybody found it disgusting. I proclaimed that my project was very much on trend, as the artist Damien Hirst had just become famous with his carcasses displayed in glass cubes full of flies and maggots. I loudly stated in class that the time we lived in needed my bones. Though, in hindsight, I must admit the drying process was somewhat smelly.

Once the bones were dry, I started the second phase of my concept. Grass seeds were stitched between two big sheets of muslin and laid out under my worktable. After watering them daily, the grass started to grow on the fabric. The watering process turned the area around my desk into a slippery road. This motivated my peers to file another round of complaints. The grass grew quickly and looked like natural grass fur. It was a marvel and beautiful to see, but it also grew mold underneath the surface, and it smelled bad too! Another detail I hadn't really thought through was that the grass would die if I dried the fabric sheets to stitch them. Therefore, I tried to stitch the wet fabric sheets, which was a mess and ruined my sewing machine. I was stopped by our technicians and had to rethink. In the end, I used the grass fabric to be displayed on the wall as a textile statement and crowned it with a big bull skull. Next to it, my two muslin looks were embroidered with bones and looked fabulous.

One more important thing emerged from this concept: a bone necklace. In 1993, on Valentine's Day, I made a bone necklace for J., accompanied by a handwritten scroll with a selected poem from Dante's Inferno. The necklace looked great, but J. did not like bones on her skin from the river Thames. From that day on, Valentine's Day was our anniversary day.

We both spent a lot of time together at the library to research new ideas. We loved to research. It all begins with research.

The Royal College had a great art and design library, and I was addicted to that space. It became once again my refuge. I disappeared for hours in those rooms and browsed through the big and small tomes on display. It was there that I found a booklet about Taoism. In Tao, there is a wise reading that compares our learning and growth with the creation of a boat. It describes how we are the creators of our own "career boat" through our skills and experiences. With this boat, we navigate the river of life. The boat is in constant flux due to our multitude of life experiences and lessons. Sometimes it is a beautiful vessel, and sometimes, we neglect it, and it becomes a wreck. Sometimes we find stormy waters, and sometimes, we find a harbor and stay on land. But we are always linked to our "skill boat" on our journey through life. This comparison of a boat, skill, enlightenment, and the journey on the river of life is and has been a very important part of my existence.

The story made sense. At night, I discussed with J. how we would build our boats together and how our skills would be able to carry us to different countries and opportunities. J. was not very fond of leaving England. On the other hand, I was ready to see the world; America had shown me how much more there is out there to see and explore. My big dream was to build, together with J., something that would be ours. Not just a family, a project far grander, a creative, art-work-family-design something. J. did not want to hear any of it; she wanted to stay in London, and so I kept on dreaming by myself of distant shores with J.

Hoping; Dreaming.

28. ROYAL SOCIETY OF ART- DAPHNE BROOKER AWARD

One of the projects in that first year was the RSA (Royal Society of Art)-Daphne Brooker Award. Daphne Brooker was a famous fashion model in the 1950s. She was a beautiful woman and the head of the fashion department at Kingston University. As a lifetime achievement recognition, the Royal Society of Art created this competition to celebrate her work and, at the same time, her retirement. The competition was newly created and a big deal. Daphne was a well-known force of nature in the fashion world. Everybody assumed it would be a Kingston student who would win since they were her protégées.

It was a design competition with 5,000 pounds of prize money to be spent on a research journey to wherever the winner wished to go. All colleges were invited, and it was a matter of prestige to win. It was the battle royale of UK fashion colleges. They all wanted to become the institution that had produced the winner. The brief was simple: create a collection concept based on the country you wish to visit. We all had to participate, the whole class. My destination was Italy. I wanted to work for Moschino; he was my hero, and I loved his work. He was more than just a designer. He added meaning to his designs. He was an artist and a painter, and he had humor—lots of it.

My concept was simple: "Pizza sweaters." It described a shop concept where you could individually customize a sweater of your choice. You decided on the toppings for your sweater, and then the sweater was embroidered with your toppings. The sweaters, once finished, were then packaged in a pizza box. It was simple, fun, and colorful. The presentation had a real knitwear pizza in a box, which took quite some time to finish. It was one of the first customizable yourself stories of those times. It was a beautiful presentation. A graphic designer helped me with the box and the knitwear department with the pizza. "Once finished, we sent it off and waited. The letter came, and I was among the finalists. I did get invited to a final interview with Daphne to explain my career plans and ambitions. The interview went well, and to everybody's surprise, I won. A Royal College of Art student had won the prestigious RSA-Daphne Brooker award. Not only did I become a fellow of the RSA, but I also became a small celebrity among the fashion colleges. The trip planning commenced immediately since my travels to Italy were meant to take place during the summer break. Since nobody had defined the spending of the prize money, I could plan as I wished. All I had to do was list the designers, museums, and cities I wanted to visit, and they established the contacts and the meetings. It was a great opportunity, and I decided I would bring J. with me. We would spend the summer together, traveling through Italy and saying hello to our design heroes. At that time, everything was happening in Italy; France was a dormant giant, and Italy ruled supreme.

Time flew by, and before we knew it, we were sitting on a plane to Linate Airport in Milan. There, we would pick up a rental car and drive up to Lake Como to start our adventure.

Finally, on the aircraft, J. was sitting next to me, our portfolios securely stacked in the overhead compartments, and we were ready to go. We picked up the car, drove to Como, checked into a lovely hotel, and had a marvelous dinner close to the lake. The next morning, we planned to visit "Mantero," an iconic Italian silk and tie manufacturer with a huge archive. Mantero was an unbelievable place. It was a historic building, a "Palazzo," and it was a lot bigger than I had ever imagined possible. We were welcomed by a friendly and stylish staff member, with whom we toured the building, visited all the different design departments, and were allowed to spend time in their archives. The archives were huge; they were full of large books with fabric swatches and textile designs dating back to the early 19th century. I don't believe anything similar exists anywhere else in the world. We were finished late in the afternoon and left to our own devices. We decided to go for a spin around the lake. Cruising around Como, taking in the beauty of the mountains, the lake, the richness of the buildings, the history, and the wealth displayed, was incredible and beautiful. By chance, we spotted an island, and it seemed to have a restaurant located on it. We parked the car, walked to a boat moored close to the parking lot, and inquired about how to get to the restaurant. The friendly man told us he would bring us over, and he assured us we would not regret the experience. He was right; the place was called "Locanda Dell'Isola Comacina" at the Lago di Como. We were seated outside under the stars and ate a fixed menu. It was expensive, but we had never eaten anything similar. The food and wine were out of this world. At the end, the owner appeared in a funky outfit with a colorful vest. He had prepared coffee for us all. The coffee was on fire, and its preparation and presentation were a spectacle on their own. He repeatedly poured the flaming liquid into a bucket and, from there, into small cups while everybody cheered and drank. Back in our hotel, we fell asleep with a big smile on our faces, ready for the next day in Milan. We had planned a week in Milan, and I was ready to meet with Armani, Romeo Gigli, Dolce& Gabbana, and Moschino. Romeo Gigli was the biggest star at that time, and he was the first on the list, followed by Dolce & Gabbana, Armani, and finally Moschino, my hero.

The studio of Romeo Gigli was an unexpected paradise. It was a fabric wonderland specialized in fabric manipulation and dying techniques. The textile studio was filled with the most beautiful fabrics hanging on racks and on the wall. For me, as a student, it was an eye-opener to see what was possible in a design studio, and I absorbed it like a sponge. Romeo very kindly asked about my work, and I was allowed to show my portfolio. The whole team was very down-to-earth and friendly—an outstanding group of talented designers. There, I realized how much I still had to learn. His genius humbled me.

Each day of the week was scheduled with another visit, and in between, we visited museums, shops, and galleries. Milan was pleasant but a small place compared with London. To get around was easy. In Milan, J. had some friends from the UK, and they showed us the town. The next day, I was meant to meet Dolce & Gabbana, but they canceled at the last minute, and unfortunately, I never met them. I think they did not like the fact that I visited Gigli first, their biggest competitor, but I will never know for sure. The day after, a visit to Armani was on the schedule. He was not my style, and I did not understand his aesthetic particularly well. I was flamboyant and loud;

Armani was stylish and understated with enormous sophistication. I was none of those things. At the office, the assistant showed me around the premises, which were out of this world. Romeo's studio space looked like a broom closet compared to this display of wealth and style. The art and interior were beyond beautiful. I quickly came to understand the talent and genius this man possessed. After two hours of touring, I was led down to the in-house catwalk in the basement, and there he was. He awaited me with a big smile and showed me his latest collection personally! What an honor! He was the friendliest man I ever met. He asked for my book and wanted to see my designs. Suddenly, I was very apprehensive since I realized my portfolio was crude and rough in this environment, but what did I have to lose? While chatting, I quickly became familiar with him, and I jokingly mentioned that my designs were exclusive and he would not be able to afford them. He laughed and agreed, and we spent an hour looking at my work. He was not much interested in my designs but more in my passion and love for the craft. He asked me everything about Hamburg, my love for art, my painting, and my pattern-cutting education. At the end, I packed up and was ready to leave when he asked me if I wanted a job. My jaw dropped. I had never contemplated anything like this. I was a German country bumpkin with no talent compared to this master and his achievements. I joked with him to be careful that I might take him up on his offer and avoid an answer because I did not have an answer. On the way out, I asked his assistant if Mr. Armani was joking, and she assured me the offer was real. Armani liked my work! Once outside, I needed a drink and smiled at the oddity of life. Later that night, I retold the story many times to J., who was, I am sure, happy when I finally went to sleep and shut up. The next morning, I got ready to meet Franco Moschino, but he was sick, and Jonathan Cheung, his assistant, received me and showed me around the building. It was amazing—his art, his paintings on the wall, the people, and their clothes. I was at home, and I knew I would fit in there. Finally, I was ushered into a room, and Jonathan looked at my portfolio. It went well, but there was no job, just a friendly "come back when you graduate" and a handshake, and then it was over. Nothing compared to Armani, but I knew this was home. I swore there and then I would be back. I loved Moschino's humor, style, color, and fun. I also admired the depth of his commitments, his investment in equality, gay rights, ecology, nature, and animal rights, and his "no" to racism. He was one of the first to advocate for all those important topics of today. He was a generous and open-minded artist and fashion designer. He was my hero.

The next day, J. and I packed the car and drove to Siena and Florence. They are beautiful cities, and I believe we had the most expensive ice cream of our lives in Florence. It was a good time.

After Florence, J. had to go back to London, and I continued to Rome, where I stayed at the "British School at Rome," up on the hills in an old Roman villa. The building was laid out in a big square with a massive courtyard in the middle. It had big stairs and columns at the entrance, and it made you feel like Cesar walking up to his palace. Located on the sides were the various studios of the artists in residence.

It was a historically imposing space, and the most fun was to meet all the artists at the dinner table to discuss concepts, philosophies, and artistic madness. A special time around a big table, which I never found again anywhere. Today, I still miss the open exchange I experienced there.

The next day, I was meant to meet Valentino's right hand in his studio.

Valentino was never quite my cup of tea, but I was in for a surprise. The building right next to the Spanish steps was massive and beautiful. Valentino's assistant was very charming and took the time to show me all the archives, early drawings of Valentino, and all his work in detail. None of the other design houses took so much time showing me everything. I became an immediate fan. Valentino's work was genius in its sophistication and elegance.

Though the most impressive part of my visit was to visit his office, I was allowed to have a glimpse into his most private chamber. The space held incredible art and selected antiques; it was breathtaking. There was a level of taste on display that I realized I would never be able to achieve, and I bowed my head with the deepest respect to this great master.

Mostly, I admired a Botero painting on the wall. There were some more art pieces by Botero throughout the building, but this painting in his office was remarkable.

Once released back to real life, I was truly impressed and admired the craft, talent, and design skills of Valentino. He taught me that excellence exists, which I would never be able to accomplish, and he opened my eyes to a beauty that is seldom found in life. He showed me "Love" in its purest form.

Back then, I realized that Valentino and Yves Saint Laurent were the absolute, untouchable geniuses of the past four decades. I also understood I would never reach their level, but I would reach mine; there was a place for my talent. On my last day, I packed my bags with a smile and with a new, never-before-felt certainty, determination, and calm. I had understood that there was a place for me in fashion.

In the evening, we had a happy, joyful farewell dinner, and then I had to leave for London.

29. THESIS AND MOVING IN WITH J.

Back in London, moving madness took up my time. J. and I decided to move in together. We had found a small apartment close to Portobello, which we shared with our friend Mark. I loved J. deeply, and it was a very happy moment in my life. J. made me complete. It was not like all the other relationships before, where my partners and I loved each other but never shared the same passion for art and fashion. With J., it was complete; she was my soulmate. I loved her smile, her high Harley boots, her plaid mini skirt, her Newcastle Geordie accent, and her humor. She was the one.

The house was small, but it was newly renovated and clean. We did not have much to move—four suitcases, a television, and a mattress—that was it. It was a special moment; it was the first time I moved in with a girlfriend. It meant a lot to me.

Living and designing at college meant we would spend a lot of time together.

We were allowed into college Monday through Saturday from 7:00 a.m. to 12:00 a.m. All of us spend every free minute at college. On Sundays, though, we stayed in bed, cooked a huge pot of rice, corn, and eggs, and watched Eastenders, loving and eating.

J. was an instinctive designer; she did not intellectually contemplate concepts and logic for hours. She just did it naturally. What she touched was beauty. When she created it, it was pure instinct and gut feeling. J. put things together, and they were beautiful. She was an incredible illustrator and sketcher. Never in my life and career have I seen such talent again. On the other hand, I was a pure intellectual designer with heavy concepts and deep thoughts. I was a good illustrator, but I had to work for it. My work was full of philosophy and research, but my designs were often heavy-handed and crude. Don't get me wrong; everybody in our class at the RCA had outstanding design talent. We were the best, but J. was better. We all knew it—Brian Kirkby and Chris Bailey included.

J. often looked at my designs and changed a few things, and magic happened. She just smiled and shrugged her shoulders. That's how she was; she saw where I was blind. On the other hand, she loved to listen to my concepts, theories, and intellectual findings. I guess she liked my stories, which I spun from art, philosophy, and life. It was a good time, and I hoped J. and I would combine our different qualities one day and create a family, life, and company together. It was a dream I spoke about often. J. always indulged me in my dreams.

While J. and I spent half of our summer break in Italy, we still had to write a 10,000-word Thesis. We had not much time left, and we started at once after we settled into our new apartment. J.'s thesis was about rewriting "Alice in Wonderland" into a fashion story set in our times. My thesis was called "Poetic Violence." I was always reading a lot, something that stayed with me from my time in the library. At the time, I found out about the "big leap" in human brain development. Nobody is certain how, but roughly seventy thousand years ago, Homo sapiens evolved their consciousness and brain function. Our human ancestors were on the brink of extinction during a volcanic winter. Then, a miracle happened, and evolution rewired our brains. Homo sapiens became a thinking and organized being. From the middle of the natural food chain, we became the number one "animal" on this planet. Our brainpower was miraculously unlocked and increased. Scientists have ever since tried to unlock our intellectual capabilities further without any success. This research led me to early cave paintings and, from there, to the history of Gods and religion, from polytheism to monotheism and the great architect. In particular, Marquis de Sade's writing drove my thesis argument that human intellect will overcome moral boundaries and that the truly enlightened will not bow to any law. I concurred that growth is always linked to pain. How does the current saying go: "No pain, no gain?" Of course, I used this argument in the context of true innovation and artistic liberty. It was a wonderful mix of theories and arguments. These were the ingredients which I linked up and combined with Taoist wisdom. To be blunt, in my thesis, I mixed it all up to conclude that humankind basically needs more wild intercourse.

It was a true tour de force. Unfortunately, I have no idea what happened to my thesis, and no copy of it is left to my knowledge. It was fun writing it, though. J. and I had a laugh.

30. FINAL YEAR

In the second year, we started our final year, the Fashion show year at the Royal College of Art. The second and last years were all about finding jobs and the final fashion show. We were ready and eager to compete, with big dreams in our heads. We wanted to be the best; we wanted to be discovered; we wanted to become rich and famous. In those days, fashion design was still a rare career choice, and many jobs were available, especially to those graduating from the UK's top schools like RCA and Central Saint Martins. We had choices and multiple job offers from top fashion houses. We were spoiled! Those were the ambitious dreams of us young designers. We were all inspired by the success of John Galliano and Alexander McQueen. We wanted to shine like them.

Before we were allowed to design our final collection, though, we first had to design a pre-collection with two finished looks. My pre-collection was called "Wake Up." I believed in the power of fashion and the impact of content. "Wake up" was linked to a simple wake-up call about the pollution of our planet, ecology, and sustainability. In those days, everything revolved around a strong message. Sustainability was the beginning of a new ecological consciousness, a fashion movement in its infancy. My pre-collection was a "wake-up" call to fashion. My fashion concept was a literal translation, alarm clocks, bed linens, pillows, duvets, and bed sheets were the ingredients of my concept. The colors I picked were horrible: burgundy red velvet and mustard yellow raw silk. Until today, I don't comprehend why none of my professors stopped me from using this color palette. In the end, I made it work, all designs worked out great, and the looks had a baroque feel to them thanks to the red velvet, gold brocade, and embroidery I added later. As it was the final year, a lot of visitors came to the RCA to find new talent or just say hello and hang out. My big heroes, for whom I hoped to work one day, were Castelbajac and Moschino. Moschino was my absolute number-one favorite of mine due to his messages, content, artistic background, and humor. I loved his style and colorful prints. I told this to anyone who wanted to hear it and to all my classmates who did not want to hear it.

To keep in touch with Moschino and Jonathan, I produced little boxes with collection design concepts and small capsule collections. They were beautiful boxes, handmade, and always contained a surprise geared toward Moschino. We called them my "teaser projects." They contained sketches, design drawings, fabric manipulations, and anything beautiful and surprising to remind them of my existence. One teaser project was all about smoking dresses, the other about my "Wake Up" collection, and so on.

Every month, I sent one box to Moschino and stayed in touch with them. Determination was the key. I wouldn't give up until I worked there. In mid-December of the second year, just before we finished our pre-collection, Gianni Versace visited the college. He was meant to give a lecture, and we were all eager to hear what he had to say. He was a big star at the time, but not everybody liked his style. He was controversial, loved, and hated equally. To me, this did not matter; I liked his attitude and flamboyant character. Once he walked on stage, he was a natural presenter and won over all doubters. He was funny and full of great stories. He was honest and forthcoming with the truth. He answered all the questions with a smile and offered support where he could. His presentation was a huge success, and everybody loved him in the end. As he finished, he wanted to see some portfolios, and he had time for four students. I was selected to be one of the four, and we ran up to grab our books. It was a big honor to present it to Gianni Versace. As it was my turn, he listened to all my concepts, stories, and designs. As we came to my pre-collection, he fell in love with the concept; he stood up and wanted to buy the collection, and he wanted me to create the outfits for his shop window in Milan. I was shocked and speechless. I did not have time for this. Gianni called up John Miles, our dean, and told him he wanted the outfits in his window in two weeks. This was impossible with our fashion show schedule. John was his diplomatic self and finally convinced Gianni not to insist. Gianni gave in and offered that I ought to contact him as soon as I graduate in May. He shook my hand and clapped me on the shoulder, and he was gone. I was still flabbergasted and speechless after all this happened within fifteen minutes. John called me into his office, and we had a quick "what the fuck just happened" moment, and he sent me back up to our classroom. The news traveled fast, and by the time

I arrived, all my peers had heard about what had happened and wanted to know the full story. I told them all while I was still digesting. After thirty minutes of talking, I decided it was time to drink and celebrate. Nobody wanted to work anymore anyway, and we went to the College bar and had a wild night.

I never met Gianni again; he was a wonderful person and designer. I still miss him very much. Those few hours in his lecture and thirty-minute interview were an incredible experience.

Life continued in the final year. We started our final collections, and we were assigned our mentors. Pepita de Foot was my mentor, and she was outrageous with her mad red hair. She was a true fashion diva who could have been part of the television show "absolutely fabulous." She kept me sane during those stressful days and helped me focus. My final collection was called "Wake up and Get Fresh." It was a further development of my pre-collection and its ecological and sustainable content. Nobody told me until later what "get fresh" meant. In a broader sense, it meant "to have sex." My title basically did mean "wake up and have a shag." My classmates had a good laugh at my expense when J. finally informed me about the underlying meaning of the title. I thought it was cool and kept it.

This time the collection had nothing to do with a bedroom but was all about washing detergents and washing symbols. I intended to wash the world clean with my collection. The garments were colorful and happy, with a powerful message embedded into the redesigned washing symbols. I had buttons made especially with those symbols and brush shoes created by one of my sponsors, "Red or Dead." I even created a bubble perfume bottle for the IFF competition (International Flavors & Fragrances, Inc.), but I did not win.

The collection was fun and geared towards landing me a job at Moschino, but first, we had to design and create the collections.

As we all came back in January, we were ready to go. Overnight, the atmosphere in the classroom changed from friendly to evil. Everybody started to work in secret.

Sewing machines were manipulated so nobody else could use them, and fabric suppliers and any helpful information were hidden. It was ridiculous, but luckily John Miles stepped in after the first three weeks of January. He came up to our studio and explained to us that we were a team, a family, and "to be negatively competitive" was not the way to go forward. We needed to understand that we all had our own styles, strengths, and weaknesses and that we could not copy or steal from each other even if we wanted to. Most importantly, he pointed out that we would need each other once we entered the real fashion world and industry. The coin dropped, and we all changed our attitudes, and the process became intense, fun, and happy. From then on, it was great to see the collections come together, with all the creativity and beauty of the garments developing around us. I have very much missed this feeling ever since. In the industry, this never happens again: the absolute freedom of creation, the creative energy in one room, the smiles when designs work, and the support to overcome failures and disappointments. Many things went wrong and were hard to digest, and we were lucky to have each other.

As the collections progressed; we had muslin fittings, then fittings of finished looks. Our mentors came and went, tears were shed, and laughter was shared. The college bar was our hangout, where we decompressed from the collection stress, and we all became brothers in arms. We knew we could rely on each other, no matter what life threw at us. During the development of our collections, it became rapidly clear that Brian Kirkby's collection was the best and most outstanding. His play on British history and "Rule Britannia" was incredibly impactful. On the other hand, Christopher had a rough time. He was the golden boy, mentored by Anne Tyrrell. Christopher had won an RCA scholarship as the best undergraduate designer out of all UK Colleges. He was crowned the best, and he was. He was very good, but his final collection did not come together as planned. He was under huge pressure and was meant to create twelve outfits for the fashion show. We only had to create six to eight outfits in comparison. Apart from the insane workload, he had an unfortunate color and print choice. As the collections progressed, more and more people tried to convince him to reconsider his colors. The more they pushed, the more stubborn he became. It was crazy to witness the number of meetings he had to attend. We all held the deepest respect for his conviction and staying power. In the end, his show was not well received, and he had difficulties finding a place to work. It took many favors to place him at Donna Karan for his first job. The beginning of his career was hard. It all changed when he moved to work for Gucci under Tom Ford, and then he became the famous Creative Director at Burberry. Chris always was and is a great designer, but we all must survive the curve balls life throws at us from time to time.

This was all later after his graduation show, though. Before the show, we were all in the same boat, and we were all fighting to give our best. We all created and worked hard, and slowly, we could see each other's collections taking shape. We could see what worked and what didn't.

Three weeks before the show, it was announced that Karl Lagerfeld would be the guest of honor at our Gala show. The Gala show was the last show in the evening. During the day, there were seated fashion shows, which were free. The Gala show, on the other hand, was a seated dinner show where fashion industry professionals bought tables and dinner plates. Those tickets were expensive, and it was a black-tie event.

Those Gala tickets were sold out in a matter of minutes, and we were all very excited because our parents would be there too.

31. FINALLY, SHOW TIME, AND MOSCHINO CALLED

The week of our fashion show had finally arrived. As with every fashion show, nobody was ready, and as always, there was still so much to do. We did fight over models; we did all the last-minute fittings; we complained about the make-up; and we were frantically looking for the right fashion show music. It was adrenaline time! We were all pumped and tired, but ecstatic about the big moment that would change our futures. Would we be discovered? Would we get a job? Would our collection please the audience? We put so much hope into this moment. Although everybody told us not to overrate the show, we still did. Next to all the stressful preparations and late nights to finish all the work, our friends and families arrived. My friends Robert, Andreas, and Anke were immediately put to work. They had to help embroider pearls on my last jacket. A tedious job, that took hours, and of course, I had miscalculated the amount of time it would take and left it until the last moment. Our parents arrived as well. It would be the first time J.'s and my parents would meet. My Uncle Yogi and Christel were there too. They were all very excited and proud to come to London to finally see Jens finish his fashion design studies. It has been a long way from Ohio to London, but I made it, and they were proud of my achievements. It was a crazy time of meeting family, friends and finishing touches before the show would start.

The last day before the show, we held the final run-through with models, and it was a disaster. The music was wrong, models took the wrong exits, shoes broke, and models refused to wear certain outfits. It was mayhem. In the end, everything came together with a lot of drama, and then we were ready. We hardly slept and returned the next day in the morning for final touches. The first show started at ten, and all went smoothly, it was a great success. The second show was at noon. For the Gala event, there was a break to change the venue. The Gala would start at seven; tables had to be put up and catering organized.

During the break, we went home, had a drink with our families and friends, and changed our outfits for the evening. Dressed up, we returned for our special night. Everything had been transformed and was beautifully decorated. We grabbed a glass of champagne, looked for our tables, searched for famous designers, and, of course, Karl Lagerfeld. To see all the flamboyant fashion crowd fill in and occupy the space was intoxicating. There is nothing more exciting than fashionistas congregating. My mother and aunt were speechless when they saw all those crazy people; they had never seen anything comparable before.

The dinner was served, and we had a spectacular time. All the stress and pain were worth it to get to this point.

We finished dinner with a drink in our hands, and John Miles started with his speech. He announced the winners for the Max Mara and IFF competitions; a lot of applause followed, and the winning students went up onto the stage to collect their trophies and shake hands. We all applauded wildly, happy for the winners. Then Karl Lagerfeld walked onto the stage and gave his speech. He was astonishingly short. He also had a few pounds too many, but his trademark ponytail and sunglasses were immediately recognized by everybody in the room. It was really him, in a short and round version. He was a good speaker and wished us all luck. We applauded loudly, and the Gala show began. To see the show one last time was very emotional for me. After nine years of pushing, fighting, and competing, I had accomplished what I set out to do. My university time and education were coming to an end. The next day would be the last. Tomorrow, another chapter will start in all our lives.

Nobody told us what to expect after the show; we were only told to bring our portfolio and not to drink too much. As the final collection by Brian exited the catwalk, John Miles once again came on stage and thanked everybody. He told us to stay seated for possible interviews. Five minutes later, I was summoned to meet Karl Lagerfeld and after ESCADA, in a separate room. Karl looked at my portfolio and asked me about my future dream job. I told him with the deepest conviction that I would work for Moschino. Not the smartest move in hindsight because Karl was not amused and wished me well. The ESCADA interview with its Creative Director, Brian Rennie, did go down in a similar fashion. He asked for a project to see my ideas for ESCADA, and I agreed to do so, but all I really cared for was Moschino. Once the big Gala moment was over, we left. Our parents went home, but the class of 94 went on a party tour, and J. and I had a wild night.

The next morning, we all hustled back to school to look at all the reviews and find out who did get a job and who did not. It was an intense moment with many highs and lows, tears, and giggles. In the next two weeks, most of us did get a call and did get jobs. I got a call too! I was invited to an interview with Rosella Jardini at Moschino. Sadly, Franco Moschino had passed away, and Rosella had taken over the reins in Milan. All my boxes, teasers, designs, and concepts had done the trick. It had taken me nearly eighteen months of preparation to land this interview. I was meant to leave for Milan in a week's time, and I wanted to take J. with me. J. did not have a real job offer yet. There were offers, but nothing exciting, and I could tell she was getting cold feet. J. had never lived abroad before, nor had she ever learned a foreign language. She did not want to leave the UK, and the coming week took a lot of persuasion to convince her to join me on my trip to Milan, but finally, we boarded the plane and were on our way.

We stayed at a small hotel in Milan, and once we arrived, I immediately prepared for my interview the next morning, my big moment. I checked how to get a taxi, how long it would take to get there, and so forth. I left nothing to surprise.

The next day at breakfast, since I could hardly eat anything, I drank a Cappuccino, which was a stupid idea since I never drank coffee because it made me nervous. It was incredibly hot, and I made my way to see Rosella at the Moschino office. It was an inconspicuous building in the back of a courtyard, difficult to find if you did not know, but I arrived on time. The office space was as impressive as the first time I visited, and after ten minutes of waiting, I was called up to the big fitting studio, where Jonathan Cheung, Alexandra Sechi, Rosella, Bill Shapiro, and Francesca Rubino were waiting for me. At the time, I did not know any of them, and Rosella greeted me with broken English and a cigarette in her fingers: "So you are the one who would not take a "no" for an answer." I smiled and said, "Yes, that's me." They asked me to sit down and show my work. I never had an interview with "Italian" style. It was sheer chaos. Everybody was talking at the same time in English and Italian. I did not speak a word of Italian. After twenty minutes of pandemonium, I was thoroughly stressed and started sweating. There was no air conditioning, and it was hot! The cappuccino did not help. I was pouring out sweat. My face and shirt were soaked and dripping. I was pouring out sweat like a water hose. I could not stop it. My sweat was dripping on my work, the table, from my hands. It was embarrassing; I had never had a reaction like this before. Rosella looked at me and asked Bill to get me some paper towels, which did not help because I became even more self-conscious, and it just made matters worse. When the interview came to an end, we stood up and said our goodbyes, and I left the office soaked and devastated. I was convinced they would never hire me after all the sweat I poured out that day. Meeting J. in a coffee bar nearby, I nearly cried. "I blew it," I told her. There was no celebration that day.

The next day, they called me back and jokingly told me to bring towels for my start at the beginning of September. We all laughed, and I promised I would. A huge weight fell from my shoulders, and I danced with J. in our hotel room. J. was not happy about the idea of living in Milan, but I managed to convince her in my excitement that all would be well. In the afternoon, I was told to come back to the Moschino office to meet the CEO to discuss my contract. He welcomed me with a smile and quickly explained that I would get an apartment for free and the equivalent of 500 Euros monthly. He shook my hand and kicked me out.

This was the worst day of my life. I had my dream job but could not afford to take it. How would J. and I be able to live off 500 Euros a month in Milan? I could have cried.

32. MILAN OR NOT MILAN; FAILURE IS NOT AN OPTION

As we came back, we started discussing all our options. J. wanted to go to New York, and I still tried to find a way to go to Milan. It was back and forth. J. was looking into jobs in New York, but nothing came up. We only had a job offer in London, but we did not want to stay there. We wanted to go anywhere but France. I knew I would not be able to work in France. My designs were too colorful, and in Paris, everything was "black cloth." I didn't wear black cloth! Luckily, there weren't many jobs in France; all the jobs were in Italy or New York. LVMH and Kering Group did not exist yet.

We had many more challenges pop up. Apart from finding a job, we had to move out of our apartment in London. Our lease was up, and Mark wanted to move to Australia. We had to pack our suitcases and gather our things. Since we did not know what to do next, we decided to move to J.'s parent's house in Durham, close to Newcastle. I had never been up north and did not quite know what to expect, but we did not have a choice. We also signed up "on the dole," and I paid off some unexpected debts that found us through J.'s credit card adventures from her previous life. Some bailiffs came knocking at our door looking for her. Luckily, I still had some money left from my father's generous monthly stipend, so I paid them. J. gave me a kiss, and we were glad this situation was finally settled. As we gathered all our things, we found out that J. had three big suitcases full of books stowed away in her old apartment. They weighed about 400 pounds. I could hardly lift one of them, so heavy they were. Furthermore, since we had no money, we had to travel to Newcastle by bus. I had never traveled by bus anywhere. In Germany, you only travel by bus on school excursions. So, we bought our tickets and had to change somewhere along the way. The journey started at 6 a.m. in the morning, and we had seven suitcases ready to get loaded onto the bus. As we arrived at the station, the bus was full, and I had to somehow manage to load our seven suitcases on the bus. It was an absolute nightmare; they were super heavy, and I had to fight to get them all into the cargo space. By the time I got on the bus, J. had secured a good seat, and we enjoyed the ride. At the next stop, we would have to change buses, and the whole suitcase-loading war would start again. One suitcase full of books did not make it; we had to leave it behind because the suitcase broke, and J.'s books were scattered all over the bus stop. Eventually, we made it to Newcastle! J.'s father picked us up, and we loaded the remaining suitcases into a separate taxi to get everything moved to the house. I was exhausted and happy that we had arrived. At J.'s house, we unloaded and said hello to her mom. Her family lived in a charming little house with a view of the sea. J.'s family was warm and welcoming, and I enjoyed our time in Durham very much. In the coming weeks, we continued to check on all the possible job options. My father was very involved and opinionated. He could not understand how anybody would even consider working for such a ridiculous salary offered by Moschino. I explained to him that it was normal for the first job and that the next salary would be much higher with the name Moschino on my resume. My father offered to give me a 5,000 Euro credit for the first year until J. found a job and we would be able to stand on our own two feet. I agreed, and it took an additional two days of berating J. until she agreed to join me in Milan. Moschino, here we come! It was decided, and we started planning for our move to Milan at the end of August.

33. MOSCHINO

Last week of August, J. and I made our way down to London with one suitcase each and our portfolio. No more jobs had materialized in New York. I was super excited, J., not so much. She was unemployed and living in a foreign country without friends, where she did not know the language. We hadn't seen the apartment either. What would our new home look like? At Milan Linate Airport, we gathered our suitcases and took a taxi to our new apartment. A friendly woman was waiting for us with the keys. She led us up to the apartment on the top floor. As we opened the door, the room before us was open and spacious, the interior was hideous, though it looked like a caravan spaceship from the seventies. It was right opposite Monumentale Cemetery and had a huge balcony. The lady handed us the key and left. We had to laugh about the house, hold each other in our arms, and be happy about our first home abroad. We unpacked and found a nice trattoria, where we ate delicious pasta and drank Italian wine. The next morning, we explored the city and shops. Milan was small compared to London and quite ugly. Nonetheless, we were happy. I popped by the Moschino office to say "hi" and find out what time I would have to start this coming Monday, and then enjoyed the rest of the week with J. We made our first Italian friend, the young owner of a bar around the corner. He made us a special deal for food and wine, which we were grateful for since our finances were scarce. The Monumentale cemetery next door was more impressive than any sculpture museum we had ever seen. It was unbelievable what had been built in that cemetery over hundreds of years. We spent many hours there wandering and discovering.

The week flew by, and Monday came, and work started. As I arrived, I was introduced to Francesca, my new boss. She was the head of Moschino women's jeans, and I was to work with her. I was shown around and introduced to everybody. Moschino was not big; it had two floors and about 25 people in total. Then, I was shown into a small office on the first floor. In the office, there was a young British girl named Christina who had been hired at the same time as me. She came straight out of college and arrived a week earlier. Christina was meant to assist with Cheap & Chic womenswear. Francesca left me to settle in, and Christina and I introduced each other. We chatted away as Francesca came back and asked me to sketch Moschino denim pieces and outfits. I unpacked my pens and pencils and started sketching. In the first year, this was my main job: drawing and sketching designs for denim or any other collection they needed designs for. At Moschino, there were many wonders to learn. Franco Moschino was a wonderful person, and his company was his family. In the nineties, it wasn't easy to be gay in Italy, and his family had broken all contact with him; only his brother was close to him. Franco spent his money on his work, family, and friends; his office was his home, and he happily mixed private life with work. His office was filled with his friends, and they had nothing to do but wander the studios, look at designs, and tell stories. Those stories were wild; they were from their good times in New York, Los Angeles, and many other places in the world. It was a crazy time; I loved to listen to all of them and absorbed their tales like a sponge. Luigi was the financial keeper of them all. Luigi was a gay man with a bad hip that made it difficult for him to walk. He came across as very rough and grumpy, but he had a heart of gold. I loved Luigi very much. Once you got to know him, he was a kind man, and he helped me more than once in difficult times. Luigi looked after all Franco's friends and paid their medical bills because most of them were HIV positive and had Aids. It was the saddest news once I realized what was happening. There was no cure; some died while I was there, and Luigi took care of them all.

Next to Franco's friends, there were the "girls." Rossella Jardini was the Creative Director after Moschino had died, and she kept the company running with the help of the CEO. There were the girls, "Rosella, Alexandra, Francesca, Luciano, Betta, and Lida." Alexandra was responsible for Cheap & Chic, Francesca looked after Moschino Jeans, and Luciano was responsible for all menswear. A very special position was held by Lida. I believe Lida was the secret female love of Moschino. She was a charismatic girl. I was admiring her very much, and I was secretly in love with her like a schoolboy with his teacher. Lida was answering to no one; she was responsible for "Marketing." Basically, she came up with whatever she liked doing and did it. Rosella was not a big friend of Lida but could do nothing to control her; Lida was her own boss and well protected by Luigi. In the office, the two power fractions were 'Luigi and Lida' and 'Rosella and the CEO.' Then there was Betta, an energetic personality with a mouth like a laser sword. Betta took care of all projects in Milan, between showrooms and fashion shows. She was a special character and a force to be reckoned with. Nobody wanted to get on the bad side of Betta.

The office was a pure design office. There were no sewing studios or ateliers like there would be in a French studio. Everything was organized through licensing deals, and AEFFE was the biggest license holder. Massimo Ferretti was the owner of AEFFE, and Alberta Ferretti was his sister. All samples and prototypes were produced in their factories near Cattolica, close to Rimini. The Italian craft man is the absolute best. I loved working with Italian producers; their mentality, smiles, and absolute dedication to beauty are unparalleled in the fashion industry all over the world. They are the best.

I was originally trained as a womenswear designer. Moschino had a small office, and often, Christina and I were summoned to join other collection meetings. Apart from sketching all day, we would join fabric selection meetings for couture or Cheap & Chic. Fittings were always a big event, and we all observed how the latest prototypes were presented and how Alexandra or Rosella would fit them. How they sketched and how they corrected the garments. All the notes were documented and recorded by the factory production staff. Most importantly, we learned how to behave and communicate in the fashion world. We were trained on how to pick fabrics, group them, and bring order to a fabric selection. In a fabric selection, it was crucial to build up a cost structure in your fabric choices, as any donkey could just pick the most expensive fabrics. It was an art to correct prints and color. Sergio and Stefania made sure we learned properly; they were responsible for all fabric orders. Picking accessories like buttons, zips, cords, embroidery, or any embellishment took careful consideration. All of this was learned by watching and observing. Moschino was heaven, and I loved every minute of being there. It was my place and my calling. Fashion shows were magical events, and we were helping, learning, and being part of every single one. They were fun and incredible spectacles.

While I was living my dream, it was not so easy for J. She applied and tried any possible opening we could find. I was constantly asking friends and any business-related connections for jobs for her. I knew if J. did not find a job, my dream would not be sustainable. I felt responsible since I convinced J. to come to Milan with me. It was not easy, but after six months, Domenico and Wiebke, friends of ours who worked at Gianfranco Ferré, arranged a meeting with Mr. Ferré, and it worked out. J. had an assistant job, and everything looked peachy for a moment. Our luck was short-lived; J.'s position was unpaid; literally no money was paid in compensation. To us, it was a shock and an unchangeable, harsh reality we had to accept. J. bit the bullet and accepted the job; it was better to have an unpaid job on your CV than no job at all. The financial situation we faced was bad, and I could not ask for more money from my father. In my desperation, I spoke with my best friend Andreas, and he came through and lent me money to survive our first year in Milan.

Not all was bad in Milan, though. We had a great time. We quickly met many new friends. Some friends were new starts like us in Milan from the UK, and some we met at work from Italy. Our Italian friends quickly introduced us to "aperitivo" time in Italy. This is the time before dinner when bars prepare a free buffet. For the price of a drink, you could eat for free! Some bars were very generous in their offerings, and our friends knew them all. At least we would not starve in Italy. Cristina, Caroline, Steffano, Mercedes, Dorota, Anna, Domenico, Valentina, and Liborio were only some of the names we met in Milan, and there were many more. If I have not mentioned all the names of those who were part of that wonderful time, forgive me! Apart from "Apperitivo" time, we were invited to all the fashion parties, which were many, and there was "Plastic," our hangout in the darkness after midnight.

After J. had worked at Gianfranco Ferré for a year, she finally received a salary of 500 Euros monthly, the same amount as mine. We were rich, and nothing could stop us. We were on our way. We were happy.

34. SECOND YEAR AND ONWARDS

During the first year, a lot of things were new, and we had to learn quickly. We met many friends, and it was an eventful and creative time. Collections were scheduled in a calmer rhythm then, and designers had time to research and work thoroughly. We settled in and learned Italian. Italian was easy to learn because everybody was happy to correct you, and they spoke slowly so you would understand. All our Italian friends were content that we were trying and helped us understand all the words we missed. Television helped, too; you could only watch Italian TV; there was no other choice available. The best teachers we had were Liborio and Chiara. After the first year and with J. finally earning some money, we moved in with Liborio and Chiara. Liborio was a friend who worked at Ferré, and Chiara was an art historian working in an art gallery. Liborio loved the Ramones and was constantly humming Ramones songs and quoting certain text fragments like 'Hey ho, let's go." Chiara was more quiet but very wise, and I loved to discuss art with her. The apartment was in an old Milanese villa with very high ceilings and old windows, which never closed properly and made you listen to the sound on the streets constantly. Italy is a very noisy country, but what a wonderful noise! It wraps you up like a blanket and makes you feel at home. The floors were old, dark brown, hardwood, scratched, and uneven through the wear and tear of time. The walls were rough; paint and wallpaper were torn and peeled, leaving a rugged but cozy charm to each room. Each room was different in color. We all had a room, and J. and I shared one room.

The living room was dominated by a huge, old dining table, and a comfortable antique couch stood in front of a big television. The television was constantly turned on, day and night. It did not matter if we had friends over for dinner or if nobody watched or paid any attention to it; the TV was on. Liborio and I loved to watch television and comment on whatever was presented to us. We would love to comment. In fact, this was where my Italian improved the most by chatting with Liborio in front of the television set.

Liborio was a genius cook. He could cook the simplest pasta, and it was divine, but he destroyed the kitchen in the process, which led in the first months to huge arguments because Libo did not care, and within days, the kitchen turned into an impossible disaster zone. We tried to convince him to clean up his mess but to no avail. In the end, I agreed to do the dishes and keep the kitchen clean if Liborio would cook for us all. I never minded cleaning anyway, and the idea of receiving one meal a day cooked by Libo was very tempting. Another positive side effect was that Libo started teaching J. and me how to cook. At first, he was horrified by what ingredients we would throw together and call edible food. He would mock us, and after the second time we prepared dinner for everybody, he made us throw our concoction into the bin. Lessons were thorough and strict, and after a few weeks, J. and I understood what good cooking meant. Liborio took us to the Italian markets, too, and showed us how to pick the right ingredients. We had no money, but we lived like kings.

Liborio and Chiara were not the only ones who looked after me. At work, Anna, a small German girl with blond hair, started coming to our office and chatting with me. She looked like a small schoolgirl with a cheeky smile. At first, she just asked me simple things about my origin and my family, and slowly, we started talking about people in the office and gossiping about the power struggles and dramas that unfolded daily. We also discussed fashion, design, and the stupidity of believing that creativity would outweigh a solid collection buildup, the childish ignorance of some, and the clear-sightedness of others. Anna was smart, and she was well respected by all. She worked with Luciano, and those two designed everything connected to Moschino menswear. They were part of a world of their own. Nobody touched them; they were quietly doing their job and doing well. With the greatest respect, Rosella left them to their own devices; it was intriguing to me how they achieved this status. Luciano and Anna both had worked with Franco Moschino for years. They were family and as untouchable as Lida was. It took me a year to understand their status in all the madness and outrageousness of the Moschino womenswear team. Another challenge presented itself during this time: J. was on the same crazy womenswear fashion show schedule as I was, which meant we hardly saw each other during those times. Menswear fashion shows had a different calendar. Without my knowing or realizing it, Anna groomed me for the menswear team and asked me at first for small things and then more often to help her design. It was a very slow process. Luciano, the head of menswear, officially did not like new people very much. He was cold and awkward at first. Only later did I find out he had AIDS and was often in the hospital for treatment. He did not want empathy or to have to explain himself to outsiders. His parents did not know, and Luigi looked after him. Moschino was his family, and I was new to him. It was hard for him to let me in, but as he warmed up to me, he became a generous, kind person with a big heart and the most hilarious humor.

More and more I was introduced to the menswear world, and one day, Anna asked me if I would like to join their team. I said yes immediately because I loved the menswear world. The next day Anna spoke with the CEO, and it was done. I packed my things and moved from the first floor to the ground floor into Anna's office.

35. MOSCHINO MENSWEAR

At Moschino, all womenswear teams were tightly controlled by Rosella, Alexandra, and Francesca, each of whom had their own team of assistants.

Rosella was not a designer by training, but she signed off on everything. Nothing escaped her control. Francesca was her close friend and always stood by Rosella's side. Alexandra was a strong character, and she designed Cheap & Chic womenswear with great success. Her collections were legendary, and it was an honor to work with her. During the design process we were invited to some meetings. You were allowed to see certain steps of the collection's development, but other steps you were not allowed to see. It was a control mechanism that restricted insight into the process. Christina and I were kept small in our growth and not included in all the relevant decision-making; especially as certain collection fittings were held at the Aeffe offices in Catolica.

At the menswear team, everything was different. Luciano was the boss, no question about it. He was in charge and called the shots. Nobody challenged him, not even Rosella. Anna was his design partner and second in command concerning menswear, and she was organizing everything. Luciano was not always available because of his treatments and had to spend significant time at the hospital. It was incredible to see how little the Doctors could do for him. He taught me a lot about composure—how you can get up each day and face the certainty of death with a smile. He was literally an angel, and his work was his legacy. He had a clear vision, as had Franco Moschino and all who had worked with him. Luciano had absolute focus and clarity about what he wanted to achieve in the short time that was left to him. In everything, he only saw the good, and he gave openly; nothing was hidden or ruled by petty jealousy.

Anna was his partner. As I started on the menswear team, I was talking all day about how to do things better, saving the planet, the power of creativity, how we must change the world, finding a cure for

AIDS, and the power of fashion. I was a self-righteous, pompous little shit from the RCA. I firmly believed that all my struggles and years of planning to get my degree from the RCA automatically entitled me to greatness. Not that I was malicious; I was just convinced that all my learning and my experiences made me special, that I held the golden key to exquisite design, and that Moschino needed my help. I believed to the core of my being that I would be the next Franco Moschino. Most of the time, Luciano and Anna listened to my rumblings about innovative designs with a serene smile on their faces. In my first year, though, Anna introduced me to how a collection was built up. How a commercial color card is constructed, and how sellable colors such as navy, white, and black have a solid function in each collection. How certain styles had to be updated so the boutiques and department stores, and their buyers, found solid, sellable pieces. That innovative piece was needed but comprised only 10% of all sales. It was an eye-opener to learn how the fashion business worked. Anna did all that and more. I owe Anna everything in my later career. She had the wisdom to see my passion and guided me towards a deeper understanding of how to bring order to chaos and become a professional functioning designer. Anna and Luciano shaped me, and I believe Luciano saw me as his final masterpiece; he poured all his passion into me. I became his living legacy and heir to his knowledge and experience. One day, Luciano could not stand to listen to me anymore and instructed Eugenio, our product manager from Aeffe, to let me design three outerwear pieces as I saw fit. There were no restrictions; I was meant to show them what I could do. I was super excited to finally blow them away. At "Milano Unica," the biggest fabric fair in Milan, I spent days finding the most outrageous and innovative fabrics. At last, I found a honeycomb neoprene mesh fabric for 80 Euros per meter, an outrageous price only allowed for the couture collection. I convinced Eugenio and Sergio to buy 25 meters, and after a long discussion with Luciano, they finally purchased the fabric. Because of this outrage, the whole design office was aware of my special mission to show them all what real design does look like. I felt like I was Christian Dior, Balenciaga, and Yves Saint Laurent all in one. I was a genius in the making, and I would show them all. I spent a week, day and night, pouring my creativity into those three outerwear pieces. Once I made my choice, I instructed Eugenio on all the details and how to produce the samples. It took three weeks before the prototypes arrived. Once they arrived at our office in Milan, I ripped open the boxes. I was ready for my applause and the golden keys to the design office. I was the new king, the heir to Moschino in the making.

As I unpacked the pieces and tried them on, my world collapsed. They looked horrible and had nothing to do with Moschino. There were three pieces I designed that cost thousands of Euros to produce and were utter shit. They were crap, not worth looking at twice. I was so ashamed, and of course, everybody knew about those pieces. In the menswear office, Luciano made me put on each piece. Made me wear them and parade them up and down the corridor. He made Polaroids and cherished every moment of my walk of shame. In the end, he put them on a clothes rack in the hallway for everybody to see. My defeat was absolute.

The garments stayed out on the clothes rack for a solid month, and every visitor and fabric representative were made aware of them. The experience was humbling and put me in my rightful place. From then on, I had learned my position, respect for the craft of design, and the power of experience. This allowed me to open up to the next level of my professional learning. I understood and fully absorbed the generous lesson Luciano had taught me. I am grateful for everything Anna and Luciano did for me in those years. I was given so much by both, and I would happily put them into paradise if I could.

36. FASHION SHOWS AND PLATON

Fashion shows, shop windows, and exhibitions have always been and will continue to be important parts of the fashion industry. Everybody was encouraged to come up with new ideas and show them to Rosella. My bag dress from my graduation fashion show at the RCA was chosen and refined, then turned into a Moschino store window. Of course, the Moschino version looked so much better than my graduation dress. My designs were also chosen for a perfume bottle. On one design, I put the Milan Duomo in a snowball shaker bottle with gold glitter. Unfortunately, the gold glitter kept clogging up the spray pump of the perfume, but I believe they finally solved the problem years later and produced the bottle.

Fashion shows were celebrated at Moschino. Womenswear had its Couture, Cheap & Chic, and Swimwear shows. All of them were elaborate theatrical productions. For the first 18 months, everybody laughed because Rosella thought I was gay and scheduled me as a dresser for the women's Swimwear show. There I was, lodged between twenty naked models, all of them flirting with me while I was handing them their whimsical outfits. When Rosella finally found out it was food for many jokes.

Menswear, though, was another dimension. Luciano loved the theatrics. While Anna was mainly the architect of all menswear collections, Luciano came up with the most outrageous catwalk concepts. He loved to work with me on those productions. One show concept was called "The Emperor's New Clothes" and was inspired by the old fairy tale where the King stands naked in front of his court, believing he is wearing the most refined clothes, and nobody dared to tell him he was stark naked. Of course, Luciano took it to new heights; he bent the story to a gay nightclub scenario with gay-related cross-dressing and transvestite performances. It was "Rocky Horror Picture Show" meets "La Cage aux Folles." Actors played the king and his court in the background while the fashion show was held on the catwalk, everybody enjoyed being part of it. Models loved to work with us because we treated them well and with respect, and they were all allowed to act and play a part. One model had to hold a goose, which did not work out well because the goose always bit him in the neck. Finally, we had to replace the goose with a chicken, as it was safer for the model's nose. We got away with murder in our productions. Another show was held in the Bocconi Olympic indoor swimming pool. There, we created a floating catwalk on water; it looked like the models were walking on water. Today, the "walking on water" concept has been repeated by many other designers, but back in the mid-nineties, those types of productions were new and much appreciated by all guests and the press. Luciano also enjoyed creating the wildest catwalk pieces. He had great ideas for silhouettes and prints; he was also a master of color and accessories. Luciano was a great designer and fun to be with.

The best and most memorable show was held in Florence during Pitti. Luciano and Pitti Uomo in Florence combined a rock concert and a fashion show. It was a huge event, and it took a great deal of time to dress and fit all the different Rock bands. "Zucchero" was there, as were many other famous acts, mostly Italian bands. They were great to work with, and the whole show took over an hour and turned into a magnificent party afterward. I am not sure if the documentation and photos are still in the Moschino archive, as they all moved when Jeremy Scott took over.

Shows were not the only means of communication, though. Publicity photo shoots and advertisements were as important. There was an external PR consulting agency to support, but mostly Rosella and Lida decided what was photographed and used as a campaign in publications and the press. One day, the famous photographer "Platon" was hired to shoot a campaign for Moschino. Platon's setup in our studio was simple. He shot in front of a white backdrop. Once the lights were set up and Platon was satisfied, he started shooting. Platon was like Robert Mapplethorpe; he only needed a few takes to get it right. The longest amount of time was used to prepare the models. A photoshoot looks simple but is a time-consuming process. After the studio and lights are set up, models are prepared by hair and makeup. Those creatives start early, usually at 5 or 6 a.m., since it takes many hours to get it right. Then, the stylist dresses the models and fits the clothes. As it often happens, concepts change during a shoot, and the shoot takes a completely new direction. Platon was shooting what he was told to shoot, but we were finished early. Christina and I were assisting; we did get along well with Platon's team, and we had a great laugh. As we were joking around, Platon looked at me and squinted his eyes, then asked me if I would shave my head. At first, I thought he was joking, and I said, "Why don't I shave a heart in the back of my head while we are at it." Everybody went quiet. I naively grinned because I believed he would take it as a joke, but he didn't. After another hour of me refusing and laughing and trying to get out of it, Platoon managed to convince me, and I finally agreed. My five minutes of fashion fame had arrived. The hair and make-up team got the clippers and shaved my head except for a big heart on the back of my head.

Platon took the picture; it took about 20 minutes, and the photo was done. Rosella loved it, and I wore the heart for the rest of the week to all the nightclubs in Milan. Later, the picture was used in books and publicity. I was never paid, but it did not matter; not many can say they had their portrait taken by Plato, maybe President Obama.

Model Jens Kaeumle, ©Photography

by Platon.

37. MILAN, BABIES AND REINVENTING FAITH

After two years, J. and I earned a salary we could survive on and found a beautiful loft in Milan. It was our first place to ourselves; we missed Liborio and Chiara very much, but we also enjoyed the luxury of privacy and space. Even better, it was close to our most favorite bar at the time, "Elephante," and our most favorite barkeeper, Fede, the cousin of Beta. Elephante was our living room, and we only had to walk 100 yards before we were home in our stylish loft with a wonderful kitchen, a free-standing bathtub, and a lovely balcony overlooking the rooftops of Milan. We had arrived, our careers made sense, and our parents were happy we could feed ourselves after all the expensive education we received. J., though, was not too happy in Milan; something did not sit right with her. Milan is not a big city and can be quite provincial at times. I never minded Milan; I was completely at home, but J. kept on pushing for New York. I wanted children and to marry, but J. refused to entertain the thought of marriage; it was out of the question. To her, a relationship was about equality and independence, not about the old-fashioned idea of wedding bells. I did not quite understand her point, but I agreed since I loved her blindly and would have agreed to anything to make her happy. I tried twice to convince her otherwise, but she turned me down every time I proposed. The thought of having children was something she agreed to, and we started trying. The first time did not go well; we tried, but nothing happened, and so after a few months went by, we were convinced it was not meant to be, and then J. became pregnant. I was over the moon, but J. suddenly had second thoughts about having children just then in Milan.

After super happy moments and very sad moments, faith decided for us. We lost our first child. It was tragic and hard for both of us.

We both suffered a lot in those days, and we did not share the loss with any of our friends. We kept it to ourselves and continued to keep up a happy façade like nothing had ever happened. As they say, "time heals all wounds," so time and nature did their miracle work and our optimism returned. We tried again, and J. became pregnant a second time.

This time, we both embraced the gift, but we still had to face a harsh reality: we did not earn enough money to start a family. We made enough to keep us above water, but we did by no means have enough money spare to buy diapers.

J. became pregnant in December; before that, we spent our summer holiday in the USA and stayed for one week in New York to interview for jobs. We had some leads; J. had a great interest in Donna Karan, and I had met Ginny Hilfiger, who wanted to hire me for Tommy Hilfiger. The experience in the USA was fun; it was easy to meet people and present your portfolio. We had learned by then to create portfolio content that was different, and we stood out from the competition. The reactions from the companies were positive, and we were confident that New York would be our next port of call. We had no idea, of course, that J. would be pregnant some months later, in December. The question then was, who would hire a pregnant designer? Our confidence was gone, and we were questioning how to go about it. Just taking a job and announcing after three months that you are pregnant was not the right way to go. The first week, we spent many hours discussing various possibilities and scenarios. We did not tell our families due to the first pregnancy ending badly. This time, though, brought us closer; we developed a stronger bond and a deep trust in each other. We stood by each other and supported each other where we could. We became an unbeatable team.

The best immediate plan we decided to attempt was to ask for a pay raise. Since J. was pregnant, she could not really ask for a raise, so I had to talk to the CEO. Rosella loved children, and Moschino supported many children's foundations and helped them financially. I was optimistic that the CEO would be sympathetic and support us. At that time, Luciano was very sick and mostly in the hospital. I had proven myself over the years to be capable of running the menswear department. My plan was to kill two birds with one stone, and therefore, I did not only present a pay raise request, but I also presented the CEO with a plan on how I would become an asset to Moschino as head of the menswear department linked to a scaled pay rise if I proved myself able and successful. I had spoken with Anna before, and she was supportive since she wanted to have more time with her new love and later husband at Lake Garda. In the meeting, though, the CEO did listen to my story and proposal with an unmoved expression. Once I had finished, he simply announced that he would have none of it—no head of menswear, no pay raise. He simply announced the pregnancy was my problem, and I could take it or literally leave it. This was an unexpected blow. That day, I had to tell J. the bad news. We were devastated, and the nightmare of desperately searching for solutions continued. One of the solutions was to approach Porsche to create a clothing line for them. I always had an entrepreneurial instinct and loved to create concepts. Mattia, a good friend, helped with the graphics, and we created a beautiful booklet with designs and a concept story for Porsche. We knew it was a long shot since Porsche had their own design offices and one of the Porsche sons had his own product design office. We believed we would have a slim chance due to my father working there all his life. After all, I had grown up with Porsche. I knew the company well, and I admit I am a bit of a car fan myself. I love Porsche. The booklet was beautiful, and my father delivered it to all the key people in the company, but unfortunately, no luck; they were already in negotiations with Hugo Boss. They were very encouraging, and it was good fun producing and developing the concept, but there was no solution to our problems there.

During the first three months, we tried everything to find jobs anywhere and had to tell our families about J.'s pregnancy, too. They were excited and supportive but did not have any real solution either; the only solution they had was moving back home. Moving back to Germany was not an option; it would have meant an immediate end to our hopes and dreams for our careers. So, we continued to knock on every open door for jobs or freelance work.

In those days, I had seen an ad in I-D magazine in which Levi's was looking for the next design manager in Germany, close to Frankfurt. Without thinking, I took a Polaroid camera, took a selfie, filled in the application, attached my CV, and sent it to Levi's. I completely forgot about it later because neither J. nor I wanted to move to Heusenstamm (a village close to Frankfurt) in the middle of German-nowhere land. As life has funny ways of opening doors right in that period of despair, I received a phone call, and they invited me for an Interview in Germany. Since we did not have any other leads, I went and flew to Germany. Once I arrived in Frankfurt, I was picked up by a driver and chauffeured to the German headquarters in Heusenstamm. The building was huge, and I was very impressed by all the attention I received. After a short wait, I was led into a comfortable office, and four smiling faces welcomed me. The head of marketing, their number two director, the head of HR, and the head of design were sitting at a table and wanted to get to know me. Since I believed I was the answer to contemporary design, I started a very cocky and rebellious presentation of my portfolio. To my surprise, they loved every minute of it, and I must admit, I genuinely liked all the people in the room. We got along like the proverbial house on fire. The head of HR told me off for my rough and unconsidered application I had sent; she stated in the room that she would not have invited me but was overruled by the others. I then admitted that she was right with the biggest, most charming smile I could muster, and after 60 minutes, she was also enjoying my presentation. It went well, and after the interview, I was shown around the building. The Levi's offices were not as opulent as Moschino and had a functional industrial ambiance, which I quite liked. Everything was very different; I was used to designing "fashion" collections, which were different each season and ended with a fashion show. Although in the last four years, I had learned that in fashion, you always have to stick to a formula (people call it the brand DNA), Moschino as well had its share of repetitive design elements: colors, fabrics, teddy bears and peace and love symbols. Creativity is not reinventing a look every season but evolving within a certain style and ingredients. I could foresee being bored at Moschino within the next two years. At Levi's, it was a completely new design angle. The product never changed. The 501 was the same for over a hundred years, but its cultural relevance—who was wearing it, how you were wearing the jeans— constantly changed. Levi's invested an incredible amount of money to consistently update and define a culturally relevant "look," and it would be my job to help define that "look." This "look" of how a 501 was worn and by whom on what occasion was a big deal to define. I had to create support material through film, photo shoots, styling, design, trend research, strategic planning, collaborations, art exhibitions, and visual presentation concepts for stores. It was a creative multimedia paradise. I was less challenged to design clothes, but I would be learning tons in all the other mediums. I loved the idea of being the driver of all those projects. I was sold. The problem was, what would J. say? I informed them that my wife was expecting, and I would be a father, and they all loved it and offered their support. The day rushed by with great talks and meeting many people in Levi's office. Finally, I was driven to the airport and flew back to Milan.

J. was not thrilled at all; luckily, Levi's had said their final decision would take three more weeks since they wanted to interview more possible candidates. While we were waiting, Beta had a connection to Gilmar, which was a production place near Rimini. They were the owners of the "Iceberg" collection. It was a collection known for its Disney graphics and Mickey Mouse sweaters. Not very chic, but commercially very successful. As we could not afford to be snobby, J. drove down to meet them in their factory. The design consultant was Marc Jacobs, who had just launched his own label with Robert Duffy in New York. To finance his label, Marc freelanced for various commercial brands, and Iceberg was one of them. Since he was based in New York, he was looking for an assistant in Italy. The job was freelance and would have been perfect for J. Marc and J. fell in love with each other, and Marc offered her the job. It was a great moment; things seemed to turn out well, and we celebrated our first job success story. Everything looked promising that night. In the coming weeks, I kept on knocking at more doors, but nothing else came up. As it happens, Tommy Hilfiger called and offered me a job in New York the same week Levi's sent me a contract informing me the design manager position would be mine if I wanted it. I was ecstatic but knew immediately that nothing would work. New York was too expensive for a young family, and the salary at Tommy was not high enough to support J. and the baby. Moschino was financially suicidal. Levi's would work best with a very generous salary but was in a completely unacceptable location in Germany. After a night of heated discussions, we agreed J. would have to talk with Marc to see

146

if she could assist him in New York, and we would move to New York. As J. called Marc, he was listening to her, and once J. had finished, he congratulated her on the baby and told her to pack her things, but not to go to New York but rather to Paris. He was the newly appointed creative director for Louis Vuitton, and he wanted her to become his assistant. J. smiled and said, "Yes." At home, I asked her if she was raving mad to accept a job in Paris, but I had to admit Marc was very generous to hire a pregnant assistant. J. and I agreed I would take the job at Levi's since the money was too good to turn down to support J. and her meager first salary. We would need a Nanny to be able to pull all this off, and Levi's compensation would allow us to do that. Our plan was that I would work at Levi's from Monday to Thursday and then come to Paris. We believed this would be a temporary solution until I found a job in Paris, and we would be together again. I informed Levi that I would accept the position but live in Paris and travel every week. Levi's was not too enthusiastic about my travel plans and predicted I would not be able to pull it off. I promised them that if I showed the first sign of not being able to deliver, we would move to Germany. They agreed, and J. and I had found our way forward. We had to admit it was not ideal, but we had no better options available, and so we embarked on our new adventure with Levi's and Louis Vuitton.

The CEO was not amused when I told him I would leave Moschino; he was outraged. He believed he could retain me for the minimum salary due to my lack of choices. He was wrong, and I enjoyed every minute when I handed in my resignation. It sent a shock wave through the Moschino office. Rosella wouldn't talk to me as I refused to negotiate further. I knew then I was done; too much had happened, and I was ready to start a new chapter in our lives. The very sad event of Luciano's death shocked me to the core three weeks later. I was devastated to have lost him; he was an incredible person, and I missed my caring mentor. But "the show must go on" as Moschino always said, and we packed our few belongings in a small van. Two suitcases, a sewing machine, a fridge, a mattress, and a television were all we had, and we didn't need more. J. was six months pregnant, we were in love, with a promising future and a baby on the way. We drove to Paris through the night with our friend Adrian as our copilot.

38. PARIS, HERE WE ARE; AND THE POPE IS IN TOWN

Two weeks before, J. had traveled to Paris and found us a lovely flat. It was sunny and centrally located at the Rue du Renard; it was an old art deco building with 90 square meters and a direct view of the Centre Pompidou at the entrance to the Marais. It was not cheap, but we could afford it with my big salary at Levi's. Our move was fast since we did not own much. Moving in, we broke the elevator by squeezing our mattress in and trying to get it to the fifth floor. Our new neighbors were not happy. In the end, Adrian and I had to drag it up the narrow staircase of the old house. Our new home, with a children's room and generous living space for us.

Once we moved in, we went out to explore the neighborhood. Paris was a stunning place, much bigger and more cosmopolitan than Milan. We did not know anyone there at all. We missed our friends from Milan; they were like family to us. Milan had been very welcoming and warm. Paris was cold, like a beautiful sculpture you were allowed to watch but not touch. It slowly dawned on us how difficult the next few months would be. We had to find a new doctor for J., and a hospital for the delivery, and we did not speak a word of French. The Parisians were not like the Italians at all; they were rude and very "French" at first. We had help, though. Morine, the personal assistant to Marc, helped J. in the first months and years to come. She became a good friend. In return, we helped her to look after Tigger, Marc's dog at the time, a Dalmatian. Morine, Marc Jacob, Peter Copping, Camille Miceli, and Jane Whitfield were Louis Vuitton's first-ever fashion design team. The first design office was a rented space on Rue du Bac, a very small beginning for Louis Vuitton. Bernard Arnault had just bought the old luggage house, and Louis Vuitton had never done fashion before. It was a big gamble for Marc, and at first, Bernard Arnault wanted to assign Marc to a different house, but Marc insisted he wanted Louis Vuitton. Marc had already established his namesake design brand in New York, and he traveled often to New York. Robert Duffy, his business partner, was assigned to Louis Vuitton as a financial advisor. Morine's first big job was to find a house and an apartment for Marc and Robert and a doctor and Hospital for J. As we arrived in Paris, there was no time to idle. J. had a big belly but was otherwise full of energy and started work immediately. The pregnancy did not slow her down at all. We both saw the new baby as part of us, and fashion design was a part of us too! Therefore, it seemed only natural to introduce the unborn child immediately to our passion for fashion. The doctor was quickly found, and after the first examination, he confirmed that the mother and child were in excellent condition and we had nothing to worry about. He also informed us that it would be a girl. We were overjoyed, and since we were not married, J. agreed the girl would have my family's last name, and J. would choose her first name. At dinner, nonetheless, we both discussed possible names until we agreed on the name Betty. Our first baby girl would be called Betty. The doctor calculated an approximate birthdate in August and introduced us to the clinic he worked at behind Trocadéro in the 16th arrondissement. It was an easy drive along the Seine and past the Palais de Tokyo.

In the first week, I went back to my parents in Germany, where I picked up things for the house, but most importantly, I picked up a white used Fiat Uno from my brother's girlfriend and later wife, Chrisi. I had bought the small car from her, and it was meant to get me from Paris to Frankfurt, where I was working at Levi's. Levi's was a full-time job, and I needed a car to get around Heusenstamm, too. Heusenstamm was outside of Frankfurt and a small town with not much to do. Luckily, my best friend Andreas and his girlfriend Anke were living close by, and I could stay with them at the beginning until I found a place of my own.

Once back in Paris, we quickly settled into our new lives, with J. pregnant and working at the small office in Rue du Bac and me driving my little Fiat back and forth between France and Germany. It took me exactly six hours from my home in Paris to my office in Frankfurt. In the meantime, I found a small apartment close to Heusenstamm and moved out from Andreas and Anke's apartment. My new flat was small and empty. There was a mattress on the floor, a TV, and a vacuum cleaner. The place was ugly in an ugly neighborhood, but it

149

served its purpose, and I didn't care much since I was convinced to be quickly back in Paris with a new job.

To be reachable, I bought our first mobile phone. A Nokia phone, which was as big as a shoe and heavy. It worked, though, and I was reachable 24/7, which gave J. a certain assurance that I would be back in time for the birth of Betty. Over the weekends, while I was back in Paris, I built a little bed for Betty and painted it. J. and I were "nest-making. We both never went to any "baby" courses but instead read books about "having a baby." I was not much of a believer in all those baby books, which scared you to hell with all the random disasters you and your baby could inflict on each other. Those books made it sound as if humans had never had babies before and that we were all going to die in the process. The only book I liked was the one my friend Robert gave us. The book described the upbringing of children by the Amazon Indians. It stated that children fare best when they are not fretted about and that we, in modern society, program our children into having accidents. The programming for failure happens when we utter the words "Don't do that, or you are going to hurt yourself." With those words, we suggest imminent failure with anything they explore and try. The book argued children would not learn by trial and error if we used the implied "failure" words- "you will hurt yourself." Children need to make firsthand mistakes to assess risk competently in their adult years. I strongly believe that with our way of "trying to help" and protecting our children from harm," we set them up for incompetent problem-solving in their adult years. Of course, if Betty tried to jump out of the window, we would stop her, but we decided the Amazon Indians had a healthy point of view, so we sat back and enjoyed the ride. Those moralistic do-gooders who sell "safety for our kids" from fictitious dangers wouldn't be able to manipulate us into panic mode. We believed we were grownups and able to bring up our children with common sense instead of fear.

While we enjoyed watching Betty kick in J.'s belly, we were happy and confident we would manage. As J.'s delivery date came closer, J.'s mom, June, came to Paris from Newcastle in the UK. June was a lovely woman, but I did not know her very well. At this point, we had only met while we were staying at her house. When she arrived, I was in the way, therefore, I tried to stay out of everybody's affairs. In our house, my mother-in-law reorganized everything to her liking and my distress. J. and her mother had a strong bond and worked well together as a team. Frankly, I was not needed for the preparations. I was happy when I was out of their way and in my car driving to Levi's.

August came and the long-awaited phone call arrived. J. would have a baby! In the morning, J. called me and told me calmly that she would have the baby the following day. She also told me there was no need to rush; just get in the car calmly and come home.

I ran out of my office and drove to Paris. I arrived home safe and sound and kissed J., and we were very excited. The Doctor assured us we had time. J.'s labors became stronger and stronger during the night, and finally, we decided to drive to the hospital in the early morning. In those days, there was no Google Maps, and we had a simple paper map of Paris to help us find our way. I had scouted the way to the hospital before, and I knew how to get there, so we loaded up my Fiat with J., her mother June, and a small suitcase. On our way, we quickly realized something was wrong. All the roads along the river were blocked. I started to panic since I did not know Paris very well, and I only scouted one way to the hospital. What was happening? We figured it out: Pope John Paul II was in town for "World Youth Day." We only heard about it because the designer Jean-Charles de Castelbajac had designed his ceremonial robes for the special event, and it was all over the fashion news. It had never occurred to us that the French police would close all the streets around the event. Now, at three in the morning, I started to panic because every turn we took was a new roadblock, and there were no police around to help us at all. It was not like the films in which you get a police escort to guide you to the hospital, and all is fine. There was nobody to help us; J. was in the back in labor and pain, and my mother-in-law, with an old map of Paris, was trying to guide me. My adrenalin level was through the roof, and I was laser-focused on getting us there. After many more dead ends and blocked roads, we finally made it to the hospital. Many years later, J. and I met Castelbajac and told him the story about Betty's delivery race to the hospital, and we joked a lot about it.

In the hospital, they rushed J. off for an examination, and all was fine. We were told to wait, and I was brought to the delivery room where J. would give birth. The anesthetist set the epidural, and it began. The Doctor was calm and reassuring. It was a fast delivery; two hours later, Betty was in this world. J. was exhausted. Then, the nurse took Betty to clean her up. I followed her to make sure she would not swap her with another baby. I stalked the nurse, who was alarmed, but I wouldn't leave her side until I was certain that our Betty was indeed our Betty and not a swap. J. told me that I watched too many films, and we laughed.

J. was brought to her room to rest as she was utterly exhausted. There was not much else to do, and June and I left the hospital and went home.

June prepared some food, and we happily had lunch in our kitchen. I was happy! I was a father! I had a family!

Later in the afternoon, we went back to the hospital and, for the first time, had the chance to touch and marvel at our little Betty. She was wonderful. Three days later, J. and Betty were released from the hospital, and we brought them both home. We had the apartment decorated, and we had a small welcome party. As a surprise gift, I bought a super expensive baby carriage for Betty. The Rolls Royce of carriages; it was huge but barely good enough for our princess. The next day, we took the baby carriage down to the streets to present our girl to the neighborhood. We quickly found out that it was impossible to navigate this huge baby carriage through the Marais district. It was too big, the pavements were too small, and getting around was impossible. We had a laugh, and J. gave me a hug for my good intentions, but two days later I was on my way to Levi's with a huge baby carriage in my car. I had bought the baby carriage in Germany, and now I had to exchange it for a more practical, smaller one.

39. VIVE LA FRANCE

The first months were tough. J. and I were young and did not know anything about raising children. We quickly forgot about the Amazon Indians. We were afraid to do things wrong, we were afraid to fail, and we were afraid to simply harm Betty when we touched her. June, J.'s mom, helped a lot. June taught us how to change diapers, how to bathe her, and basically how to get used to having a baby in our care. I was not home very often as my life as a "nomad father" had begun anew. We believed this setup would only last for a year until I found a job in Paris. In Milan, we were together most of the time, but Paris demanded a new rhythm to survive. Every Sunday night, when I drove back to Germany, we were saying goodbye with a kiss and a tear in our eyes, and we were happy when I came back home again on Thursday. It was strange to be alone in my empty apartment in Germany, knowing Betty would wake up every day without me. It was a lonely time, but I had no choice; I had to earn money as J.'s salary would not cover the rent back then, let alone finance a Nanny to look after Betty. We had a long discussion, in which I tried once more to convince J. there would be a way to survive with freelance work, and I proposed a second time and asked J. to marry me, but the offer was refused once more. We stuck to the original plan, in which both of us continued our careers and followed our dreams of "fashion." Both of us loved our work, and J. was right; she was not a mother who would thrive without her independence. I understood and supported her with her ambitions as much as I could, and I made it as easy as possible for J. to return to work. June could not stay forever since her husband, Bob, J.'s father, was alone back home in England, and so we slowly learned to organize our lives.

40. DENISE AND ALBERT

J. was on mother's leave for nearly three months but returned much earlier to work to not miss important meetings. We realized we would need a Nanny quickly. Although both our parents, J.'s and mine, were very supportive, they could not look after Betty all the time. We needed someone who was free and able to adapt to the crazy hours of the fashion world. We put an ad in a local ex-patriot paper and waited. To our surprise, we received twelve applications, and we were happy to have received so many. As we sat on the couch in the evening studying the various CVs and applications, we quickly sorted out the too-expensive candidates. In the end, we settled on four possible choices, and I started interviewing them. They were all interesting, but only two were left in the end who could really do the necessary job for us. A young girl from Portugal about 22 years of age, and Denise, who had a son, Albert, a year older than Betty. In the evening, I told J. all the funny stories about the interviews and showed her the gifts some candidates had brought with them. One girl had brought a ring for Betty. It was a very sweet gesture, but it put me in an awkward position when I had to turn her down and return the ring to her.

J. and I organized a second meeting with the girl and Denise. Both interviews went well, and we finally settled for Denise. Denise was a kind person, and it would be a good solution for Betty to grow up with her son Albert. Albert was coming with Denise, and Betty suddenly had an unforeseen older brother. This agreement worked for all of us, and it would allow Denise to be more flexible with her working hours. We agreed on general terms and a salary, and the following week Denise started. Denise and Albert were with us for 24 years. We owe Denise for her kindness and devotion to all our children, Albert, Betty, and Stanley (Stanley's birth is still to come; patience). We think of them as three.

Albert graduated from the Royal College of Art and currently lives in London.

We are still in close contact with Denise, and we couldn't have been luckier. Thank you, Denise, from the bottom of our hearts!

41. A FIRST FOR LOUIS VUITTON

Our lives slowly developed a "normal" rhythm, which was not normal in the least. Both our parents and friends thought we were crazy. Nobody believed we could keep up the pace, with me leaving Monday morning at 2:30 a.m., driving for six hours in a Fit Uno to Frankfurt to start work at 9:00 a.m., and J. having the insane schedule Marc Jacobs brought with him by working on two collections, his own in New York and Louis Vuitton in Paris. J. and I were in love, motivated by our success and our daughter Betty; nothing could have stopped us. Anyway, we believed it would be for no more than a year, and then I would be with them in Paris. As I started looking for jobs, we quickly realized there were not many opportunities in Paris. In those days, Milan ruled supreme, and Paris had only a few fashion houses like Gaultier and Castelbajac. All the famous designers from the 1980s were in dire financial situations.

Bernard Arnault had just refinanced Dior, and John Galliano was the big star. Alexander McQueen was the new kid on the block as creative director for Givenchy. Marc Jacobs was first asked to take over Givenchy, but he insisted on Louis Vuitton. A big gamble on his part because Louis Vuitton was an old luggage name with no fashion attached to its history ever. I believe Marc was motivated to have a clean start with no big shoes to fill from his predecessor, John Galliano.

All this did not help my situation in finding a job in Paris. The small opportunities that came up on those tiny design teams were rare and mostly filled before they ever became proper opportunities. The biggest challenge was my salary, though. Levi's paid very well, and we needed the money to finance our expensive overheads. Betty, our flat, and Denise needed a certain amount of income, and the assistant designer jobs only paid a pittance. Nonetheless, we kept on fighting and believed in our luck.

Marc Jacobs and his small team of Peter, Camille, J., and Morine were all getting to know each other. Robert Duffy tried to keep Marc in line, who had a wild party habit at the time. It was great fun, though. The new design team was not located in the main Louis Vuitton building but in a tiny flat on Rue du Bac. The first thing Marc installed in his office was a bed, in which he often rested during his insane working hours. Louis Vuitton was a big question mark, and everybody had a different opinion on what it should be. There was no history to lean on but luggage and a dusty image. Marc did not care. It was one of his strengths to blend out all the pressure and opinions that people and the press tried to impose upon him. Together, they were a great team, all with incredible energy. Marc's biggest strength was not only to design fashion but also to design a team around him. He knew his strengths and weaknesses very well and managed to surround himself with incredibly talented designers who complemented him. Marc would have been able to put together the Beatles with his eye for talent. They were all having fun and creating the first Louis Vuitton fashion show ever, and finally, the day came for the first show. They all worked day and night, and Denise quickly learned firsthand what it meant to work for a crazy fashion family. The day came, and the first show was presented to the public at Paris Fashion Week. It was a disaster. Marc's vision was not at all what all the CEO's wives and press had expected, but most of all, there was not a single bag in the show. Marc and his team had, for some reason, neglected or simply forgotten that Louis Vuitton was a bag company. Bernard Arnault was livid with anger and gave Robert and Marc a very clear idea of his first impression, which was not a good one. The whole team was upset and worried about what would happen next. In his first show, Marc's style was very minimalistic and needed adjusting from New York chic to Paris chic. After the first show, we all went for dinner, and I was invited too. Although the collection feedback was a crushing reality, it became a fun night, and many friends came by to cheer them up. The after-show dinner became a tradition in the coming years, and I spent many hours discussing design and fashion with Marc. Mostly because the others were too tired and they had spent too much time with Marc designing the show, and I was fresh and full of stories and gossip, which Marc liked to hear.

The next day, the team took a break from each other but quickly went back to designing the second show.

42. LEVI'S

As J.'s and Betty's lives fell into place, my career at Levi's was off to a good start too. I was young, and the little sleep I got every night did not bother me much.

Coming from Moschino, I was used to designing collections within a six-month cycle. Most work there did not require travel. The technicians from AEFFE came to Milan for sample launches, fabric orders, and fittings. Sometimes, we went down to Cattolica, but rarely. Eugenio, the head of Moschino product development, became a good friend and handled most details concerning prototypes by himself. The Italians were very fond of their designers and supported them by preparing the prototypes to a very high standard. Fashion shows were the celebration of excellence and style and the reward every designer hungered for.

At Levi's, everything was different. The main product was a five-pocket denim jeans with the famous number 501. All the details were almost unchanged for 160 years. It was an incredible product. The main fascinating secret, which most people do not know, is that the 501 is still side-graded. At least it was when I worked there. To explain what "side graded" means, we must look at a leg pattern piece. To grade the basic pattern measurements to the next bigger size, the extra room was added only to the side. In regular grading, you would add extra room on all sides. The 501, therefore, only gets bigger to the side; this means all the other measurements get out of proportion. To speak in layman's terms, the 501 does not fit. That's why they invented the slogan "Levi's 501; no two pairs are the same." This was literally true in the 501's case. When you went to a store, the chances that your first pair of jeans would not fit you were huge, but the chances that you would find a pair that would perfectly fit you were huge, too. This paradox manifests the biggest success story in fashion history: a product that is inconsistent has the biggest following and has a reputation for individuality like no other. I was absolutely amazed by all the history. There were so many stories linked to Levi's, and I was eager to learn them all. Surprisingly, those stories were rarely written down. They were passed on from worker to worker, and whenever you traveled, you would find another nugget of wisdom.

When I first arrived at Levi's, I was not a Levi's man; for exactly that "side grading" reason, they did not fit me! To be honest, I never kept trying them on until I found a pair that fit me, but now I did, and to my surprise, I found a pair that fit me perfectly. This fitting happened in week two. I was kindly told to wear Levi's to work because I wore Diesel Jeans to two meetings with our CEO, Felix Sulzberger. I only owned Diesel jeans! At Moschino, corporate dress rules did not exist. At Moschino, you were free to wear what you felt and wanted, but here, you had to become a Levi's man. My rebellious nature did not accept this corporate pressure at all, and I refused. I based my argument on the fact that the 501 was made by rebels for rebels, and I stated that I am a rebel for not wearing Levi's at Levi's. It was a stupid argument, of course, but I was young and still felt superior to Levi's by coming from Moschino. Trine had much patience with me, and together with Michaela, they gently made me try on Levi's denim to teach me the history and the different key fits in the collection. By trying on the product and hearing the side-grading story about the 501, it grew on me. I fell in love with the brand. Occasionally, I do wear other brands, but now, in my heart, I am a true believer that there is only one denim in this world, the Levi's 501. Trine was very open and showed me some vintage "Big E" 501s from the archive. The big "E" was from a time before 1971, when the tab on the back pocket spelled the brand name Levi's with a big "E," LEVI'S. Those denims value a lot of money to collectors. They only existed in vintage, and you had to dig for them through mountains of vintage denim in vintage stores like you would dig for gold in the Klondike Gold Rush.

A funny twist on history: the first gold diggers wore Levi's, and now Levi's is treated like gold. Trine, in her generosity, made me wear some of the unofficial big "E" 501s, which were constantly collected and brought back to the office but not yet certified. One fit me perfectly, and she gave them to me as a present. My first perfect 501 I ever wore was a big "E.." Trine and Michaela were proud, and Felix joked when he first laid eyes on me and my new pair of 501s.

Once again, the denim did not just fit me; Levi's and I were a perfect match. I loved it there—the people, the culture, and the work. Moschino will always be number one in my heart, but Levi's instilled awe in me for its history, products, and content, which I did not know before. Moschino was a strong believer in all his messages, and I was too, but Levi's went so much deeper into the culture of our everyday lives. At Levi's, I realized I would be able to literally change the world, as Levi's had done for more than 150 years. It was unimaginable to fathom the creative possibilities with a product that did not need designing.

My first weeks at Levi's started with one meeting after the other, and I wondered when the designing would be done. It was all very interesting, and many subjects that were linked to designing were discussed, but when would I sit down and draw a collection? My main job at Moschino was to design, draw, research, select fabrics, fit, and create a fashion show. Now there was no drawing, no fabric research, no fabric vendors coming to the office with gorgeous fabrics, and no fashion show. There was none of it.

43. DESIGN MANAGER

My new title at Levi's was design manager. Before my arrival, the design manager at Levi's was Michael Michalski. Michael was by himself a PR machine and had made his Levi's role very reputed throughout the German press and the denim industry. He was a powerhouse in the German design scene. Michael had left Levi's to become the Design Director at Adidas. I did not know him. The German design scene was irrelevant on a global scale. Apart from Joop, Jil Sander, and Klaus Stockhausen (a famous German stylist), there weren't many German designers known internationally. The biggest German design export was Karl Lagerfeld. It's not that there weren't any good designers in Germany, but this phenomenon was rooted in the German fashion businesses. They were profit-driven mass-market operations ruled by money with no interest in design.

All my life, I had tried to leave Germany for that reason. America, the Royal College of Art, Italy... always restless, traveling and searching for a culture that would understand the deeper meaning of design. I had found it in New York and at Moschino, but now I was in Germany. My move to Levi's was not logical in my career, and I was fully aware of the challenges I would face once I chose to move on to another fashion company. In fashion, you do not jump from the "fashion" level to the "denim" level. It was considered a flaw, like failing.

The Germans did not care for fashion design. It was not an important part of German culture. Germans were logical engineers, scientists, philosophers, doctors, and artists; they considered themselves deep thinkers, and fashion was a shallow business in their eyes.

Luckily, Levi's was different.

I also realized Levi's could become an important step in launching our own fashion brand, J. and me, a plan and dream that I had had for many years. J. and I were an unbeatable team. We would become our own fashion house together. A House for Art, family, and Love, as I had witnessed at Moschino. He had created his House to design fashion, but it became so much more. Not just a house but a home for many. Moschino saw fashion as a medium to do good and literally change the world.

If they could create a paradise for work, family, and friends, then we could do it too. It was my dream, my fuel, to do anything to get there, to build "Our House." It never crossed my mind that it might not be J.'s dream.

At Levi's, I had big shoes to fill. Michael Michalski had done a great and impressive job. So, I set to work. As I mentioned before, Levi's was completely different from how I had worked at Moschino, but there is one rule valid for all designers. "Whatever you do, it has to be beautiful and desirable"! Since I believed in this rule, I started to reorganize my design team. The team had worked differently before and complained to Trine, but Trine saw the logic in what I did and supported me, and our first adoption meeting with the sales team was a great success.

An "adoption meeting" was new to me, too. At Moschino, salespeople and showrooms saw the new collection on the catwalk on the day of the fashion show for the first time and were then told to sell it. At Levi's, a collection was developed in a collaborative effort with marketing, merchandising, and the sales team. It was an intimidating meeting because the sales team had strong opinions concerning the collection. They had to deliver on their sales budgets and were afraid that crazy designs would ruin their chances of success. Therefore, trust had to be established between me, the "new design manager," and them, "the sales team." To them, I presented a threat since my background was "Fashion" and "Fashion shows." They all knew I had never collaborated with a sales team before, and they were ready to fight and establish their dominance. Levi's had a big sales team. My collection was responsible for Germany, Austria, and the German-speaking parts of Switzerland. We had the biggest sales volume in Europe. Globally, we were number two after The United States; we were massive. The annual turnover was about 600 million dollars, and now I was responsible for growing that number further. The sales team was made up of seasoned veterans who knew the denim market well.

I, on the other hand, was the new designer who had never worked in the denim industry before.

My first adoption meeting was approaching fast. An adoption meeting is a meeting where the design team presents their first concept stories, design sketches, fabrics, and colors at an early collection development stage, around week five in a collection development cycle. Those concept stories are linked to delivery drops. Usually, there are three drops and an additional summer or winter capsule, depending on the season. In the Fall or Spring season, each drop or delivery has to be designed with regard to regional needs like climate, Christmas, summer holidays, or special festivities. Those market needs must be considered and incorporated into a commercial collection. The reason for an adoption meeting is not only to inform people about the latest designs but also to lead, motivate, and, most importantly, instill courage in them so they will believe in the "new." If a sales team does not believe in "you," the designer, they will block your collection. If a sales team is not motivated and does not understand the new concepts, they will not be able to successfully sell and will fail.

My role, therefore, was much bigger than designing a collection. I had to take the convincing lead for a collection making 600 million dollars in turnover. Our CEO, Felix, and all the relevant department heads were also present at the meeting. They wanted to see if I could pull it off. Would I sink or swim? I was a big gamble, after all, "The fashion designer" from Moschino.

Trine and Michaela were by my side. They had thoroughly explained all the necessary steps and formalities, and I had prepared quite the spectacle for them all. To introduce myself, I gave a brief glimpse of my life and career. Where I grew up, how I fought to become me, how I traveled the world, and how I had learned to make dreams come true. How to define a collection and form a vision to guarantee consistency and success, how to work as a team, and how to lead a market

In my presentation, the key to success was a detailed trend analysis of the fashion market and the denim market in particular. It was very specific and logically conveyed what the market will need in the coming months. It showed where the influences came from and what we intended to do to satisfy those market needs. The Levi's team had never seen anything like it. Usually, they were told a trend would be a certain color or fit, and that was it. Nobody ever connected all the dots and explained the background stories of how those trends came into being. I informed them about music trends, the latest films, spectacles, fashion fairs, architecture, parties, and people to watch. I became a magician at storytelling and presenting, a talent I did not know I had until that day. Once I had their full attention, we surprised them with a small fashion show. Nothing big, just some models presenting a first glimpse of the new collection.

In the weeks leading up to this meeting, I had driven our factories into despair. They were close to revolting due to my insane prototyping requests in a very short amount of time. It was worth all the effort, though. The impact of the show was incredible, and the sales team was smitten; they were believers. I was the new kid on the block at Levi's, and they believed in me. It was a great feeling. My first adoption meeting was a great success, and my denim career was promising to be a fun ride. I loved my new life at Levi's.

44. LEARNING AND TRAVELING

My new position at Levi's was a revelation in so many ways. At the time, most career advisers thought my move into the denim world would be career suicide. Their opinion was that I moved too quickly into the commercial world. I disagreed with them. I saw an opportunity to grow and to learn. What is life if not for learning? A career should always make you better. The new job was fun, but it was not easy. I was used to an international fashion world and not ready for a small town in Germany. There was a price to be paid. The downside was the location of the office in Heusenstamm. It was a tiny provincial town in the middle of nowhere. Once the job was done, there was nothing left to do.

During the week, my new home was a tiny apartment with a mattress on the floor. There was nothing else but a mattress on a gray industrial carpet, a portable TV, and a kitchen corner. The windows were facing the neighboring buildings, which were gray and bleak too. The bathroom had white tiles and a shower cabin that was functional and sterile. I had no spare money to buy furniture; all my money was needed for our life in Paris. Therefore, the flat never received the caring interior love it so desperately needed.

There was only one way out, and the solution was "traveling" on Levi's business. At Levi's, it was all about traveling. The European Levi's headquarters were in Brussels. At the time, the London office was considered the design center for Europe. London was the coolest Levi's office in Europe. I learned that research (which meant vintage shopping) was an important part of the collection development process. At Moschino, research means looking at books or art. We never traveled at Moschino; we invented and designed things with our creativity and imagination. Copying or looking at other designers' collections for reference was highly frowned upon. We were creators, and we were proud of it. At Levi's, the design reality was somewhat different. Research and shopping for competitor samples was expected. The idea of designing was "to be informed and inspired" by the market and vintage samples.

A 501 had hardly changed for over a hundred years but the rest of the collection did. Garment design and innovation did happen, but mostly in the "tops" collection. The bottom line was stable and did only evolve except with new programs being added like the "STA-PREST" program or the "engineered denim collection." The traditional five-pocket styles were updated rarely. The denim styles received updates through their washes, which were developed meticulously and with great effort. Furthermore, designing meant not only creating garments but also designing social context.

The cleverness at Levi's was to define social context, culture, and what happened on the street. Who was wearing it? How could you wear denim? Tight fit? Loose fit? Unwashed? Selvage? Ecological? Levi's was always at the forefront of every cultural evolution, from workwear to rock and roll, hippies, punk, you name it. Levi's favored the "rebel" and was part of every "rebel at heart" wardrobe. Levi's was embracing sociological changes like no other fashion company on this planet. They were cool because they embraced change. They understood that not only the innovation of a garment is relevant, but also the new "wearer" and their values. This is not the "customer" who comes to the store; do not confuse the customer profile marketing uses with the aspirational figure we created and are talking about here. We were constantly redefining and researching the "dream" of a new generation. We were very much part of shaping and forming a new world. We were transforming minds and habits. How does a new generation live? What furniture and music would they listen to? Where do they live? Countryside? City? The moon? What were their beauty ideals? In the 70s, we dressed differently than in the 80s or 90s, and so on. Each time has its own values and aesthetics, and Levi's understood this through their long-lasting success and company history. Levi's not only observed but was instrumental in shaping the ever-evolving cultural landscape.

To comprehend Levi's influence, you must "time travel." Look at Levi's commercials over the last 50 years on YouTube and how they evolved. What models they used and how they embraced equality, race, religion, and environmental issues. Especially the "girl-boy" attraction, the same-sex attraction, or any "attraction" for that matter, was explored and incorporated into their visual communications. The use of models was important. What was the new "type"? All sizes, skin tones, sex, etc., were considered, and Levi's explored anything and everything; there was no limit to researching the world and its thoughts and ideas. I loved every minute of those research moments. I embraced the intellectual component of my new job, it was fascinating to learn about all those streams in life, sociology, and novelty of thought. The new digital world interested us especially. There was much hype and talk about our future. Levi's had invested in an e-commerce platform (This was 1998). They were one of the first, but the market was not ready. It was too early, by about 15 years. Not many know that Levi's was one of the first companies to launch an e-commerce platform next to Amazon in the mid-90s. Levi's was planning to achieve what Amazon later did become: a leading digital marketplace. The advantage Amazon had was the simplicity of its product. They sold books, and Amazon only needed to display a book cover, whereas fashion had a tactile and fit issue that proved too challenging to solve at the time. The idea of selling clothing on the internet was not yet accepted by the world. The consumer of the 1990s was not open to the digital revolution in the fashion world. It was considered too intrusive and "Orwellian." People thought buying on the internet would lead to a totalitarian state because "Big Brother is watching you." Most were opposed to it.

"Research" became a new priority in designing clothes, and our research needed to be shared with the rest of the company.

Especially with our CEO, marketing, and sales teams. The "cultural values" were the "Gold" Levi's dug up to create visions of how their product would shape a new generation. Levi's understood, like no other fashion company, the power of this knowledge. The tricky part was how to communicate all this in a comprehensive manner. A written report did not do it; there were too many possible misinterpretations in language and written words. Images were also tricky to find since we were defining "the new" and existing imagery represented a status quo we hoped to redefine. Communication was key and challenging. Presenting was not a designer's strength. Designers were often useless in presenting and preparing a presentation so that a uniformed audience was able to follow. Designers were not able to explain their research in a logical and understandable manner. Levi's acknowledged this challenge and spent a lot of money on "presentation training," but they could not transform the "bird" into a "horse" either. You had it, or you didn't. I discovered I had it, and I was very good at breaking down "trend" information. The word "trend research" does not do justice to what Levi's did; it was so much more.

My new personal discovery was that I was very good at presenting in front of an audience. At some point, I presented to more than 300 people. I loved it and still do today, I enjoy motivating and exciting an audience to teach and inform. My obsession with research absorbed my work, and I had to consciously make time in my daily planning to fashion design and create compelling collections. Ultimately, I managed both. Levi's Germany became the most successful "denim rocket" ever built, and we were all a phenomenal team. I learned and understood what chemistry can do for a team.

To accumulate the necessary research, it required many trips. I had to travel to museums, concerts, vintage shops, etc., all over the world, from Tokyo to New York. Those vintage shops were not your traditional flea market shops; they were specialized warehouses. Companies that did specialize in curating vintage garments for professional clients. The general public is not aware of this hidden part of the fashion industry. Those warehouses are museums, and the owners create "riggings" in which they depict color and garment stories. A "rigging" is a staged garment display with vintage garments and props, like a window display in a high-end department store or film set, and you could purchase all of it.

As you can imagine, there were many research trips to escape Heusenstamm, and I used the opportunity as often as I could. My "nomadic" airport life had begun, and I exchanged my lonely apartment with hotel rooms and airport lounges around the world.

One part of the presentation medium Levi's used was film. For every new presentation, we produced a video. A video was about 3-5 minutes long and formulated the latest trends. A video contained words, music, and visuals; it was the most impactful medium to communicate and motivate. Those videos were produced at ARRI Studios in Munich. The mecca of German film production. They were the best. Florian Seidel was our film specialist hired to support me. Florian was a fashion photographer and filmmaker. Our task was to compose our own Levi's trend video, it was like remixing music but with far more ingredients than just sound. We even incorporated "smell" experiences long before Abercrombie & Fitch perfumed all their stores.

I usually spent a week in Munich, and we produced the video there. The production of the video took many long nights. We filmed nightclubs, theaters, and art shows from our seats with small video cameras. The videos were for internal use only and were never used by outsiders. Therefore, we were completely free to use any material we could find, and the ARRI studios had epic archives. I had never directed videos before, and it was more fun than working on a fashion show. The impact of those videos was unparalleled; it was a powerful tool. Making videos with Florian Seidel in the Munich ARRI Studios was a highlight each season; I loved to create and cut our trend videos there. Cyrill Gutsch was part of the Munich team. He and his golden Rolls Royce were legendary. Cyrill was a graphic designer and brand developer. He later moved to New York and created, with his wife, "Parley for the Oceans."

To develop and design the denim collection was more complex. To create the basis of each collection, we had to work with Brussels, the European Levi's main office. Brussels did not have any commercial sales power; they did not have a market to sell to, but all denim "5 pockets" had to be sourced through them. The Levi's denim and vintage denim teams were located there. They were the denim wizards, but unfortunately, they did not produce any direct sales results as the other European countries did. They were only sourcing denim and overseeing all financial operations. Brussels was not too happy about this set-up. They were kings without a kingdom or any real influence.

Brussels was boring, but it was the main office. To meet with all the other European design teams, we had to meet there. The five-pocket denim collection had to be established in accordance with all the European design offices. In Brussels, all the washes and new developments were presented to us designers, and there, we had to pick our collection in agreement with all the other countries. We were allowed certain local choices, but about 70% of the five-pocket denim washes and fabrics had to be agreed on by all European countries. It was good fun. We were a great team, and we rarely disagreed. It was exciting to meet them all and work together. Once the five-pocket collection was established, each country developed its own top collection as each market saw fit.

There were huge differences in style and look because we all had slightly different consumer profiles. The UK was the edgiest but also the least successful commercially. Germany and Italy believed a 501 should be worn by all "young at heart," the Porsche-driving entrepreneur as well as the skateboard kid on the streets. Our collection was selling like hotcakes, and we ruled the European denim market.

The Levi's denim market was well positioned. In the German market, we sold our 501 for about 120 dollars a pair, and it was considered luxury denim. In the US, Levi's denim was considered workwear and sold for around $30 a pair. This was a huge difference, and it allowed us Europeans to develop high-quality products without worrying too much about cost and prices. The Brussels denim meetings always ended with dinner parties, which were a riot. We were on the company budget and could expense literally anything, so the parties and dinners were legendary. Many hotels would not have us anymore once our "design meetings" came to an end.

45. LOS ANGELES, THE CITY OF ANGELS

The most spectacular trip happened twice a year. It was the photo shoot for our catalog and PR needs in Germany. Ela, our Art director responsible for all graphic design output, organized this event, which took place in Los Angeles. As with everything at Levi's, we were working with only the best. Ela oversaw all the planning and logistics. She sourced our location and model agents. Those agents sent us their research, and we discussed the best options for our needs concerning the collection and marketing. Models were pre-selected, and a casting was set up. Once the general setup was in place, the collection had to be shipped to Los Angeles, which was a headache because of the tedious customs declaration needed.

Ela went first to get all the relevant licenses and shooting permits. You had to pay to shoot on the streets or anywhere around Los Angeles. Ela did all the red tape, and then we, the design team and marketing people, flew in. At Levi's, every flight longer than six hours was business class; therefore, all of us were flying business class. It was mayhem. As soon as the plane was in the air, we started to party, and everybody was misbehaving. The stewardesses were not amused, but we were misbehaving with a smile, and in the end, they shared the fun with us. As it was time to disembark, we forgot one of our colleagues on the toilet. He was fast asleep and had himself locked in. As soon as we realized he was missing, we had to go back, unlock the door, wake him up, and take him with us.

During the flight, somebody must have filed a complaint, and by the time we landed, an official note had been sent to our travel agent and head offices in Germany. At the hotel, a stern message from our boss awaited us. She was not amused by the details in the complaint. She made it clear that we would have to answer for our behavior once back in Germany. We were worried for about half an hour, had another drink, and went to bed. All of us were wrecked from our adventure in the air and had loads of work to do the next day. We were lodging at the Sunset Marquis in West Hollywood. The best rock and roll place in town. The Chateau Marmont, which was around the corner, was still a dump and had not been refurbished to its old glory. The Chateau had a great terrace for drinks, though, and we hung out there quite often. The Mondrian Hotel was not yet built. The Sunset Marquis was an inconspicuous motel-type complex with a two-story building in front and private bungalows in the back gardens. The rock and roll elite and actors were renting the bungalows to party over the weekends. We met the Red Hot Chili Peppers, Bruce Willis, and Leonardo di Caprio there. The place "to be" was at the hotel bar. It was very difficult to get in, but if you stayed at the Sunset, you had free entrance. We did fit right in; the crowd was creative, mad, and wild. You were free to do as you liked as long as you respected each other's boundaries. I will never forget one time as we came back from a shoot in the desert, smelly, dirty, wanting a drink, and we ended up right next to Leonardo di Caprio. Rina, sitting next to him, had nothing else to do but take his hand and doodle her designs all over it with an ink pen. He did not care, and to be honest, we did not recognize him at first until one of our models started kissing him. They knew each other from some previous filming endeavors. It was a good laugh, and Leonardo did not mind, neither the doodles nor the kisses.

The next day, we woke up bright and early and had breakfast with Ela. She updated us with the latest news, and then we met our scouting and modeling agents. The casting was not until later in the day, so we set out to visit the remaining locations to finalize everything. It was great to cruise around LA in a convertible 1967 Mustang from Rent-A-Wreck. The Mustang was, as the name said, a wreck but super cool, and we wanted to use it as a prop for one of the shoots. While we checked out all the locations, we got to know LA quite well. It is a beautiful city; we were very lucky and saw amazing places. I especially liked the desert around LA and its landscape. LA itself also held marvels and wonders the common tourist would never see. Our location guide knew everybody, and we were granted access to anywhere we wished. Later in the afternoon, we had our model casting and selected five models. The chosen talents were three boys and two girls. All young and matching the rock and roll grunge image we were looking for. They were cool characters and did fit with our photographer, us, and the rest of the LA crew. In total, we were about 15 people. We had two RV vans for all our equipment and the

Mustang convertible. In the beginning, everybody wanted to drive the Mustang, but after the first day, the drivers nearly had a sunstroke. The sun was too strong, and quickly, nobody wanted to drive the Mustang anymore. We tried to put the roof up, but it did not work. The air conditioning was broken too; it was an oven in there, so much for the cool factor.

All the styling of the looks had been prepared beforehand, and at the actual locations, there was little to do for us; still, we had to make sure every look was fitted correctly. Once make-up and hair were ready, we dressed the models, perfected the looks, and then let the photographer and Ela do their jobs.

The designing of clothes was the trade every designer had learned and was trained to do. At Moschino, that was my main job: designing the clothes, choosing fabric, choosing trims and sundries, fitting the prototypes, and making sure the garments arrived on time for the fashion show. The styling, though, was rarely done by us designers but by an outside stylist who brought a fresh eye to the collection and knew what stories the magazines and press were planning for their next editions. I had done styling before in Hamburg, but most designers are not trained to create looks for the "camera." Styling is quite different when you style for a location and not a catwalk.

At Levi's, it was part of my job, and with my team, we pulled it together successfully. All the looks were pre-prepared in Germany. We arranged the garments and pre-imagined the model type and possible location. Once we arrived in LA, the reality was often quite different. We had to react on the spot to get everything right. The fit was especially challenging because the key was to create novelty. Should the style be worn tight? Loose? Pulled up high? Hanging? For key looks, we had complete size sets, which meant we had multiple sizes in key colors to ensure we would be able to create the perfect silhouette for the photo shoot. Those samples were produced exclusively for our photoshoot; no expenses were spared. Altogether, it was great teamwork. It was hard work and long hours. We had to get through a lot of different looks and locations. Per day, we had easily 12- to 14-hour shoots. It started early with the sun rising, then shot all day. In the evening, we selected the best pictures in the hotel bar and prepared for the next day.

The two weeks flew by, and we had to say goodbye far too quickly. Back in the air in business class, we celebrated as it was our custom, and once we landed in Heusenstamm, Lufthansa nearly banned us for life.

We did get a big "well done" for our pictures but a huge telling-off for our in-flight behavior. The result was that we were not allowed to fly in a large group anymore. Only two of us were allowed to travel together at the same time, and Anja Sziele, head of marketing, became our designated chaperone.

Our shoot in LA also had a Levi's baby as a result. Two of our models fell in love, got married, and lived happily ever after.

46. LINE OPENINGS

Every six months, Levi's opened the market with a big line-opening event. This was new to me. I had never prepared a line opening before, only fashion shows. In the denim world, a "line opening" was the fashion show. At Levi's, I was introduced to a new presentation format. The opening lasted two days of events and presentations; it was a big deal, and much money was spent.

Levi's expected me to explain the collection to all our sales teams. I had never explained clothes before. Either clothes were beautiful, or they weren't, what was there to explain? Trine and Michaela patiently introduced me to the concept and showed me video recordings from past line openings.

Line openings traditionally comprised short "fashion show" presentations, followed by tedious workshops until everybody was bored to death discussing every rivet on every style. This time, due to my arrival, we restructured the line opening completely. We turned it into a Levi's fun fair. We planned a two-day spectacle. Since I hated to be told what to do, Trine gave me free rein to change the format as I saw fit. We all worked together to create a dream. It all started with all our country teams arriving at a beautiful hotel close to our office. To their surprise, the Hotel had been turned into a denim winter wonderland. The hotel was like a snowstorm had hit New York and all the cool kids were out in the snow celebrating the first snow. In New York, when the first snow arrives, everybody gets on the street to have the first annual snowball fight. Vintage cars with fake snow and display forms rigged with the coolest outfits were everywhere. It looked like a setting for a film. That year, the line opening would be in our main office. We completely transformed our main building for the coming two days, too.

Levi's had a large reception hall with a big stage, which we changed into a catwalk with a cinematic screen as a backdrop. It could accommodate up to 2,000 guests. During normal office hours, it was our canteen with a big kitchen attached to it.

The first day started by welcoming all the teams and congratulating them on their phenomenal sales results. Levi's, during the last 150 years, has learned the ups and downs of the fashion market. In 1998, Levi's was rocking the boat and dominating the European denim market; nobody was even close. Our commercials were a much-anticipated highlight in the fashion world, and the new Levi's commercial was always part of the line opening. The new ad was revealed and unveiled during this event. Felix and Trine started with last season's results, achievements, and numbers and pointed out areas for improvement. Then, the main Directors from Austria, Switzerland, and North-, Middle-, and South-Germany presented their markets in detail. This took all morning, and then we took a break for lunch while we prepared the room for the next spectacle, the new collection. My team and I were ready to razzle and dazzle our guests. We started out with my trend report, a multi-media event like they had never seen before. I explained what was happening in the world—in music, art, fashion, theater, food, nightclubs, concerts, big cities— anything that was new and cool. Then, we shifted to interviews. We had filmed cool kids on the streets. We recorded those short commentaries during our visits to Munich, New York, and our photo shoot in LA. The medium constantly changed from PowerPoint, photography, animation, slide shows, and verbal presentations to film. Then, we showed our trend video and explained our seasonal Levi's concept stories. Once all the concepts had been explained, the catwalk lights came on, and we presented the new collection of models in a real, live fashion show. It was a professional production, impactful, and grabbed you by the balls. The audience's reaction was instantaneous. The sales force loved it. They were fired up and couldn't wait to get their hands on the new collection. The dinner following the first day was a happy madness but still controlled. The second day was still to come, and the new Levi's commercial had not yet been presented.

The next day started with workshops. The teams could touch and discover the new collection with their own eyes and hands. We surprised them with a new element in those workshops. The teams had to style looks from the new collection, which were then photographed in a professional setting. Afterward, each team had to present and explain their looks to the whole crowd, with many comments and much laughter, a great team-building exercise. Though the highlight of the second day was the launch of the new publicity film. Once all the workshops were done, we came back to the big presentation theater and were ushered into the darkened room. The big screen was up, and Felix announced the arrival of the latest Levi's advertisement for the coming season. The lights went out, and we watched the video. It was a huge success, and we watched it twice. Once the film was finished, we were all sent back to our hotels to prepare for the big party, the final event of the day. A nice break to digest all the information from the last two days. During the break, the reception hall was completely transformed into a snowstorm denim world. As we came back, it was a big surprise to find the transformed theater ready for a party. There was delicious food, drinks, and, later music. Everybody was dancing the night away. The launch was a big success. The design team and all involved were happy.

47. ALL GOOD THINGS COME TO AN END

There were rumors, and the rumors became reality. The main office in San Francisco had decided to create three global headquarters and three main markets. The three markets to be were the Americas, Europe, and Asia, with the new headquarters in San Francisco, Brussels, and Tokyo. This meant only three collections were needed. No more individual country collections with individual positioning in their respective markets. First, we did not believe this would become a reality since the individual country approach was financially very successful. In comparison, the American and Asian markets were slow and less profitable. Felix and Trine were in many meetings with all the other country CEOs, stating their case and defending the current model, but to no avail. The owner and CEO, Bob Haas, had selected a new brand director, which we called "The American." Together, they decided this would be the right way to go forward. We understood the logic of the plan—one collection and one image would be easier to control—but the reality was somewhat different. Europe and its individual country's needs were different. It was a decision based on financial figures without comprehending the complexity of the European markets. In the following months, we were informed that there would be only one design office for Europe, and it would be based in Brussels. At the time of the announcement, we were told the transformation process would take a year, and we were all encouraged to apply for design positions in Brussels. If we decided not to apply, we would receive a generous severance package. We were quite upset about the news; it did not make sense to change a winning formula. If we had been struggling, we would have understood, but we were the most successful business globally. We were the absolute number one in the denim market. Nobody was even close to our market share. The day came, and The American was visiting our German office to share his concept and future vision for our branch. He arrived with two "life coaches." He had an older hippie couple following him, who were preparing his food and coaching him mentally for his success. They were his shrink, parents, and constant companions wherever he went. They were in every meeting, and it was a strange dynamic. After a day of meetings with Felix and Trine, a general meeting with all the directors was scheduled. He arrived with a huge roll of paper in his hands, and by welcoming us all, he unrolled a massive sketch he had made himself. In his infantile sketch, which was taped to the wall by his two coaches, he depicted the unfolding of his plan. He had drawn up the unification of the European market. The artwork depicted how we all had to go through fire to achieve the construction of a successful new Levi's. In his final words, he confidently announced that he would not accept any criticism but only positive comments about his plan. With a big smile, he welcomed us to his new utopia. To finish off his circus stunt, the two coaches clapped in applause, and then the room fell silent. We were speechless, to say the least, and stared at him with open mouths. We had heard that he was eccentric and very self-absorbed, but this was insanity to the highest degree. After the meeting, we were ushered into another room where drinks and nibbles were prepared. It was The American's idea to get to know us in this informal setting. He shook all our hands and asked about our families, our responsibilities, and so forth. Very bizarre. When it ended, nobody knew what to say, and we were left with nothing but uncertainty. In the following weeks, The American installed himself in Brussels and started conducting interviews. First, with all the CEOs. Felix and Trine were the first to announce they would leave the company. I was not really interested in working in Brussels. While I was contemplating the possibility of applying for a design job, Brussels headquarters sent a booklet to all European offices. The document contained details on how the new market positioning, products, and collection would look. They encouraged us to give feedback. The booklet was geared toward skateboarders in skinny jeans and "Indy" rock bands. A pure "youth-teenager" image with very little commercial sense. We were all shocked, but mostly, our sales team was devastated. They saw their livelihood going up in smoke. There was no way they could satisfy their market's needs with this niche collection. Maybe it was possible to introduce the new image on a marketing level only, but on a product level, it meant absolute brand suicide. The sales team had an important bonus program linked to their sales, which was a substantial part of their income, and they could not maintain their sales numbers with the new collection. Panic broke out in all the European offices, and this time, it was not only doubt; it was PANIC. All European CEOs met in an unofficial meeting to discuss how to reply. They decided to create their own booklet in which they would explain their market, collection positioning, and product needs. They all understood they could not stop the centralization process, but they needed a product that would allow them to maintain their numbers and budgets. As Felix came back, it was my responsibility to assemble the booklet for Germany. I began by researching who had created the Brussels booklet in the first place and discovered that Brussels had already hired designers from the UK and Scandinavia. Those were the edgiest and trendiest markets, but they had hardly any sales to speak of; they were minuscule markets compared to Germany and Italy. Those designers had created the first directional booklet, which was approved by The American. In response, we created our German booklet and sent it to Brussels, as did the other markets. We explained in our booklet that we had a large variety of customers, from the denim-wearing businessman to a skateboarder, and that we catered to all rebels and "young at heart." The booklets were sent to Brussels, and a week later, we received another booklet back from Brussels. There, they stated what Levi's "is" and what Levi's "is not." They had taken all the booklets sent to them and rearranged the images to show what was good and what was bad. Almost all images from Germany were in the "bad" section and were used to describe what is "not" Levi's. We were furious and disappointed about the reaction and ignorance of the new directors. We also realized that we would not find employment within the new design team since we were responsible for all the "bad" images in the latest booklet. Trine immediately flew to Brussels and tried to reason with the new management. As Trine was still in Brussels, she reported back to us and informed us about The American's disappointment in the German team. He considered us obstacles and ordered Trine to clean up and create a supportive new team. As soon as we heard this, we were very upset. Later that evening, I drafted a letter in which I stated how stupid and ignorant I believed the new vision to be. My letter was blunt and direct since I realized I would never be part of the new design team. My email hit their mailboxes before dinner time. Immediately I had Trine on the phone; my career at Levi's was finished, and I did not care. I knew I did not have a future in this wonderful Levi's world that The American was creating. The letter was like an atomic bomb. It contained the truth that we all believed the new concept would ruin the European Levi's market. After a few months, everything calmed down again, but we were resigned to the fact that we could do nothing to change their minds. My contract was extended for six months to help with the transition period. I was happy to do so, and I started looking for a new job. It was time to move to Paris and be with J. and Betty, both of whom I missed very much.

In the following year, The American and his Brussels team continued implementing their product vision and created the first collection with the new positioning. The German market could not sell the new product. It was a disaster. Switzerland and Austria even created their own products secretly so they could satisfy their customers' needs. Of course, Brussels found out and fired within the first year most of the German, Austrian, and Swiss sales teams. All those redundant sales agents were immediately snapped up by the competition. They then replaced all the new Levi's collections with the new brands they were working for. They knew every shop, store, and boutique owner and convinced them to substitute Levi's with products from different brands.

The market in Europe and the treatment of the Levi's teams did not respond well to the new vision. Within the first year, the European sales volume had dropped by 50%. The Levi's market in Europe has not recovered until today.

48. JOB HUNT, JASPER CONRAN AND FIGHTING FOR SURVIVAL

As the six months of transition progressed, I had to sit by and watch how the German Levi's office was dismantled. It was heartbreaking to see how every month, more people packed their bags and left, and simple executional staff was hired. There was no more heartbeat in the German Levi's office; the once-thriving, motivated team became a soulless operation. I needed a job urgently. I had contacted every headhunter of repute. Most of them knew me well and wanted to help, but there weren't any jobs available that were right for me. Especially since I hoped to find a job in Paris. I had enough of traveling. I wanted to be with my family, J., and Betty. Levi's was generous, and I received a 6-month salary severance pay. Luckily, this gave us money to survive since J. still did not earn any decent money. J. was not aware of our financial situation; she did not care where the money for childcare, a babysitter, and rent came from. We had an expensive "family machine" that needed feeding. The day came, and I had to pack my things and leave Levi's. A hard goodbye since we all believed in Levi's but were cast out. Once in Paris, I was happy to be back and started settling into our Paris flat. It was a nice flat, and I bought a desk, which I put up next to our bed, and it became my workstation. A new Apple computer in a colorful bubble was the next of my acquisitions, and my office was ready. But what to do? I became an intruder in my own house. J. left every morning for work and did not come back until the evening. Denise and Albert came to our apartment to begin their day, and I was in the way. I was sitting at my desk responding to e-mails, searching for jobs, sending out the occasional "teaser projects" and waiting. I started walking the streets of Paris and became an expert in Parisian fashion windows and merchandising displays. The cinema became my place of escape. Down in the caves of Les Halles was a big cinema complex, and I spent many afternoons there. It was a way to escape, but it was brutal when I had to reemerge from the depths of a cinematic wonderland and go home. Paris was still at the beginning of its fashion awakening, and there weren't many jobs. J. was happy in her bubble and doing well, but she also had no time for me. Again, I was alone, alone in my own home. Neither a happy family nor a happy job life happened. Since I could not change the job market, my entrepreneurial spirit took hold of me. One morning, I decided it was enough time to spend waiting for a job and launched a T-shirt line. The concept was simple. I wanted to create T-shirts that gave the wearer different skin sensations. I printed tactile patterns on the inside of the T-shirt so it would create the feeling that you were touched and caressed. I imagined my T-shirts were "making love" to you, a great concept, and it was funny to explain. The product execution was somewhat more delicate. Once I had the inside tactile print patterns sorted, I realized that I had to double up on the shell fabric to hide the print pattern showing through from the inside. To make a long story short, the T-shirts were two in one and my ingenious T-shirt design cost double the price. My idea and concept doubled the final asking price. To make things even worse, in my creative madness, I decided on the metal box packaging. The boxes were not cheap, either. To meet the minimum, I had bought 5,000 boxes, which were stored at my Italian manufacturer, CAMAC.

CAMAC is the best jersey manufacturer in Italy, and Magali and Signor Tosi helped very much with my first steps into the luxury fashion market. They helped me source and produce my first collection. Since I was quite persuasive and sure of myself, nobody dared stop me as I created a product that was insanely expensive. The price for a metal-boxed T-shirt was more expensive than a cashmere sweater. To top it all off, the T-shirts were calculated with a ridiculous 20% profit margin. It was commercial insanity, but since I was a designer, I believed in the power of the "new" and insisted this would be the "new"—a clothing line that made you feel "love"! The company I created was called "JAEL." The company was registered in London since Paris was still very alien to me, and I did not speak French. I spoke Italian, English, and German and used those countries to set up my future enterprise. Bernd Schneider, my friend from Hamburg, did the graphic design; Dr. Grossmann was my lawyer in Germany; CAMAC was my production based in Italy; and Dennis looked after the financial and tax sides in the UK. It wasn't an efficient setup, but it worked, and it kept me sane in those lonely times in Paris. J. was aware of my new project, but she did not show much interest. I was like a little child trying to impress her, but I failed. She did not react as I had imagined. I hoped she would get excited and that we would start working together. I hoped she would see that this fledgling company could become a future project for us both. I convinced myself that once success set in, she would come around. It never crossed my mind that I could fail.

The first months passed quickly, with me working next to my bed and Betty, Albert, and Denise playing in the living room. We experienced a happy coexistence and got to know each other better. June, J.'s mom kept coming over from the UK, and we were a happy mix. I continued to travel between Germany and Italy in my Fiat Uno. The mad fashion designer in his white tin box. The final missing part was a showroom. I was able to win over Riccardo Grassi from Studio Zeta in Milan to represent me. The first season was a success for my image, but not financially. We had great shops, and the crown jewel was Harrods. Harrods had made a decent order, but otherwise, we had great customers with ridiculous quantities. The metal boxes became a problem too because you could not see the product once you stored them. You had to open all the boxes and search for the right size, and some customers refused the box. The biggest challenge was my 20% profit margin and exorbitant wholesale price. My first collection did not produce a salary I could live on. I had learned a lot in the first season but also used up the relevant resources I needed to live and pay rent in Paris. In my young innocence, I assumed I would immediately make millions and live as a celebrated designer. All I had achieved so far were bills upon bills and people expecting payment. Luckily, CAMAC stepped in and gave me a helping hand until the second season came around. Riccardo and Mauro from Studio Zeta helped, too and gave me a crash course in how to break into an international market with a small T-shirt brand. It was quite different to fight for yourself with limited resources. I was used to spending money through a big company like Moschino or Levi's.

At home, our financial situation had deteriorated. I had no more money left, and the T-shirts would not produce an income for some time in the future. J. was happily working at Louis Vuitton and sleeping well. I did not tell J. about our financial situation. I will never forget the last week before the money ran out. There was nothing left. I was sick. We would lose everything, must pack up, and move back to my parents' house. My father was aware of the situation. In this last week before our bankruptcy, I did not sleep much and stood most nights at the window looking down on the empty Parisian Street and the Centre Pompidou opposite our balcony window. The Centre Pompidou became my friend on those nights. It was the absolute worst time I had experienced in my life. The knowledge to have failed, to have failed my family, J., and Betty; worse still was that J.'s dream at Louis Vuitton would end too. We were broke and would have to start again. No more Paris and the big fashion world, but back to Leonberg and my family's house. I had spoken with my father, and he invited me to join them in Saalbach, Austria, where they were on holiday, to discuss the next steps. I was meant to stay for the weekend. To travel there, I borrowed one of J.'s Louis Vuitton bags and flew to Austria. As I arrived at Salzburg Airport, there was no more Louis Vuitton bag. At the Paris airport, I had checked in my travel bag, and the bag never resurfaced in Austria. The luggage people just informed me with a sad smile that only a madman would put a Louis Vuitton bag in the luggage hold since they regularly get stolen. This was the cherry on top of my misery; not only was I penniless, but I had lost my luggage too and had nothing else to wear but my father's clothes. I rarely cry, but I cried then. My parents were very supportive, and I explained everything over dinner. The next day, we all went to the lake nearby for a swim. As I was lying there in my father's swim shorts (not a sexy sight!), my mobile phone started ringing. It was Joanna Neicho and Julius Schofield from Indesign, a fashion design headhunter in London. Joanna politely asked what I was up to and if I was interested in a job in London. My heart skipped a beat, and I said that I would be very interested in a job. Joanna was not aware of my desperate situation. She then confirmed Jasper Conran was looking for a design assistant, and if I wanted the job, it was mine. After carefully inquiring about the salary and quickly calculating if it would be enough to allow us to continue our lives in Paris, I said yes. This was the second time in two days I had to cry. On the very last day before bankruptcy, Joanna would change my life, I was saved by Joanna and Jasper

Conran. I shared the news with my father, and they were relieved about the good news. Then I called J., who was not fully aware of the severity of our situation. J. was not too happy about her lost Louis Vuitton bag and the prospect of me traveling, but she also understood that it was time for me to work again. It was a bittersweet pill for both of us. That evening I went to the local church, lit a candle, and thanked the Gods in heaven. Even though I'm not religious, the higher powers in the sky deserved this candle.

49. BACK IN LONDON

As I arrived back in Paris without my luggage, I could not wait to get home to see J. and Betty. The worst had been averted, and we would continue to build our lives in Paris. I had not managed to find a job in Paris yet, but we had enough money coming in to survive. In the evening, I explained everything to J. and then calculated all the costs and expenses. Jasper Conran was not paying for my travel, and I had to work five days a week, not four as I had negotiated at Levi's. It was a full-time job, and they did not care that I had a family in Paris. I was worried about the time commitment, but as explained before, I had no choice. As I added up all the expenses, it quickly became clear that I could not afford a flat in London or a room. Travel and Paris would absorb most of my income. J.'s sister Lyn and her husband, Colin, offered help. At the time, they had a house in Reading that stood empty because they were living in India and working for British Gas. Colin suggested I could stay there rent-free until I found something more suitable. Reading was an hour's train ride from London, not ideal to get to the office every day, but it made sense financially, and as they say, a beggar can't be a chooser. Time flew, and it began; within a week I had to start, and I became quickly acquainted with Eurostar travel. The Eurostar was still new, and the daily commute of the masses was not happening yet. The concept of traveling to work from Paris to London daily was not yet conceived. I was one of the first. I started Monday morning, leaving Paris with the first train headed for London at 6:00 a.m. The whole train was empty, only occupied by a few commuters. We could spread out and sleep comfortably in the seats. We arrived around 8:30 a.m., and I rushed to the office close to Kings Road. I was about 15 minutes late every Monday morning and got told off every time. Jasper knew very well that I came from Paris on Monday mornings, but in his eccentricity, he would not see the reason why I could not make it at 9:00 a.m. sharp. It became a habit of his to wait for me on Monday mornings when I arrived late. It did not bother me much, as I assumed it was part of his character to be unreasonable. Jasper Conran and his father, Terence Conran, were legends in the British design world. Jasper started his company early with outrageous designs for evening gowns and minimalistic chic. At the beginning of his career, his boyfriend, John Galliano, worked with him. Later, John moved on to start his own career. Jasper's collection had the same problem my t-shirt collection had. It was incredibly expensive, and to finance his catwalk collection and stay afloat, he signed multiple licensing deals. His most lucrative collaboration was with T.K. Maxx (known in the U.S.A. as T.J. Maxx). T.K. Maxx had approached him to create accessible designs at the mass-market outlet level. It was a t-shirt with sparkling Jasper Conran logos printed on the chest. T.K. Maxx and Jasper had a trial run, and it turned out British ladies were crazy for those items, and Jasper was hungry for the extra turnover, so my position was created. Jasper needed a designer who could redesign these sparkly logo t-shirts a thousandfold, and this was my new job. I had an assistant who helped me prepare the mood boards and designs. Every week, the T.K. Maxx buying team would turn up and select the designs they wanted, and we produced them. It was a crazy business that was very successful but exhausting. Designing was not the challenge, but the little time window we had between each drop was ridiculous. We were a fun team, and crazy Jasper could be quite entertaining in the office. It felt every day as we were in a film set for "Absolutely Fabulous."

The word "Darling" was used a lot.

He had great style and incredible energy. I loved working with him. The offices were beautiful, and he deserved every bit of fame he accumulated. He was a good guy, and I liked him apart from his "Monday morning complaining about me being late." He was obsessed with making money and thoroughly believed the world owed him millions, and T.K. Maxx did just that. After the first month of traveling with Eurostar, taking the train from Reading every morning and night, and working long hours, I was exhausted. I had to get up at 4:30 am on a Monday morning, then travel to London to work until 7:00 p.m., then rush to catch the train to get to Reading. I had to eat something on the way because I did not feel like shopping or cooking at home in the deserted, empty house. At the time, Waterloo Station was a horrible station. It was dirty and neglected, and I developed the habit of grabbing two cheeseburgers on my way home, which was my dinner. At home in Reading, I watched some TV and collapsed onto my bed. Since the house was not really meant to be lived in while Lynn and Colin were in India, it was cold, and I started sleeping in front of the gas fireplace on the floor in the living room. Not a comfortable life, but it kept the lights on in Paris. If I went for a drink with friends after work, I always ran the risk of missing the last train to Reading. If this happened and I missed the train, I stayed at the Wellington next to Waterloo station. The Wellington was a nice pub, but their rooms were out of a William Burroughs novel. The trains were constantly running by, and it was apocalyptic. I loved it in a weird way. I always felt like I was in a Franz Kafka novel and would turn into a bug lying on its back. All in all, I did get very little sleep because I had to get up at 6:00 a.m. every morning to make it back to the office on time. None of this bothered me; it was fun, and the team was great, but I knew that this was not a career anyone could build a life on. It served a purpose, but I had to continue to look for a job.

As I was in my third month at Jasper, a call arrived. Emanuel Ungaro in Paris was looking for a head of menswear design. The Maison Ungaro was all over the fashion news because it had been bought by Ferragamo, and Giambattista Valli was the new creative director. Giambattista was a powerhouse; he had transformed Maison Ungaro in the two years of his reign. At the same time, Hedi Slimane was rocking the menswear world at Yves Saint Laurent in Paris. Now, Ungaro wanted to establish their menswear presence and grow their business further. I was super excited about the call and immediately sent my CV to Giambattista. Within a week, I was invited to meet Giambattista and Laura Ungaro. Laura was the wife of Emanuel Ungaro, and she oversaw everything in the House apart from design. Both were friendly and charismatic characters who were very passionate about the future of Maison Ungaro. We had a great interview; I presented my portfolio to them, and they shared their ambitious plan concerning menswear with me.

At the end of the interview, Giambattista asked me to create a project for them in which I would envision the new Ungaro menswear. This request was common after an interview, and we agreed on a date to present it to them again in two weeks' time. I was super excited at the prospect of working for one of the last fully functioning couture houses in Paris. Only Chanel and Dior had bigger couture studios in the whole world.

At last, an opening in Paris! Not only was it a great job opportunity, but it also meant I could be with my family. Now I had to get the job, though. I was not the only one applying for this opportunity; everybody wanted that job, and it was a golden ticket. The next challenge was the short time I was given to create this project. Working for Jasper did not leave much room for extra design activity. I also still had my T-shirt collection, which needed attention. Luckily, J. saved me and agreed to help; she accumulated most of the research images, so I did not have to spend hours in bookshops researching for pictures in books and magazines. Once the mood boards and fabrics were in place, the design of the collection was quick. All in all a stressful situation because if I failed to land this job, I would have had to return to London, and God only knew when another golden opportunity in Paris would come along.

Time flies when you are having fun, and in no time, I was sitting in front of Laura and Giambattista again. It was a friendly hello, and then they wanted to see the project. I had a special book made for the occasion, and it was beautiful to touch and to present with. Laura and Giambattista listened with curiosity and concentration; it was quite intense to present under their focus and scrutiny. As I showed the last page and answered some last questions, Laura looked at me and said, "Welcome to Ungaro," and Giambattista laughed. I could not believe it, but I had done it; with the help of J., we had done it! It was an incredible feeling. After I left the Ungaro offices on Avenue Montaigne, I was exhausted and had to sit down on a park bench to take it all in. Then I stood up and walked home, which took me about an hour. In this hour, I was in a world of ecstasy and, for the first time, saw Paris. I absorbed it all. I had arrived in Paris!

50. PARIS, UNGARO, JASPER IS NOT HAPPY AND NEVER GIVE UP II

In the evening, we had a big celebration. The world was whole again, and we were all happy together. The next day I had to get back to London because I only had a day off and I had to be back in the Conran office pronto. The next few days were all about finalizing the contract. The headhunters and lawyers checked all the details, and then I signed the document and was officially the new Head of menswear design at Ungaro, Paris.

The tricky part was that they wanted me immediately, within two weeks. This was a very short notice period for Jasper.

Now I had to go and tell Jasper. He could be quite emotional, as we all knew, and I was dreading the moment. I made an appointment with his assistant and entered his office. He knew something was up, and so I told him straight that I was going to leave Jasper Conran to go back to my family. He was furious, and he demanded to know for whom I would work next. I knew he would find out one way or another, so I told him I would be the new head of menswear at Ungaro. He went ballistic and threatened to sue Ungaro, the headhunter, and everybody in between. He asked me to leave the office immediately.

In the evening, the headhunter called and informed me that they had managed to calm Jasper down. Jasper insisted that I would work the final two weeks and that I had to pay him back his headhunter fee he had paid just three months ago. Ungaro would not cover the expense of Jasper's headhunter fees, but I did not care; I was happy to pay since I was again on a generous salary and could afford it. We all agreed on the terms, and my final two weeks in London commenced. Jasper made sure to make it absolute hell, but as with all things, those two weeks passed as well, and I was finally in my new office at Maison Ungaro Couture on Avenue Montaigne, Paris.

51. COUTURE AND MENSWEAR

Maison Ungaro was a special place in Paris. Monsieur Ungaro was born in France, but he was of Italian origin, and his wife was Italian too. Therefore, the languages spoken in the office were Italian and French, which suited me perfectly since my French was still basic. Most of the collections were produced and developed by Vesitmenta and Ferragamo in Italy, and we traveled frequently there. As I arrived in the Ungaro office, there was still a menswear team in place, which was all French origin, and opposed the changes Laura and Giambattista were introducing to the traditional Couture business. They believed the old-fashioned model was still valid, and they were neither helpful nor welcoming to me, the newcomer. This did not bother me much. Giambattista had already assembled his own team, and I was allowed a new assistant too. There were still some licensing deals with Asia, and the old team took care of those while I started Collection "0." This collection was meant to be the start of the menswear catwalk collection. There was a lot to prepare, and I started immediately. In the first months, I also found my new assistant at the Royal College of Art, Daniel Kearns. Daniel was straight out of school from the RCA as he joined Emanuel Ungaro.

Our office was right across the hall from Monsieur Ungaro's couture studio, and we were lucky to see all the new couture outfits walk by our door. Monsieur Ungaro loved to stop by our office to see how we were doing and initiate us into the world of Ungaro. He was happy to share his love for prints, African art, and African objects, which he collected with addictive passion. His most interesting stories were about Armani, though. Giorgio Armani was once his apprentice; he learned the trade and couture techniques from Monsieur Ungaro. At the beginning of the 1960s, Monsieur Ungaro did develop his trademark soft shoulder. It was a particular way to cut the armhole to give a tailored jacket a soft shoulder with a tight, fitted armhole. In Monsieur Ungaro's collections, with the colors and printed patterns, it was never as evident but present. Once Armani left Maison Ungaro and founded his own house, he presented this elegant Italian tailored jacket for men and women, which became the legendary Armani style.

As Monsieur Ungaro showed us how to cut the shoulder and armhole, he always claimed Armani's look was really the Ungaro look and that one of his biggest legacies to fashion was that he created Armani's soft shoulder.

Monsieur Ungaro and all his staff in the Couture studio were an incredible source of craftsmanship. They were the real thing; they could do anything with fabric and their bare hands. They looked like an army of scientists because they all wore white lab coats to work. Along the hallway were all the prototypes on rails, and we could touch and examine them as we pleased. They were not stitched but pinned, with thousands of pins, which were pinned vertically. They were all pinned by hand, one by one, and they stuck out like cactus spines. Incredibly beautiful to see the absolute perfection, attention to detail, and cut. The embroidery samples from Lesage and other wonders could be observed in the presentation rooms next to the big fitting studio. A treasure trove—Aladdin's fashion cave. Every day, the couture-fit models had to wait in the hallways until Monsieur Ungaro was ready for them. Monsieur Ungaro did not sketch. He designed draping straight on the body in front of massive mirrors. While waiting, they loved to hang out in our office and share the latest gossip. They not only fitted for Maison Ungaro but for other Couture houses as well, and there were many stories to tell. We loved to listen to the fashion grapevine, which was very educational to learn about all the little scandals among the couture clients and staff. While we were absorbing all the latest gossip, Monsieur Ungaro was creating in his studio.

Monsieur Ungaro was a kind and elegant man. He had a magnetic personality with sophistication and style. He was cultured and well-educated—a Gentleman through and through. He abhorred fast fashion and the sloppiness of its cheap production.

He had a temper, though, and was famous for throwing things at his staff if they did not pay attention. He demanded discipline in his studio and work.

Giambattista was like Monsieur Ungaro; he also had a fiery temperament and did not suffer fools gladly. The structure was simple: Monsieur Ungaro created the couture collection (Giamba helped of course), Giambattista created the pret-a-porter collection, and I did pret-a-porter men. Only Monsieur Ungaro's Couture Collection was developed in the Paris couture studios; everything else was produced in Italy with Vestimenta.

The fashion shows generated the most excitement. I was used to fashion shows in Milan from Moschino. At Levi's, I was mostly used to making and presenting films rather than fashion shows over the last few years. Finally, I was back in the wonderful world of models and catwalks. I loved fashion shows. Line openings and parties had their charm, but fashion shows were royal; they were special, especially at Ungaro. Monsieur Ungaro did not believe in small shows; he invited everybody. In those days, it had become more fashionable and exclusive to only invite smaller crowds to give those spectacles a more intimate feel, but not at Ungaro. The couture show held at the Louvre under the Pyramid was attended by up to two thousand guests. Spectacular events and Monsieur Ungaro's clothes and robes were outstanding. Giambattista's shows were not much smaller but had a more contemporary feel to them. I felt honored to be part of the magnificent Maison Ungaro and its creations, to be able to see and touch the ancient art of French couture filled me with awe and wonder. We were part of something sacred.

52. PARIS LIFE AND STANLEY WAS BORN

Not only did Maison Ungaro become part of our life, J. and Louis Vuitton had developed into a powerhouse too. Marc had found his place, and the Louis Vuitton board was happy with his fashion collections and shows. His winning angle was his ability to create "it" bags. Marc quickly understood that the road to success would be Louis Vuitton bags that sold in the thousands. He was very good at bringing artists together to create wonderful pieces of accessory art. My favorite collaborations of his were with Stephen Sprouse, his American fashion design friend, and Takashi Murakami.

They had moved out of their small studio at Rue du Bac and were part of the Louis Vuitton offices close to Pont Neuf. The new offices were understated but very chic, and the whole fashion team was now fully integrated. J. had made it and was part of the new fashion powerhouse.

Marc designed his own line in New York as well, and he was constantly traveling back and forth between the US and France. It was a grueling schedule for him, and he often arrived at the office, where he collapsed in his small bed in the corner of his room and slept. When he awoke, he started working. This was a difficult arrangement for the team because they had to be available 24/7, especially before the fashion shows. J. had to go on a four-week lockdown in the Louis Vuitton offices before the shows. The rhythm was demanding, and we needed the help of our parents often. J.'s father had died in those years, and J.'s mom was alone in the UK. We needed help, and Denise could not be around all the time to help. June offered to come to Paris and help with Betty (and Stanley, who was born in 2002). She was coming often and was staying with us in our small house in Paris. At first, for me, this was challenging—being around my mother-in-law all the time and having to behave. It did not take long until we realized that we were a great team, and we went everywhere to all events and parties together. June was a true party animal and well-appreciated by all our friends. Best of all, she never complained about me driving fast, which I adored, and which horrified J.

Between my parents, June and Denise, we had the perfect setup.

We even looked after Marc's Dalmatian dog, Tigger," from time to time. A real "Villa Kunterbunt."

Dior and Givenchy were still the headliners, but Marc Jacobs and Louis Vuitton were clearly making their mark in fashion history.

Marc was very kind, and I was always invited to the Louis Vuitton shows, after-parties, and dinners. Marc and I liked to talk on those occasions; we both loved art and were happy to discuss the latest artists we had found. Life was good. I was sleeping in our house and had a normal life. No hotel rooms, sleeping on floors or empty apartments, and no airports, at least not as often as before (of course, I had to fly to Italy). I was home with my family. Betty was growing up and going to kindergarten in the Marais district behind our house. A nice life, and we had many friends and dinners. As Betty grew older, we increasingly realized how difficult it was for her to play on the small playgrounds available in our arrondissement. We needed more space, too; my collection boxes started taking over our bedroom. After three years, J. and I decided it was time to look for a house with a little garden. In the Paris fashion world, we were the only ones with children. In fashion circles, there were not many children among fashion designers. Our friends were from all over the world, but we did not know any French people. We lived like phantoms in Paris. We had lots of foreign friends, and the city was full of people, but we could not find our place among them.

On weekends, we started by driving around Paris and searched for parts of the city that we could hopefully afford and liked. We knew the center of Paris, but Paris was a big place with a multitude of different facets, which we intended to discover. We scoured magazines and internet sites searching for estates to buy. Once we found a house we liked, we made appointments to visit it. It became our weekend occupation: breakfast on Saturday morning, and then off we went to visit houses. Like unwrapping presents at Christmas, you never knew what you would find, what houses you would see, or which areas we would see next. We did not have a big budget, but Paris was not as expensive then as it is today, and it was still possible to find incredible opportunities if you were patient enough. To entertain ourselves, we also booked visits to houses we could never afford. There were beautiful apartments, and we hoped to become rich soon. Apart from expensive houses, we looked for dilapidated gems we could transform to our liking. One of those rare finds was an old hat factory in the 20th arrondissement. The area was horrific, and the buildings around it depressing, but the hat factory, which was a hundred years old, was a diamond in the rough. It had a huge surface and cost more than we would have been able to afford. We tried to buy it with Aisling and her husband, but we could not make it work financially in the end. I always wondered what happened to it. I hope they did not tear it down and build another ugly Highrise. Weekends passed by, and finally, it became two years that we had spent looking for a house. Nothing! We could not find anything we liked and could afford. We started further outside Paris towards Versailles and St. Cloud, but there, we also did not find anything we wanted to call home. We wondered if we would ever find a house we liked. In the last year, another miracle happened. J. became pregnant again, and we were overjoyed. Nine months later, Stanley was born, much to our delight.

Stanley's birth was not as dramatic as Betty's, but there was a story too. J. was pregnant with Stanley, and Stanley's birth was not meant to be for another three weeks. The doctor had advised us that this night, the 3rd of December, would be the last night to go out before we had to get J.'s suitcase ready and wait for her labors to set in. Graci, a good friend of ours, decided that she would take me out to town before the waiting began. We went to all the bars and clubs and came home at 2:00 a.m.; to our surprise, J. was waiting in the living room. J. told us that Stanley was on his way, labor had set in, we had to go to the hospital, and the doctor was already waiting. We sobered up immediately. Graci had to stay in our apartment and look after Betty, and I ran to find my car keys. There was no traffic, and we made it to the hospital quickly. By 3:00 a.m., J. was wheeled into the operating theater, followed by me. Stanley's birth was uncomplicated, and three hours later, Stanley came into this world. As I did with Betty, I stalked the nurse to make sure she would not switch our precious child. Once I had ensured that our Stanley was our Stanley, I looked at my watch and realized it was close to 6:30 a.m. I gave J. and Stanley a kiss, told J. to get some rest and that I loved her, and left for home. At home, I proudly told Betty and Graci that Stanley and J. were healthy and resting and that I would have to take a shower. We had a quick breakfast and at 8:00 a.m. I drove to my office because I had a fitting at 9:00 a.m. with Giambattista and Monsieur Ungaro. Everybody in the office congratulated me, and the fitting lasted until noon. At noon, I made my way back to the hospital to see J. and Stanley. I was super happy, fully sober, and exhausted. Back home, I collapsed onto our bed and slept.

Stanley was our "party" child, and we were and are still overjoyed to have him with us.

We were very happy and needed a bigger place more urgently than ever. On one of our excursions to the countryside, we found Montfort-L'Amaury. One weekend, we all went swimming at the Étang de Hollande, close to the Forêt de Rambouillet, a gorgeous lake in the middle of the wooded area around Montfort, and on our way back, we had lunch there. As it were, we walked by the windows of the local estate agents, found charming properties for sale, and were surprised at the affordable prices of farmhouses and manors in the area. J. stated that it would be too far from Paris and that Denise and Albert would never move to the countryside, but I convinced her that it would not hurt to have a look. The next weekend, I had Stanley in my car with me; he was only a few months old, but he loved to travel in the car, and we were on the road to see two houses. They looked lovely in photographs. The first house was nice; it even had a Sauna, but it was too close to the main road. The layout was also not right, but it was a huge improvement over anything we had seen in Paris over the last two years. Stanley was clapping in his Maxi Cosi, but I told him we had to wait for the next one; him being a baby, he just smiled back. Once I had him strapped back into the car, we drove to a small village close by called Auteuil le Roi. It was close to Thoiry, which was home to a famous wildlife park and zoo. It was a lovely drive through country roads and fields, and finally, we stood in front of a big metal gate. Hugues and his wife Maylis, the owners, greeted Stanley and me and laughed about him smiling out of his Maxi Cosi. As we walked through the houses, there were three houses, a courtyard, and a back garden. The three houses consisted of a main house, an atelier, and a barn, which still needed restoration. Ample place for us, the children, my t-shirts, and my artistic ambitions. That was the house we were looking for; it was like I was struck by lightning. The price was right too; it was on the expensive side, but we would be able to make it work. I was so excited and could not contain my emotions—not a good basis for negotiations. I told Hughes and Maylis not to sell it and that I would be back with J. the next day, Sunday.

Turning the car around, I hit a nail on the street and had a flat tire in front of the new house. I had to jump out and ask Hugues to help me change the wheel, and to his amusement, I told him that even the car wanted to stay.

Back in Paris, I was like a whirlwind, laughing and dancing and telling everybody about the great house and that we would move to the countryside. J. was less excited about the prospect of moving to the countryside. She did not drive in Europe, and the commute to work by train each day scared her. She often had to work late hours and weekends. I told her to wait and see if she would like the house. The next day, all four of us seated in the car, we drove out to Auteuil le Roi. It was a perfect sunny day, and we were curious to see the house and if we would all like it. We arrived to a friendly greeting, and J. and Betty walked silently through the house. Maylis was a perfect tour guide, and J. and Betty followed her through all the rooms with big eyes. Maylis and Hughes had done a marvelous job restoring and modernizing the house. They mixed a contemporary open floor plan with the historic features of the house. The house or parts of it were built in 1831, and the house had thick stone walls. Often, those old buildings were dark and gloomy inside. Not this house, it was well-lit and full of sunlight. Downstairs, in the kitchen and living room area, they had poured concrete floors, which added to an industrial loft feel with a Moroccan touch. A gorgeous and unusual house; it was an artist's house full of charm and happiness.

This was a huge change from our 90-square-meter apartment in Paris. As the tour was finished and Betty was happily playing with the dogs in the courtyard, we sat down on a bench, and I looked at J. with a big question mark on my face. "Do you like it?" I asked her expectantly, and she just replied, "It's perfect." I hugged her and gave her a big kiss, and we told Hughes and Maylis that we would buy the house.

53. FINANCES, PARIS, FASHION SHOWS, ART, JAPAN, AND WHAT TO DO?

Buying a house is easier said than done in France. As we drove back to Paris, we slowly realized all the problems we had to sort out. First, we had to ask Denise if she and Albert would or could move to the countryside. A big move for them too, and Denise's husband had a job in Paris that he would have to change. J.'s driving skills were also a big challenge. J. always claimed that she was a good driver, but to be blunt, she had never driven a car, neither in the UK nor in France, in years. The next big question was where we would get the down payment of 10% of the asking price. We had no savings; we spent all we earned instantly. All those questions piled up in the car on our way back to Paris, and a gloomy realization of having bitten off too much to chew set in. In the evening, I called my father and my Aunt Christel. Christel was a banker and dealt with mortgage loans, my father, because we needed collateral. My family was great as always, and my aunt opened a line of credit for 100,000 euros so we could pay the down payment, cover lawyers and administrative fees, and buy a new car because the old one was dead. My father, in return, had a new mortgage on his house in his name, which J. and I had to cover. This was a fast and swift process due to my aunt's help. The next challenge was Denise and Albert. We spoke with Denise Monday morning, and it turned out Denise was quite open to moving to the countryside since she was tired of the noise and dirt of a big city and was hoping for a cleaner life with fresh air for Albert too. As things looked doable, we called Hugues and told him we were ready for the "Promesse de Vente" to be signed at the "Notaire." It was an official meeting where we had to show our passports and sign a document that stated that we would pay the full sum of the asking price in three months' time. If we fail to do so, the seller will keep the 10% down payment. We signed and realized that we still had to secure a bank loan in France, and I did not have an aunt or father to support us here. The next challenge was the realization that Denise would need a car and a place to stay. We started solving all the issues and challenges one by one. Our friends helped us quickly find a bank that agreed to support us.

They gave us lots of documents to fill out, and we sat at the kitchen table in the evening and accumulated all the necessary proof of income and bank statements. It was a lot of paperwork, and luckily, Morine helped us. She was used to dealing with French bureaucracy, which was a nightmare. The biggest issue was that I was not paid in France but through my newly-founded design office in the UK. In the end, I had to put my work contract in our request to the bank as proof of income. We had to omit some facts in the process. Of course, we did not tell the bank all our expenses and cost of living. We did not mention a word that we also had to pay for Denise and an extra car. As all documents were in order, we did get approval for our mortgage loan, and we had another small celebration as we had secured the funds to pay for the house. The most important part was solved and done. The next step was to find a flat for Denise. Again, we had to look through magazines and local ads to find a place, and we got lucky once again. It was a small place, but it had a garden, and it would work for starters. The car was found quickly in comparison, and I realized that Denise was as unpracticed in driving as J. was. I spent many hours practicing driving with her in the zoo's parking lot in Thoiry in the coming months, and Denise improved. J., on the other hand, was another challenge altogether. J. refused to drive flat out, and Denise and I had to drive her about in the countryside for the next 10 years. It took us ten years to get J. to drive a car, and finally, she overcame her fear and became an independent driver. Today, she is a small "Niki Lauda" and a secure and passionate driver. What a pleasure to see her race through Paris streets, honking at other cars with British confidence.

In three months, we managed to move two families, train two lady drivers, buy two cars, buy a house, and find the financial resources to do so. We were happy!

The moving was easy since we did not own very much, and to J.'s delight, she was able to go shopping for new furniture with the little money that was left from the German loan. The house looked gorgeous, and we had found our first home, which we owned together. The next tricky element was paying the bills every month. As time passed in the last two years, we managed to look for houses, bring

Stanley into this world, and establish a life in France. J. was soaring at Louis Vuitton, and her career took off, but she was still not earning very much money. My job, on the other hand, was well paid, but my job prospects had turned sour. We had created the famous Ungaro men's collection "0" and had created more collections and documentation, but Vestimenta and Ferragamo did not agree on the licensing deal. A nightmare. Everything was ready to go, but we did not get past the financial dealings between production and the owner. Giambattista, Laura, Monsieur Ungaro, and I were fighting to get the deal done, but to no avail. We weren't idle during that period, we had enough to do with the other licensing collections, but we were hungry for the promised catwalk show. The old menswear team had left, and it was Daniel and me working in the menswear design office only.

Then, many things happened at the same time. Not only did we buy the house, but also, in my professional career, I took charge and rearranged possibilities. Since it was not clear what would happen next with Ungaro menswear, I decided to expand my t-shirt collection and create my own fashion show in Milan. Because of Maison Ungaro and a possible conflict of interest, I could not hold the show in Paris, and we decided Milan would be a great place to do so. The collection was renamed from "Jael" to "JENS," and we started to get the balls rolling. We registered the "JENS" collection with the "Camera Nazionale della Moda Italiana-Milano." JENS was accepted and received an officially scheduled calendar date. It all sounds easy, but it took a lot of documentation to get on the official Milan fashion show calendar. Once we had the date, we had to design the collection and get our set-up in order. A good start.

Next, we had to find more freelance work because J. and I did not earn enough money to cover all the new expenses we had accumulated with our ambitious dreams.

In those times, our friends Stefano and Carolyn were of invaluable help, and I will be indebted to them eternally. Stefano was a magician at organizing fashion shows out of nothing, and Carolyn was building a design consultancy office with well-reputed clients. Carolyn's connections helped us connect with a Japanese brand called "Five Foxes," who were looking for new design input for their multiple brands in Japan. The very exciting part was that we and six other designers were invited to fly to Tokyo, Japan, for a weeklong test exercise. This was a very generous interview opportunity, and we were all super excited. We all knew each other, and the week in Tokyo promised to be a wonderful experience and a generous gift from Five Foxes.

The day came, and we all boarded the flight to Tokyo in business class! I already had a cold but quickly developed a dry cough, and my lungs hurt. As we arrived in Tokyo, we were picked up and transported to our hotel. The first day was reserved for us to settle in and acclimate. The only meeting that we had that first day was with Five Foxes at their headquarters. There they explained the expectations of the design exercises and tests they wanted us to complete. They wanted us to create a small capsule collection within two days for a concept story set by them. In ordinary circumstances, there was nothing wrong with the brief; it was a straightforward design exercise, but I had developed a strong cough and was coughing throughout the whole meeting. This was considered rude in the eyes of the Japanese, or better yet, unpleasant, and distasteful. I could not help it; I had developed a slight fever, too. In the hotel, I ordered medicine and pills, which I usually take when I have the flu, but they did not help. It was my lungs. I could not breathe properly, especially on the left part of my lungs. I felt like no air went in. I had to turn the hot shower on to humidify the hotel room and turn it into a steam room, much to J.'s dislike. The night before the test, I could not sleep. I locked myself in the bathroom and pressed a towel in front of my mouth while coughing so I would not wake up J., who needed her sleep. I dosed off now and then, but the morning came far too early. I had no choice but to get into the shower and pump myself full of black tea and medication during breakfast. Completely drugged up, I made my way to the Five Foxes offices to start the test. The design concept and brief were easy, and we were well prepared, and everything went smoothly except for me coughing and sweating away. We all finished our tests, had many dinners, and discovered Tokyo while I was coughing, not sleeping, and sitting in our bathroom with a towel in front of my mouth. In hindsight, Tokyo was a blur, a crazy dance with flu, fever, coughing, jetlag, and designing clothes. As the week in

Tokyo came to an end, we all climbed aboard our plane and flew back to Paris. The next day, I was in our doctor's office and did get an x-ray of my lungs. The doctor proclaimed that I had a severe lung infection called pneumonia, and a less healthy person would have died under the strain I had put myself under. My whole left lung was a huge, infected cloud on the x-ray. She gave me antibiotics at a strength suitable for a horse and sent me home to rest. It took two rounds of antibiotics to shift the pneumonia and recover. Luckily, Five Foxes did choose us for a consultancy, and we could secure the extra income we needed to cover our extra expenses. We did get lucky.

Things in Paris developed in a positive way. I had found new friends, a great group of people who had started an "art-fashion collective." Like the factory once founded by Andy Warhol in New York. It was a Paris office and store that created concerts, art exhibitions, and fashion in all its crazy forms. They later opened a showroom and a fashion fair. Jeremie, Aldric, Rajan, Gordon, Juliette, and Vidya were the key drivers, although Vidya joined later. They called themselves "Surface to Air" and I met them at their opening party for a young artist called "Banksy." A crazy team, and I was mostly linked to them through their art exhibitions. Through Surface to Air, I started buying and collecting art. Rajan and Gordon were my advisors. I bought mainly art from FAILE, Maya, and Alfredo Martinez. They often had DJs and parties in their store and exhibition space. Often, I went with Betty on my shoulders to those Parties while J. was working. Betty was five years old and happily joined me in partying with the cool crowd in Paris. There, Betty became famous for her wriggly moves on the dance floor.

Surface to Air had its own fashion collection too. We connected with my JENS line, and they became my French agents for a short period of time. Vidya became our first assistant, helping us with our consultancy work for Five Foxes, and Jeremie Rozan, who was a filmmaker and CEO of the team, became a great friend and business advisor. Later, I invested in Surface to Air and became a shareholder.

54. JENS

In those years, we had a lot of fun, work, and many other things going on at the same time. The fashion world slowly changed. Paris and the LVMH group became global fashion royalty, and LVMH made Paris the fashion capital of the world once again. Italy and its fashion houses were stuck in an old business model of mixing creativity with commerciality. The one breaking out of the norm was Gucci, under the creative direction of Tom Ford. Gucci was later transformed into the Gucci Group under Pinault and became the second French force in fashion. LVMH and Gucci Group (later known as Kering Group) revolutionized fashion. They bought all the well-known French luxury houses and focused on creativity. From the 1930s to the 1960s, most French fashion houses were owned by textile companies. The textile industry understood that to sell fabrics in quantity, they had to team up with designers, and therefore, most French design houses were founded and financed by textile producers in those early years. This all changed to a new business model when the Italian "licensing deals" with fashion designers took hold from the 1970s to the beginning of the 1990s. The Italian designers understood that to be creative, it was a lot easier to separate design creation from production and selling clothes. Those licensing deals allowed a fashion designer to concentrate on designing. The design offices had no more "Ateliers." Ateliers were sewing studios in which the first prototypes were created in-house under the direct supervision of the designers. Now, all the sewing of prototypes, showroom samples, and complete production resided within the factories. None of the "stitching," invoicing, and delivery troubles were part of a design studio anymore. The fashion design teams did the original research, sketching and designing, fabric selection, fashion show production, and marketing. It allowed the designers to concentrate on creation alone. The drawback was that you made less money as a designer, but for many, it was worth it to live worry-free from the mundane hustle of manufacturing, selling clothes, and dealing with tedious fashion clients. Now, under the new licensing business model, fashion houses like Moschino or Dolce & Gabbana were design offices with designers only, and all development and production were handled by a different entity like AEFFE. The Design houses took a percentage of the profits, usually between 10 and 15% (10% royalties on sales and 5% marketing budget); the rest of the profit belonged to the producer. The rights to the fashion brand name usually reside with the designer. They left the business side of handling and selling a collection to capable businessmen.

LVMH and the Gucci Group changed the model once more and transformed the fashion world in the 1990s. They were investing in young, charismatic designers and allowed them to create with complete freedom. The fashion shows became marketing tools, and only the PR impact was relevant, as they did not care if the collections sold. The big money was in each brand's or fashion house's core products like accessories, bags, shoes, and cosmetics. At Louis Vuitton, it was the "monogram bag" series. This product group was a lot easier to sell than catwalk fashion, and the profit margins were much higher. The best thing about the new model was that a "monogram bag" was a "non-seasonal" product, which meant you could sell it all year round, year after year, and your stock would not devalue after one season like it did with fashion garments. Those core essentials hardly changed and were produced in the hundreds of thousands. So, Bernard Arnault and the Pinault Family saw this golden opportunity to turn creative fashion shows into a marketing tool and concentrate on selling non-seasonal core products to make an absolute killing. The French model conquered the fashion world at the beginning of the 21st century.

In all those shifts from Milan to Paris, I was in the middle of it all. My JENS fashion show was in Italy, and my Ungaro show was in Paris. The only trouble was that Ungaro's menswear did not move. Ferragamo did not want to invest the amount Monsieur Ungaro demanded, and Vestimenta would not start producing until everybody agreed on the financial expectations. Giambattista did not help either because, after the first 5 years of his success, he demanded the label inside all garments change to "Emanuel Ungaro by Giambattista Valli." Monsieur Ungaro was furious about this request, and so Giambattista and Monsieur Ungaro were continuously quarreling. To make matters worse, Giambattista always threatened to leave if his demands were not met, as did Monsieur Ungaro. Poor Ferragamo was in the middle of it all and had to deal with both prima donnas constantly.

While they were fighting the "Ungaro" war, I realized that Ungaro menswear would not be on the Ferragamo priority list. Daniel had the chance to become the designer for Galliano menswear and had left, and I assumed all the designing for the Ungaro licensing and the free travels to Italy. This suited me well, as I did not have to pay for the flights, and I could focus on my JENS collection and its first fashion show. In Milan, to get on the fashion calendar during fashion week was an achievement, but it also meant failing was not an option. My friend Duccio had helped with finding suitable Italian factories, so I started designing and creating the first JENS collection, a big step from t-shirts to a complete line. The focus was on a streetwear look mixed with fashion elements. Most importantly, it was a gender-neutral collection; we showed male and female models equally, it was a mix of everything: race, sexual orientation, size, and gender. A fresh and different collection. I mixed all my experiences into a fashion-streetwear look, a new "casual designer look." Only Undercover from Japan and Surface to Air in Paris did anything similar.

Stefano and Liborio were incredible helpers. Liborio because he let me stay at his house and provided stability, food, shelter, and styling support; Stefano because he created the show without any budget available to him. We had no money to spend. My time in Paris became less and less, and my traveling and sleeping with friends started again. My family life and Paris career slowly faded away, and I became Italian again. J. was not very interested in my fashion line. She helped design when I was stuck, but she never came to one of my shows. While my family life suffered under the new arrangement, my fashion life was thriving. What a thrill to oversee your own fashion show and fashion line, which was a lot of work and took many hours. Suddenly, I had to do everything: designing, marketing, press, production, and selling anything, and everything else that popped up. The first show was styled by Sheila Single and Liborio Capizzi, and Christian, Sheila's boyfriend, helped with make-up and hair. The show was simple; we rented an old exhibition hangar in the heart of Milan and had only money for one massive spotlight, which looked super cool with the massive space and this one focused beam of light. All our friends were modeling, and it turned out to be a great event. Unfortunately, it was before social media was available, and the filming and recording of the show were lost and gone. We had a decent turnout of buyers and press visits and were hoping for a good sales season. In the evening, we had a celebratory dinner with everybody involved. For the next few weeks, we waited anxiously for the sales results from our showroom. The result was okay, but not enough to earn money, only enough to keep going. It was disappointing, and CAMAC helped and supported me massively. We were positive, though, that the next show would yield a better return, and we focused on the next season. The next fashion show was in an industrial glass house with dancers, both modern and classical. Where the first show with one single spotlight had a rougher and punkier feel, this one was more playful. The dancers were not only dancing; they were also wearing fake fur animal costumes in pop colors and interacting with the models, a dance and animal fashion spectacle. Alastair McKimm did the styling.

It was wonderful to see the presentation. Alastair McKimm was the stylist from then on. Alastair was just at the beginning of his career, and I believe JENS was the first fashion show he styled and supported as a stylist. Alastair became a good friend and did a lot to keep it all together. Dirk Seidenschwan did all the photography, and one of our best shoots happened on a motocross track with Cross bikes and models. We had many great people helping, and we made the best of nothing. We were getting known for funky invitations and clever gifts too. We had emergency cards from planes redesigned into funny "how to wear" cards, iron-on gold logos, chrome stickers, pin-on buttons, and sticky tape with funny slogans.

Part of my duties was to sell the collection, so we decided to use sales fairs held during fashion week in Paris and Milan. In Paris, we participated in "Who's Next" at the "Bourse de Commerce," which has become a museum and houses the Pinault art collection now. A beautiful space and a well-selected mix of emerging designers were curated there. The space was regal and great to set up. You only needed to bring clothes, hang them on the provided rails, roll your collection into your booth, and sell. You had to hang your posters and display images to make your stand attractive and show the look of the collection. We played a show video and created impactful lookbooks. The creation of sales books and the production of order forms was a hustle, but we managed. Selling was an important learning curve because many clients gave feedback on their needs and collection expectations, which helped us fine-tune our offer.

In Italy, we did get accepted into the biggest and most important fashion fair, "Pitti Uomo" in Florence. This was a place where you wanted to impress. The most relevant and important menswear collections came twice a year to Florence to open the menswear season globally. It was the first major event on the menswear fashion calendar, and everybody in the industry flocked to Florence to see and touch the latest collections.

My friend Robert had flown in from Hamburg to help me. He was an industrial designer and interior architect. He had worked on many fair set-ups before and knew what he was doing because I didn't. It was June, and we were allowed to enter Fortezza da Basso 48 hours before to set up our stands. Entering the Fortezza was already a nightmare; it was an old fortress built with huge defensive walls and only one entry gate. Everything and everybody had to enter through that door. We had a small truck, and it took us two hours to get to our pavilion to unload. Once unloaded, we realized there were no electric power lines in place yet, and we could not use our equipment to set up. We set off and searched for the fair technicians in the general chaos, and after another five hours, we finally had electrical outlets and started working. Being one of the hottest summers on record, it was easily 50 degrees Celsius in our building. Everybody was topless and sweating buckets. We had a simple construction in mind. We had brought transportation pallets borrowed from CAMAC and wanted to construct a wooden shell on which we would wallpaper yearbook images from my year in the US on the walls. The aesthetic was a punky, preppy, streetwear, and skater feel. A mix of Andy Warhol's factory look and Sex Pistols on skateboards. The conceptual drawings and simple plans we had drafted looked great, but the reality of putting up the stand in 30 hours with two people was a daring strategy. We did not care; we had to get it done so we would get it done. After 18 hours of work, 10 liters of water each, and no food, we finally collapsed on our hotel beds at four in the morning. After three hours of sleep, we were back at the Fortezza to finish our stand. It was brutal, but it was worth it. We just managed to complete our stand on time and had a nice dinner in Florence before the fair started for real the next day. The feeling was overwhelming to walk into the Fortezza on opening day. When we left it the night before, it was still a warzone, but now it was all clean and professionally lit. The stands were polished fresh, with all their collections and their wares on display. Pitti Uomo is not a selling fair like many other fairs. You did not sell your collection. Customers browsed and looked to make appointments with the respective showrooms later. It was all about making an impression and getting their attention. Every important department store, shop, and boutique from all over the world was there. Especially Japanese clients, which were vital for us since 60% of JENS clients were based in Japan. The highlight of our first day was a visit from Tommy Hilfiger himself, who complimented us on our stand and collection. We chatted for a while and joked about my yearbook pictures on the wall. The fair flew by, and it was a great success. We received a lot of positive feedback and appointments in our order book. The packing up of our stand was a lot faster than the initial building, and we quickly left through the only exit gate once more and went back to Milan. We made a slight detour for the coast, where we dipped our toes into the sea, ate seafood, and were content with life.

55. FREELANCE

As all things happened at once, it soon became too much. For me, the saddest realization was that J. was not interested in the JENS collection or fashion shows. I understood back then that my dream of "us" building a fashion House together would never happen. J. was in love with someone else, and that someone else was her career at Louis Vuitton, a crazy "ménage à trois J., myself, and Louis Vuitton, and I was losing ground quickly. This realization made JENS an empty dream. All the work would not be worth it if J. was not part of the dream. J. would never leave Paris, and a fashion show in Milan did not matter to her. Apart from my dream coming to a crashing halt, my biggest challenge was our finances. We had bills to pay, children to feed, and mortgages to honor. My JENS collection did not make enough money. All the money we earned, which was little, was immediately swallowed up by the next collection. I needed to find more freelance work quickly because my job at Ungaro ended abruptly. Giambattista and Monsieur Ungaro could not agree on who's name should be on what label. The power struggle had become a tedious fight, which created a sour work environment, to say the least. One day, Ferragamo had enough and announced they would sell "Emanuel Ungaro" and that they no longer wished to be associated with the house. Everything happened quickly, and within three weeks, Monsieur Ungaro retired, Giambattista resigned, and I decided it was time to leave, too. We all three went our ways.

Now, a big question mark had appeared in my life. What to do next? I had a fashion line that made me happy, and created great press, but did not make enough money. To find another well-paid job would mean moving away from Paris and my family, which I did hope I would not have to do again. There was a big question about where and what to do with my career. Paris had very little to offer, especially for my more relaxed preppy sportswear street style. I loved color, and Paris menswear was "black cloth." I did not do "black cloth." Going to New York was initially our dream when we left Milan, and Paris was only meant to be a stepping stone, for a few years only.

Now, the idea that J. would move to New York was not an option either. Although J. loved New York, the reality was that Louis Vuitton had become such a global powerhouse, and J. had become too successful to move anywhere else. She had the best fashion design job on the planet. It was difficult to compare her position to anything else in the world. Louis Vuitton was the absolute number one on a global scale, and J. did well there.

J. had a great career ahead of her. We had bought a house, had two great children, and had a wonderful fashion life with Louis Vuitton, Five Foxes, and JENS. The brutal reality was that we needed more money quickly. Once more, I was contacting all headhunters to drum up more work, but it did not go fast enough. Carolyn helped and put me in contact with Uli, who needed a freelance designer to help with the newly introduced "Liz Claiborne" European fashion line. Liz Claiborne US had just acquired the Mexx Fashion Company, based in Amsterdam. The plan was to introduce the Liz Claiborne collection to the European market using the Mexx platform. Uli oversaw the project and needed help from a designer. We did get along well, and it was fine with Uli that I would do most of the design work from Paris. The Liz Claiborne European collection had two main segments: The main clothing line and a "plus size" collection for women. The main line was easy. I was aware of the "plus size" market segment, but I had never before designed for a "plus size" market. It was new to me. I cherished the challenge and looked forward to learning and getting to know this very relevant part of the fashion world. The job was great, and I loved working with Uli. We became a well-oiled machine, and our team was successful. I learned the ins and outs of a plus-size collection and enjoyed designing for this market very much. J. was a great help, too. Louis Vuitton was planning a collaboration with "Bathing Ape." A young, cool Japanese streetwear collection designed by Nigo. Nigo and Marc had met and dreamed up this project. J. suggested I design the clothes, and Marc happily agreed. It was a leather puffer jacket collection where the leather was printed in a particular "Bathing Ape monogram" design. They were super-high-end leather puffer jackets. Produced by one of the best leather manufacturers in Paris. Life was good again. My new career was my freelance design office, and we had Louis Vuitton, Bathing Ape, Liz

Claiborne, and Five Foxes as clients. In the end I had to stop JENS because it was not producing enough money, and I needed all my available time to design for my paying clients. Adriano Sack, who helped me with the press, scolded me for stopping JENS, but there was no other way. My private life consumed too much of my resources, and I could not indulge in a money-losing dream anymore. J.'s career became a priority. She earned a decent salary and was stable. I happily organized my freelance work around our children and her Louis Vuitton schedule.

56. AMSTERDAM

The new freelance setup suited me well. Once I had closed JENS, everything became easier. I could focus on design and not have the constant challenges of a fashion brand to deal with. No more complaining, nonpaying boutiques, quality issues, delivery issues, or cash flow problems. Now, I enjoy the occasional flights to Amsterdam and design only. Amsterdam was a great place, and I enjoyed the new environment. There was a lot of work but well paid, and I enjoyed seeing the children at home and getting to see them grow up. In those days, I spent a lot of time with June, while J. spent most of her time at work. J. had immersed herself completely into her LV job and left the house and home to June and me. Freelance work is great, but freelance work has one tricky element: if things go wrong, you are very quickly out of work. A volatile setup that is not secure. Companies can change their minds quickly, and then you are no longer needed. First, Louis Vuitton and Nigo could not agree on terms, so the collection, which was already prepared and sampled to be presented to the world, never saw the light of day. I did get paid, but the project was never released to a public audience. The Liz Claiborne US office also changed its mind on how they wanted to introduce their collections to the European market. They wanted to guarantee constant freshness and introduced the "twelve-drop" collection model to the market. Every month of the year, twelve times, they decided to deliver a new capsule collection on the shop floor to guarantee freshness and a new product offer. The idea is not bad; it is easy to design and produce, but the challenge presented itself in the delivery velocity and shop floor management. It was utter chaos between new arrivals and markdowns. The department stores could not handle the twelve garment drops. Liz Claiborne was not the most decisive company either, and I felt sorry for Uli, who had to constantly correct and adapt what had been planned and decided. There was a constant change, and everything was in flux, including my position. In my contract, I was paid by the number of designs that were selected to be produced. This amount constantly changed due to the latest shop floor concept. I had well-paid months followed by meager months. This was not a stable income situation at all. Before we moved to Paris, we spent a couple of weeks interviewing and looking for jobs in New York. On one of those occasions, I interviewed with Ginny Hilfiger. Ginny was the sister of Tommy Hilfiger. We did get along well and became friends. She was a flamboyant character, full of energy and curiosity. We stayed in touch, and we met up either on my trips to New York or when she was in Paris. Ginny introduced us later to Spencer, who became a good friend too. Both of them together were a riot, and we had many funny dinners and conversations. As I was freelancing for Liz Claiborne, Ginny told me that Tommy Hilfiger was currently setting up a European office in the Netherlands. Carolyn already designed for Tommy Hilfiger womenswear in Amsterdam, and I asked her to introduce me to them for the menswear line.

Carolyn was so kind and talked to Alice. Alice was American and was sent to Amsterdam to help set up the European fashion lines. Avery was head of Marketing at the time. Tommy Hilfiger was a great American Sportswear brand, but it was not well known in Europe. Tommy Hilfiger Europe was new to the European market, and there, the new licensees did correct the positioning that obstructed growth for Tommy in the U.S.

Tommy Hilfiger was positioned oddly in the USA. They tried to establish their signature preppy style but somehow failed to succeed. Europe, on the other hand, was a small startup licensing deal headed by Fred, and they were very successful. Their positioning was sophisticated sportswear in the affordable luxury market segment. The key difference was the target customer. In the U.S., it was a young clientele, in Europe, it was a more mature audience. The famous story was that Fred had started Tommy Hilfiger Europe in a Pepe Backoffice with one box of Tommy clothes. He had done well, and from initially importing American products, they had evolved to designing and producing their own European Tommy fashion collections. In Europe, the biggest challenge for American products was fit. The American product was too big and badly cut. There were three main lines introduced at this point in time: men's, women's, and Tommy Jeans. Alice was great, and we got along well from the start. When I met Alice for the first time, they were not ready for a menswear designer yet, but she told me she would let me know as soon as there was an opening. As it happened, Alice called just as Bathing Ape and Louis Vuitton could not agree about their collaboration, and I now had time and was available. I was happy to be introduced to Tommy's leadership team, and Alice asked me to prepare a small project, one capsule collection. Sometimes, the timing is perfect, and I fully immersed myself in the Tommy Hilfiger project. Instead of one capsule collection, I prepared three and sank all my energy into them. I thoroughly enjoyed the assignment, and I realized that I was made for Tommy.

The day of my project presentation, Alice met me in their Amsterdam office in a conference room with a big center table. We chatted for a while, and then she asked me to present the project to her. I took my time and presented all three collections and their concepts. I had created three concept stories that were printed on heavy paper, movie poster size. They looked like "Robert Rauschenberg" collages (a famous pop art artist). The first story was a "red, white, and blue " story, very Tommy and preppy. The second theme was about utilitarian styles and was based on a British car rally through the desert. Fancy classic cars and motorcycles. This second story was kept in khaki and white with some subtle pastel highlight colors. The third and last story was colorful and about a sailing trip in the Caribbean. Lots of prints and fun beach summer styles. Those posters looked fantastic in the big showroom. Additionally, there were fabric, color, and print boards accompanied by eight colored illustrations each. The illustrations were A3-sized and artistic in their style and execution. It was impressive, more like an art exhibition than a fashion presentation.

Alice was excited and told me to wait as she went to fetch some people who would want to see this too. As I was seated and wondered what would come next, the door opened, and four men and a woman entered. Initially, I had no idea who they were; luckily, they introduced themselves. It was Fred, Ludo, Michael, Iris, and Daniel, the leaders and winning team of Tommy Hilfiger Europe. They were an energetic group, and they bombarded me with questions and comments. There was a tsunami of opinions and within 30 minutes, all of them ran out again with lots of smiles and shoulder clapping. Then Alice asked me to meet one more person, and she introduced me to Hans, the VP of Tommy Hilfiger Menswear Europe. Hans was more serious; he grilled me in our conversation and wanted to know many commercial details. He wanted to know how I would integrate commercial core products, plan a collection drop, and manage price buildup, margins, and merchandising.

Luckily, I managed to answer everything to his satisfaction. My unusual career had prepared me perfectly for this meeting. Experiences in Fashion, Denim, and Couture had taught me all the references I needed to successfully banter with Hans.

Once Hans left, Alice and I chatted some more, and she told me she would be in touch in the coming week and smiled at me. Out of the office and back on the streets of Amsterdam, I did not know what to think. There had been such a whirlwind of different people and characters that it was impossible to judge. There was no time to reflect, though; I had to rush to the airport to catch my flight back to Paris. Back in Paris, I concentrated on my work and waited for Alice's phone call. To my surprise, she called me the next day and asked me when I could start and that everybody loved my concepts.

57. TOMMY HILFIGER EUROPE

I was over the moon and could not wait to tell J. the good news, but then it dawned on me that I would have to travel again. I knew Tommy wasn't looking for a freelance designer. It would be an exclusive position, which meant I would have to stop all my other freelance work. When J. came home, my excitement was somewhat diminished, and we talked about the possibilities. Being separated again was not something any of us were looking forward to. I suggested once more that we might go to New York, where we could both work and be together, but I saw in J.'s eyes that New York was not an option anymore. J. had found a home in Paris; I, on the other hand, did not fit in and was struggling. With heavy hearts, we both realized that traveling would be the only way to maintain our calling, careers, and love. The realization that we could not both maintain our career dreams and be in the same city at the same time was hard. The next day I called Alice, and I told her we would have to discuss my new contract to make it work. She agreed, and I flew to Amsterdam and discussed with Hans the reality and needs concerning my new job. I told them that I wanted to stay freelance and not become fully employed. They had to pay for my flight tickets between Amsterdam and Paris, and I could only work for three days in Amsterdam, Tuesday to Thursday, Monday and Friday in Paris. Alice looked at Hans and said it would be fine with her; Hans also agreed, and so I became the new head designer for Tommy Hilfiger Europe.

J. was happy that I was not gone for the whole week. A bearable compromise had been found. I had to stop all my other freelance activities and work exclusively for Tommy, though. I was happy about the flexibility offered by Hans and Alice and couldn't wait to start.

The Tommy offices in Amsterdam were very basic; since the company evolved so fast, they did not have time to decorate them in a friendlier manner yet. Their showrooms were spectacular, but the design studios were basic, bare, or nonexistent. I shared an office with Ilan, the head of production. He is a great guy; we got along well, and I loved him. Hans introduced me to the other directors on his team, all great characters with a no-bullshit attitude: Thorsten, Nick, and Koen. My early design team consisted of Aniela, responsible for fabric and shirt designs, and Leon, who helped with all the other design duties. Aniela designed 90% of our shirt patterns and colorways in Illustrator. Those graphics were then sent to our factories, and they created the first handloom swatches for us to choose and perfect. Tommy shirts were not only about the patterns but also about the inside details and trims. Each shirt had a special inside design. They looked better and were visually more impactful than ordinary shirts due to this "point of difference." This was the very beginning of Tommy Hilfiger Europe, and nothing was yet as established as it had been at Levi's, Moschino, or Ungaro. It was the "Big Bang" of a company. Everything had to be shaped and created from scratch. Those were exciting times; anything was possible, and there was no stopping Fred and his team. Tommy Hilfiger Europe was a rocket ship ready to take off, fueled by Rock and Roll. The first few months, I had to call in a lot of favors from friends to get the new collection sorted. Aniela, Leon, Thorsten, Nick, Ilan, and Koen were magicians, but we needed designers to help get the huge menswear collection going. The collection consisted of three deliveries and 1400 garment options in total, roughly 550 styles. This was a lot of work, and then there were the in-between seasons, too. For the first year, I mostly stayed in hotels since it was the easiest to organize. I hoped to never live in a lonely apartment by myself again. I was still traumatized from my "mattress on the floor" apartment at Levi's. The workload was intensified by my three-day work schedule. Of course, I could work from Paris too, but the reality was that I had to squeeze five workdays into three. I did not care; this was the job I had been waiting for all my life. My new job was entrepreneurial, creative, and growing fast, and I was in charge. Best of all, it was my favorite team ever; those people were the best I had ever met, especially Fred. All the CEOs I worked with before were great, but Fred had such an incredible personality; he was one in a million. His support team, consisting of Ludo, Daniel, Iris, and Michael, was unparalleled, too. Nothing would have been possible without them, and then, of course, Hans. He was our fearless leader. The magic was that we all understood each other; we liked each other's company, whether it was at work, after work, or at parties; it was a family, and we all helped and supported one another. The publicity concept of the Tommy family was not just a marketing story; we lived it naturally. The possibilities made available to us were unheard of. If we needed more people, flights, travel, presentations, equipment, research, more space, or anything else we asked for, we got it. As we needed more space for our collection development, we turned the corridor into our design space, all the designs were stuck to the walls and laid out on the floor. Anyone who walked by could comment. Some comments were stupid, and we had a laugh, but some were very valid, and we adapted immediately. This effectively meant we had an adoption meeting every minute of the day. If prototypes arrived, we asked the next best person who walked by to put them on and fit the garment there and then. Even better, we did get feedback from a passionate potential customer. It turned into a project runway game, and we asked all the girls in the office if they fancied our "walk-by" model in the new garments, and they happily replied. It was a great atmosphere— open and respectful. Hans was very passionate about modeling our first prototypes, and the corridor quickly turned into a catwalk. This, of course, only works if you work with a great team; if you work with idiots, this system will kill your company in a season. Luckily, "cancel culture" and "woke inquisition" did not exist, and people were still having respectful fun, had a good sense of humor, and were able to laugh.

Fred empowered us to become true entrepreneurs. Every single one of us was thinking creatively and entrepreneurially. We behaved as if we had launched Tommy Europe ourselves and took full responsibility for all aspects of the business. We all learned that if we combined our creativity, we could find powerful solutions together. Fred had positioned Tommy Hilfiger Europe skillfully. While everybody in fashion was constantly hunting the latest youth generation whims and quirks, he understood that those kids had parents, and they had two of them, which made the market double as big as the elusive "next generation" youth market. The secret was to sell the dream of "youth" to all ages and genders. Selling "youth" was the key.

This magical "key" I knew well because Levi's Germany was doing exactly that until it was turned into an "Indy Rock-Skateboarder" brand. Fred was cleverer than all of them. For the first time, I learned what the word "to see" meant. Fred could see what others could not. A fashion house is like a garden; you need a variety of trees, bushes, flowers, and grass. Some grew faster, some slower, but together, they built beauty and magic. Fashion was a garden; you had your core product, which grew on a different scale and, once fully matured, was as solid as an oak. Then, you had your seasonal fashion items, which grew and withered as fast as roses. Fred understood all of it; he was a true visionary with enough experience to not be fooled by whims and trims within the fashion market. Marketing, press, economic climates, customer needs, and their lives and dreams were the sun and rain, the ever-changing weather. He understood that fashion journalists who had never worked in the fashion business printed "news and trends" only to stir the masses without grasping the basis of the industry. He knew how to harness all those powers and directions to create the perfect weather for his Tommy Garden. I felt like a little boy in a toy shop, to which he gave me the key and told me "Go and play," and I did; we all did. Hans was a passionate man, very driven and ambitious. I loved working with him; he was amazing, and together we created our first collection. There was no high expectation for menswear because everybody expected the menswear market to have linear growth potential, unlike womenswear, which could grow exponentially if given the right climate. To all our surprise, our menswear rocket took off. Our collection hit a market segment that was starving for new products. We managed to grow the sales volume by an average of 20% each season, which was massive given the size of our market. We did not enter a virgin market. We had to push out and be better than our competition to achieve those numbers, and we did. We understood the two basic rules for any successful business: "increase profit and reduce cost." We were good at it, and it was a blast. The bureaucracy was reduced to a minimum, and communication was instant and immediate between all of us. This only works if everybody is speaking the same language. Fred was a pirate captain on a fashion spaceship traveling at light speed. All normal rules were obsolete, and we were acting and reacting in a new creative world built by us.

In the first two years, we managed to not only increase our sales numbers, but our design team grew from two to twelve designers. It was a pleasure to see it all grow. Menswear was incredibly successful.

At line openings, the event presentations grew more spectacular every season. First, we were all in a hotel outside Amsterdam. All the European sales force and the Amsterdam office. Soon, the hotel was too small, and we rented huge fairgrounds to introduce our new collections. Hans and I were enthusiastic presenters, and our sales force enjoyed and trusted us. I believe in our main season, we presented to 500 people in the audience.

Since Hans and I did well, Fred decided to give us control over women's wear as well. Hans and I were entrusted with the creative direction of the European Tommy menswear and womenswear collections. It was a great compliment from Fred to promote us to oversee both collections. Those two collections combined represented an enormous sales volume.

As Tommy Europe was thriving, the American Tommy market had declined rapidly to a disastrous level. The product was cheap and sold in outlets, but even cheap," nobody wanted it. The US management had to take drastic measures and had decided that Tommy Hilfiger Global needed to be sold to save the brand from ruin and bankruptcy. This was a shock to us since we were doing so well, but Tommy Europe was still nothing but a licensing deal that could be revoked at any time. We heard rumors of the most impossible suitors wooing Tommy Hilfiger in the US. The sharks had arrived, and the feeding frenzy had begun. I thought to myself, "Here we go again," the idiots have arrived and will ruin another great fashion brand. Once more, luck had run out, as it had happened at Levi's and Ungaro. We were all downtrodden by the constant bad news that arrived from America.

On one of those nights, Fred and Ludo had a now-famous dinner at which both hatched the plan to buy Tommy Hilfiger. Tommy Europe would buy the mother ship, Tommy USA. This was not immediately shared with anyone. They secretly secured funds and investments through APAX partners and a substantial bank loan. Once in place and approved, they started negotiations with the US, and in good old Fred style, he succeeded.

58. APAX AND BEING AN OWNER

Fred could never resist a good Rock and Roll party, and true to style, he announced the takeover with a huge celebration. We were amazed at the balls the man possessed and could not believe we were the new Captains at Tommy Hilfiger. "We" had bought Tommy Hilfiger! The "tail was wagging the dog." Fred announced the following week that the directors and management team would be allowed to invest and buy shares in the new ownership deal. A very generous offer for us to acquire shares at the value of the takeover deal. The finance department trained and schooled us in the modalities of all the necessary steps to becoming an investor. After four weeks, I was the proud owner of Tommy shares, the first shares I had ever possessed. The sweet part of the deal was that if we reached a certain target, the shares would multiply a hundredfold. I learned a lot about shares in those weeks. We learned about possible IPOs (Initial Public offerings) or stock launches versus private acquisitions. APAX Investment wanted to resell the company in five to ten years. That meant clear financial targets and the repayment of the bank loan were in place.

We learned about possible evaluation models concerning our stock, the importance of our job positions, and our performance. This was a very interesting new topic because I had never heard of the "lifecycle" of a creative leader before. All and everybody were evaluated and risk assessed. We all had to take thorough medical exams to ensure our fitness and health for the coming five years. This was not new and made sense, but our performance had an expiration date that I did not know. I learned that any big company linked to a creative process had to renew its creative directors every seven to ten years before they became repetitive and stale. This process was revolutionary in the fashion design world and had been introduced by LVMH and Kering Group, as both business models were built on creativity and surprise. Fashion served as a marketing vehicle to sell their non-seasonal core product, and the cool factor of a brand needed to be constantly updated for the fickle, fast-growing consumer generation. Now, fashion was not only the constant creation of new products but became entertainment which led to the constant replacement of creative directors.

Their financial models did not allow for their creative impact to ever slow down. This meant fashion houses, once reliant on style continuity, now changed styles every seven to ten years. Fashion houses changed style, aesthetics, and creative directors as people changed their underwear. This was visible at Gucci, Balenciaga, and Dior, where designers were regularly replaced to be fresh and entertaining. Everything was constantly updated in the name of novelty. I learned that in five years' time, once the company was sold, I would most likely be replaced. This did not bother me in the least because if I had learned one thing from Fred, it was that you must become creative to find solutions. I understood I simply had to reinvent myself, and I intended to do just that, but my reinvention was a slow process, and it took four years.

Now, we celebrated that we were the new masters of the universe. We had changed the game, and there was a lot to do to secure its success. Europe had to continue to produce record sales numbers, or all would come crashing down. The first step was for America to be reduced and turned into a profitable business. Fred left us to create our successful collections while the US team was restructured into a skeleton crew. All wholesale businesses were shut down; only Macy's remained as the single major customer and key account in the US. All retail stores were closed except three flagship stores, which only held European merchandise. This was not communicated to the world. Tommy Hilfiger has remained an American brand true to its heritage. America needed time to clean up its marketing message. Tommy Hilfiger needed time to reposition its product perception in the eyes of the general public. This would take time, and a slow preparation of the market started.

Effectively, this meant America was a field that could not be harvested for some time. Fred needed to generate more income on a global scale to make this possible. To do so, he had another trick up his sleeve.

The Asian market was a separate license and had not been part of the direct purchase of Tommy Hilfiger USA. To buy the rights to the Asian market, Fred needed to raise more money. He knew of an asset most had overlooked. Tommy Hilfiger Europe and Tommy Hilfiger US combined had an enormous product quantity that needed production every season. These were millions of garments that held a substantial production value. This production value was fragmented throughout various factories all over the world, and nobody paid much attention to who produced what and where. The general perception was that many different factories were beneficial to negotiating better prices. The idea of divide and conquer was a common business practice.

Fred, though, saw an enormous advantage in combining the total product quantity and selling this value to one production company. This company was the sourcing platform "Li & Fung" in China. Li & Fung was revolutionizing supply chain practices and was eager to become the number one producer for Tommy Hilfiger globally. Fred and Li & Fung struck a deal in which Li & Fung would possess the totality of Tommy Hilfiger production for a certain amount of money, which allowed Fred to acquire all the Asian Tommy Hilfiger licenses. It was a "win-win" scenario for both companies. Now, Fred owned the Asian market, which was guaranteeing the growth needed to rest the US market, and Li & Fung was the number one supply chain manager in the world.

Those were business matters taken care of by Fred and Ludo, but we also grew creatively. Tommy Accessories, Tommy Tailored, and Tommy Sport became sizable entities. Everything grew fast, and we had to hire new people constantly. The design team for menswear and womenswear reached 30 designers, all managed by Hans and me. It was an insane number of designs that we processed daily. We traveled the world constantly, and sometimes, we had no idea where we were.

Hong Kong, London, Amsterdam, New York, Tokyo, Los Angeles, Düsseldorf, Berlin, Paris, Istanbul, Milan, Madrid, Stockholm, and anything in between. The rhythm of airplane lounges, flights, hotels, taxis, chauffeurs, work, dinners, and jet lag was a crazy aphrodisiac of success. We kept on producing and smiling.

The first four years had successfully passed as planned, and we had celebrated four incredible Tommy Christmas parties.

Now, it was time to prepare the company for the planned resell. APAX wanted to move on.

59. WHAT TO DO NEXT?

After six years at Tommy and having been a part of creating one of the most powerful brands, it was time to transform again. Tommy would be available on the market once more. The big discussion was about IPOs or private ownership. Fred was not a big friend of a stock market IPO because the company evaluation was a gamble, whereas a private sale guaranteed a certain price. On the other hand, he had to look for the best possible financial outcome for all shareholders. A possible match was needed to understand our company culture, too. We were wild and not the conventional corporate deal.

We were ahead on our credit payments to the bank, and Tommy Global had solid results. It was a healthy company and an asset to any suitor. Tommy Europe had achieved record results in those six years. We trusted Fred and were not worried that he would find the best solution available.

Meanwhile, the company went through an internal evaluation process. Outside independent accessors were hired to scrutinize and check on all eventual red flags in the process. In the Tommy Europe business setup, each division (Men's, Women's, sports, accessories, tailored, and jeans) was organized as an independent unit with its own budget. They were run like individual companies within a big company. The first red flag was that Hans and I were running men's and women's under one leadership position. Men's and women's needed to be separated. Hans and I were not happy about it, but we saw it coming a while ago. To be honest, it became too big to be handled by us alone.

Another red flag popped up, to my surprise. It was the position of Tommy Hilfiger himself. Apparently, it is a "negative" in the evaluation process if the principal designer and holder of the company name is still alive. In terms of a sale, this presents a risk factor. If the owner has an accident or, God forbid, dies, it will have a negative impact on the company's results. In a worst-case scenario, it could bankrupt a brand. The solution was to put the "next generation" into place, a successor to secure stability for the future. Michael was the next in line. He already ran the US fashion show and was working with Tommy in New York, but they both did not get along and often quarreled like little school kids. Tommy had a creative heart; he was a designer. Michael, on the other hand, had incredible taste but was not a trained designer. He had no design track record; it was unlikely the press and fashion world would accept him readily.

I knew Fred had to deal with the dilemma of finding a successor and putting somebody in place. It was time for me to reinvent myself and break out of the seven-year designer life cycle.

I proposed to Fred that J. and I would be a suitable match. This was highly irregular, and under normal circumstances, Fred would never allow a couple to hold a key position at Tommy. The risk of a "divorce" was far too great and presented another risk factor. Nonetheless, the idea of having J. from Louis Vuitton and myself as the next generation was appealing. The press would love it. It had something romantic, and it would give Tommy Hilfiger the luxury credibility it was lacking with us being in our mid-thirties. We were also young enough to not threaten Tommy's position, and it was easy for him to "adopt" us.

Fred saw the potential and agreed. He then discussed it with Tommy, and Tommy agreed, too. Tommy wanted to meet us both.

Now, I had to discuss this possibility with J. This was not an easy adventure either. Over the last seven years, J. and I had drifted apart. My constant traveling and her growing in her position had created a rift. We still loved each other, but it was clear by then that I would not find a position in Paris. J., on the other hand, loved Paris. For us to work as a couple, we had to eliminate Paris. It was the only possible scenario. We discussed various options to fix our relationship and our family. One option was that we both quit our jobs and travel the world for a year or two. We both loved the idea but lacked the courage to do so since all our advisors told us it would be career suicide. The other possibility was that I would stop working and become a "houseman." Another idea was that we would open a hotel and stop fashion altogether. Many dreams popped up in our attempt to save our relationship, but deep down, we knew we both loved fashion, and we both loved our jobs.

At Louis Vuitton, Marc Jacobs faced the challenge of his expiration date as creative director presenting itself. His quarrels with Bernard Arnault became more frequent, and rumors of his resignation grew louder every week. J. and I knew that Louis Vuitton was not a stable entity anymore and that J. had to prepare herself for new possibilities.

In our attempt to find solutions, there was now a new scenario on the table: both of us at Tommy! Arriving in Paris, J. had had time to reflect because I had explained on the phone the new possibility of living in Amsterdam and working together at Tommy. I guess it was my version of reviving an old dream of mine to create a "house" together. Since it did not work with my JENS line, I hoped becoming a leader at Tommy Hilfiger might be an enticing option for both of us. We had dinner and discussed the possibility in detail. What would J.'s role be? Would she oversee the fashion show? Could we be living in New York? Would the contract guarantee succession? There were many valid questions I did not have the answers to. As those questions were communicated with Fred, he was hesitant with his answers, to my surprise. J.'s biggest worry was that she would end up as creative director for womenswear only and commit career suicide. Since Fred was hesitating, I was not sure either. J. had a point.

Hans and I had to fly to San Francisco for research and were meant to pass through LA and then back to New York. J. told me to go on the trip and that she would think about the offer and let me know. Hans was aware of the discussion, and he was eager for J. to accept. This change would have affected his career and position, too. He believed it was a dream offer, but he did not know J. as well as I did. I will never forget the phone call. While we were on a street corner in San Francisco, my mobile phone rang, and it was J. J. told me she would be happy to move to Amsterdam, but she had to decline Tommy's offer. We spoke for a while longer, and I tried, in a last attempt, to change her mind. I tried half-heartedly because I knew deep down that J. would never leave Paris. J. had her career, and working with me was not an option.

As I put down the phone, I took a deep breath and told Hans J.'s answer; he was furious. The swear words following were of epic proportion. For Hans, this was a betrayal, and he took it very personally. Something broke between us that day, as it would with Fred later, too.

It was a once-in-a-lifetime offer, and we blew it.

After the outburst, which lasted about 5 minutes, Hans turned and rushed off, leaving me standing on the street corner in San Francisco. He just told me that he would call Fred and let him know "our" decision. This was the key point! Hans said, "Our" decision! Fred would see it the same way as Hans: "I" had said "no" to Tommy Hilfiger, too. My reinventing had failed, and my career had come to a sudden end. The reality sank in. It was brutal. There were some cataclysmic events in my life, and this was one of them. All collapsed within me, ambition, love, hope, dreams, and faith were all wiped out, and there was only an empty, functioning shell left of me. All planning was for nothing; I had lost my ability to operate my brain; I was an empty entity unable to grasp the total and absolute annihilation that had just happened. The worst part was that my "home" and its secure haven had vanished; it was only an illusion now. I had lost all trust in my relationship and all we had built. The security of having a partner who loved and protected me was no more.

It was the proverbial supernova, the black hole with no escape, no reinvention, no salvation.

I looked for the next bar and got drunk.

The next day, Hans and I traveled to Los Angeles. He informed me that Fred did understand and that all was well, but I knew something had broken in the last 24 hours. I wondered to myself how deep those cracks would go. Cracks with Fred and cracks with J. How would I be able to repair any of them?

60. IT IS NOT OVER UNTIL IT'S OVER

Two years passed, and PVH became the suitor who bought Tommy Hilfiger in the end. As the company went through another evaluation process, new bonus schemes were put into place to retain key personnel. I was not among them. This was understandable; Fred had extended his hand to make an exception for me, and I didn't deliver. There would always be a place for me at Tommy, but my career had come to an end. It was time to rethink and refocus once more.

As PVH officially took over the reins at Tommy Hilfiger and we all received the gains from our shares, it was time to leave. I did not have a job lined up, but I had enough money and did not need to worry. I was picky with new job offers because I wanted to find something in Paris. I had enough of airports and hotel rooms. I had traveled for twenty years; it was enough.

I had started to paint again, and I enjoyed it very much to create my art in my atelier in Auteuil. Collecting art and painting were my new-old passions. It kept me alive. Art and driving my cross-buggy through the French countryside became my salvation.

A friend of mine, Hugues, had bought a Parisian fashion company, and I, too, had invested and bought shares in his company. In the long run, I hoped to be able to work there and create a stable base for my Parisian career. I also had invested in "Surface to Air" for the same reason. I wanted to be able to work in Paris and be with my family. Once again, I was planting seeds to survive in France, it looked like a promising move, but neither worked out. Both investments failed in the end and had to be closed. Both investments were lost, and I had to admit that my wishful thinking of a career in Paris had clouded my judgment enough to not see the dangers in those companies. I just shrugged it off with the attitude "You can't win all the time," but I knew deep inside that I had entrusted my future into the hands of other people, which was stupid. Since I did not know what to do next, I had hoped friends would fix "life" for me. It was a dumb assumption.

A few months after I left Tommy Hilfiger, Carlos called me. Carlos was an important businessman in fashion. He owned Pepe Jeans, Tommy Hilfiger showrooms and distribution centers in Spain. We knew each other well through Tommy. He was a good friend, and I liked Carlos very much. He is an incredible businessman and has had his fingers in many fashion pies. Lately, he had bought Hackett and was in search of a creative director because his recent director had left for New York. The job offer was great, and I was super motivated to work for Carlos and Hackett. Hackett was a fashion brand founded by Jeremy Hackett, who was still alive and the brand ambassador. He was a true British gentleman with sophistication, class, and style. Hackett was meant to become the European Ralph Lauren. A bold plan but doable in my eyes. The product was of very high quality and was currently concentrated on menswear only.

The job was based in London, and since all my Paris efforts did not produce any opportunities that would sustain me, here I was, packing my suitcase again, traveling to London and Florence every week. The main office was in London, but all production was handled by "GBS Italy" and "Prima." These were incredible Italian manufacturing companies based in Florence and close to Venice. I loved Italy and London and agreed to Carlos's offer. The current CEO was Vicente, a blood relative of Carlos, whom I liked very much. He was a great boss.

J.'s career also had its changes. Marc had left Louis Vuitton, and J. had found a new position at Chloe. The job was good, but it was not Louis Vuitton. The chemistry on the team was not the best either, and it was evident it would not go anywhere. The experience lasted a year, and luckily, J. did get introduced to Nicola Ghesquière and Natacha Ramsay-Levi, who was his right-hand assistant. Both famously brought Balenciaga to its newfound glory. Nicola was a legend in the fashion world and well respected. Deep down, I was always hoping J. would find a job outside of France, but it was not meant to be. J. had found a new position at Balenciaga, and she was thriving there. She got along well with Nicola and Natacha, and they were a great team. As it happens, Nicola and his management team did start to quarrel, and after another year into J.'s career, Nicola left Balenciaga. A sad moment to see him leave. Alexander Wang was his successor, and Natacha and J. found themselves working with a new creative director. Alexander had a tough time finding his place in the Parisian fashion world. J. and Natacha were trying their best to introduce him to the French fashion system, but it was not as successful as they hoped. In the meantime, Nicola was approached by Louis Vuitton through Delphine Arnault. Delphine wanted Nicola to join Louis Vuitton. After months of negotiations, he was finally announced as the new creative director at Louis Vuitton and started assembling his new team. His first phone calls went out to J. and Natacha. Without hesitation, both handed in their notice at Balenciaga and started anew at Louis Vuitton. After a two-year detour, J. was back at Louis Vuitton. In those years, Betty started University in Brussels, and Stanley was on his way to becoming a grown man too.

61. PARIS, LONDON, AND HACKETT

We both got our careers back on track. I had my fingers in many pies. I had invested in two Parisian businesses, was painting in my atelier, collecting art, and was the new creative director of Hackett. Betty and Stanley were doing well and had become young adults, and we were proud of them. J. was back at Louis Vuitton and did very well for herself. Since Stanley had to continue his schooling in Paris and J. had to work in Paris too, we bought a small apartment on the Boulevard St. Martin together. We found an old building with an abandoned attic space. The attic apartment was for sale and had great potential because of the hidden space under its roof. The whole apartment needed to be restored, and J. loved the challenge. We had found a small jewel in Paris. The flat was hidden in the back of two courtyards, and you did not hear any noise. Being high up, you could see all the rooftops of the quartier. At the same time, it was very central, and it was easy to get around. J. did a great job renovating the apartment.

Compared to Tommy, Hackett had a small office, and things were slower. As I began my new job, Vicente had started to present the Hackett collection during London Fashion Week. I attended the first Hackett fashion show in the first week of my new job. I was very excited since it was a proper show presented to the public. At Tommy, the company had grown too big for me to be involved in every aspect of the collection. Hackett was smaller, and I enjoyed working on all the different details of the collections: tailoring in the high-end Mayfair line, the Aston Martin line and all its technical elements, the casual chic of the Hackett main line, the authentic quality of the accessories, and the playfulness of the children's line. I especially admired the British quirkiness, which was everywhere. Jeremy Hackett, who was collaborating often with us, had a great sense of humor and an incredible eye for detail and style. The collections were well positioned, and Carlos and Vicente had planned a solid retail expansion to grow Hackett in Europe and the USA. Retail and brick-and-mortar stores were essential growth drivers. To make a retail expansion work, you have to understand risk assessment at its finest.

If you open one new store per year, the chances of success or failure are 100%. If the store works, you are 100% successful. If your store fails, you lose 100% of your investment. If you open 10 stores per year, the chances of all 10 stores failing are slim. If one or two stores fail, you lose 10 or 20% of your investment, an acceptable risk. Easy math. The challenge was to have enough money to open 10 stores annually. Carlos and the other Hackett investors had enough money. Hackett was thriving.

Wholesale growth was difficult due to the elevated price points of the collections. Department stores did not buy deep enough to secure the growth figure needed. The investment model was like Tommy's; Hackett had to be sold within 5-7 years. Carlos and Vicente planned to resell the company within the next five years, but first, Hackett had to become a shining star. The team was once more special, and we started to rock the boat. In the following years, we were to create three noteworthy fashion shows. The locations for the shows were incredible. We managed to show at St. Paul's Cathedral, the Free Masons Hall, and the original Billings Gate Market in London. Paul Hunt from JN Events and William Gilchrist created unforgettable moments, but Carlos did not see the value in fashion shows concerning Hackett. They represented an expense with a questionable return to him. Carlos and I started to see the growth of Hackett differently. Fashion shows and an expansion into a women's and denim collection were my dreams. Carlos did not engage. He had other plans, which he did not share with me. Carlos had many investments, and I did not push further, trusting his decisions and business acumen.

After two years, we had grown Hackett, and Carlos announced they would sell it. I had hoped for more time to create a true market impact, but the management was eager for a resell to raise more equity to grow the brand further. They organized an evaluation process like Tommy's to put Hackett on the market. We all had to be vetted again. The positive side was that we were given the possibility to buy shares once more, which we all did. We would make extra money earlier than expected.

236

62. M 1 AND "WHO AM I?"

Over the last four years, J. and I had further drifted apart. I guess it all started when I launched my JENS line, and J. was not interested. She did not come to a single JENS Fashion Show, but I had been to every single Louis Vuitton show. As much as I hoped, there was no "us" between J. and me. There would be no marriage. In our relationship, my role had been to help J. realize her goals, and I was proud to have done so. J. was thriving. Our children are amazing and an important part of J.'s and my life, but we could not ignore the cracks anymore.

The separation process did not happen overnight; it took me ten years to realize that I was living somebody else's life.

Since J. had returned to Louis Vuitton under Nicola's reign, I was not invited to any Louis Vuitton shows anymore. I was not invited to parties or dinners. J. had found her Parisian life, and I lived my life in London and Florence. When I came home to Auteuil, we slept in different beds, and J. often escaped to the Paris flat when I was back. We did not talk about the elephant in the room. Since the "no" to the Tommy position, we have accepted the reality that J. would never change her life to fix "us." Therefore, I never asked anymore. This left me in a challenging new position. I had to decide what I wanted for myself. So far, all my decisions have always been based on the well-being of my family, the children, and J. The Jens and J. team, who once had many dreams, had disappeared. There was no dream. My "boat" was literally stranded in the middle of the river of life. I had neglected my skills, my career, and my friends, and I was stranded on a sandbank.

At Hackett, Carlos had stopped all fashion shows, and it became evident we had different visions for Hackett. I believed in a collection structure that was inspired by Ralph Lauren. A structure that would have expanded Hackett and introduced a denim and womenswear collection. We already presented our Hackett man with a woman in every advertisement shoot. The denim line would have allowed us to enter a more lucrative market and price segment. The women's line was challenging, but the denim line would have helped to massively increase our finances. The infrastructure was already in place because Carlos owned both Pepe Jeans and Hackett.

Carlos would not have any of this. He and the board members insisted that Hackett should stay a true menswear brand. He wanted Hackett to stay a core product brand. Which made my creative director position empty. To update the same core product every season did not hold much appeal for me. I wanted to build a brand and make a "dream" come true. Carlos instead wanted to sell the "dream" to the next buyer. He used the "dream" to increase the company's value by showing "plans" but no real action. He was like a property developer who sold houses based on drawings that were not yet built.

Carlos's answer to growth was a strong retail expansion. Another new initiative presented itself: E-commerce. We pushed for a digital expansion. An e-commerce platform to conquer the world. Fashion had evolved once more; the digital "direct-to-consumer" sales model was fresh and immediate. Social media was the new fashion show, and we wanted to be part of it. Retail stores were great, but we needed a digital reality, too. Unfortunately, the project was only executed halfheartedly, and the Hackett website never made it beyond a basic platform, which was both unattractive to consumers and underperforming.

During those heated discussions about growth initiatives, a suitor appeared who was interested in buying Hackett. The group was called M1, an investment group based in Lebanon. They specialized in mobile networks in the Middle East but, for some reason, had acquired "Façonnable" in the past. Since they did not know fashion, they tried to turn it into a luxury brand inspired by Dior Homme. They ruined the brand in the process, and there was no turnover left to speak of. Façonnable was a casual sportswear brand like Hackett, and Carlos knew that. He convinced M1 that Hackett and Façonnable combined would be an unbeatable force predestined to make them all a fortune. He explained that once Façonnable was repositioned to its true place in the market, it would excel once more. Since M1 had deep pockets and no idea of the fashion industry, they believed Carlos and bought

Hackett. The only stipulation was that Carlos and his team would take care of Façonnable and return it to its previous glory.

63. M 1 BOUGHT HACKETT

After the sale, Hackett and Façonnable were managed by Carlos under the new ownership of M1.

We all sold our shares and made a decent profit. At the same time, we were asked to reinvest our newly earned money for ten more years into the new Group we had just created. Since Carlos and I had very different ideas about the future of Hackett, I declined. This, of course, created serious questions that were quickly answered by my replacement. I had made my money with Hackett and was happy to leave. I loved Carlos, but updating basic products for the next ten years was not my calling. I still helped with the first steps of repositioning Façonnable, but my heart was not in it.

My heart was not much into anything in those days. Everything was falling apart fast. J. and I had hit rock bottom.

We were both turning forty-nine, and our 50th birthdays were around the corner. People call it the midlife crisis, but I refuse to acknowledge this part of our lives as a crisis. I call it the unknown, which everybody tends to ignore. In our lives, we get prepared and taught about most things, but nobody ever mentions the big void that presents itself once your children are grown and have left the house. We get taught about school, University, career, marriage, and children; everything has a place, but once you reach the point where you have had a career, had children, have married, gone to university, etc., what then? You still have about 20- 30 years left to live. I had tried retirement when I was in between jobs, and after six months of sitting at home doing all the things I always wanted to do, I found it boring and self-destructive. Retirement being fun is a myth. You are left with 24 hours each day to be filled with nonsense. Meeting friends and playing golf—no thanks. The question I had to face was: If I had a chance to take a second career, what would I do? 20 more years to create and play was a huge gift. Choosing a different path was a valid option. This was not a crisis; this was a chance to start once more, to get busy dying or getting busy living. The question was, Will J. and I start to build a second life together? Things were not going in the right direction. We were in "couple therapy" and tried to save our relationship and family. It was a dark time. There was no logic to the situation in which we were living. I did not see it as a chance for a second life yet. I only saw myself as an absolute failure. All the things I had believed in were no more.

I had made enough money with Tommy and Hackett not to be worried about my immediate future, but J. and I would have to come up with a plan, or we would fail. Becoming a "houseman" and having J. support me for the rest of our lives was not an option. Betty was living in Brussels for her studies, and Stanley was starting his IB in Paris. The children were on a stable path and were mature. J. and I had to come up with a vision for our life. We had been together for 23 years and had been through many good and bad times, but it was about to come to an end.

Why did our love die? I often asked myself: We were a great team and navigated many storms together. Faith and our successes didn't allow us to continue, though. J. was on a secure path, while I had to redefine myself. We could have done this together with a very high risk of failure. All the solutions I investigated always came up with the same outcome.

We would fail together. J. would have to leave her job and follow me down an unsecured road toward a questionable future. We would have to start again in a new country with a new life. In the end, I am convinced it would have destroyed us.

The realization was hard that I would eventually break our family and that me being me was the obstacle, the spanner in the wheel. J. was stable and would be until her retirement. She had enough money and no need for reinvention. The same was true for our children; they did not need a new beginning; they were on solid ground and thriving. It was me; it was all my doing. I concluded that I had to break it all to keep them all safe.

J. and I did not manage to find a future for "us," and after a year of couple therapy, I decided to leave.

64. JENS "I AM"

I am gay, I am lesbian, I am trans, I am intellectual, I am boy, I am girl, I am man, I am woman, I am animal, I am nature, I am pain, I am angel, I am devil, I am chaos, I am order, I am swan, I am queer, I am song, I am dance, I am son, I am daughter, I am father, I am mother, I am old, I am young, I am art, I am science, I am religion, I am love, I am who I am, I am all.

All is one. Peace of mind, smiles, and harmony. Everything has its place in one's mind. Accept the many. Enjoy the many. No choice is needed. "I AM."

A friend once called this state "translectual." I always liked that word.

For me, fashion design and being a fashion designer has always been a sanctuary. Here, I must stress not the fashion industry but the fashion design world. The fashion industry has job segments that are highly "unfunny" and judgmental, unfortunately.

Fashion design is a place for all the misfits and "different" ones. In this fashion design world, we can all be free. Being different was never our choice but was given to us. Seeing things in a different light and being different happened by nature. We still fit in, though, with a smile. We like to live, and we hate being told by others how to do so. Nonetheless, we are very forgiving because we know that to succeed, you must experiment, you must take risks, and play with the new and unknown, and this means you must fail, too.

Fashion design is a "gay" world, and I mean the word "gay" not only in its queer interpretation but the original meaning of "gay" as "happy, fun, or lighthearted." We are fun-loving people who love to celebrate life. One thing is certain: we are never boring! We are social animals. I believe no other design segment is as playful as us fashion designers. Our mantra has always been "work hard, play hard." Some might find our ways offensive, and to those, I apologize and guarantee that everything we do is in good faith. We never meant any harm. In our lives, we understood to leave those imaginary cages behind and learned to be confident in choosing to be ourselves. To us, the earth is alive and kicking, and we embrace all challenges with love, humor, and respect.

Inclusivity, compassion, sacrifices, and kindness will define our future. We are not equal, but we deserve equal respect. In our modern society, we must relearn the meaning of respect, human interaction, and community, and sometimes, all it takes is a tiny shift of perspective to see something familiar in a totally new light.

Today, each day, well-meant decisions restrict our lives a little more. By being saved from all the bad things in life, we are cheated of joy, fulfillment, and happiness. Therefore, to all "woke" and "cancel culture" aficionados, please get a life and start living. In the famous words of Ted Lasso: "Be curious, not judgmental!" Governing bodies must realize they cannot decide and protect individuals from life. Life cannot be "safe" and fulfilling at the same time. Otherwise, we are condemned to live a domesticated existence like cattle. We need to be free to experiment.

Freedom means that we can decide for ourselves what to do with whatever life throws at us every day, and individuality means that each and every one of us has a unique life, and we all have to deal with it in our own very personal way. This makes life special.

I believe we can learn to shape the future through creativity. History shows us that the most creative periods happened in challenging environments like natural catastrophes, war, paradigm shifts, political uncertainties, and obsolete regimes. You must look at it like "It is a precipice." A high place from which you can fall. At a precipice, one sees things better. Danger awakens the slumbering mind. Things become clearer. This clarity will open the floodgates of new thinking, starting a new Renaissance. This is fashion design and art to me. Let's start "new thinking" and play again.

Those were all important reflections of mine, but the day I moved out was the saddest day of my life to see all those years of dreams and hopes gone. There was no other way. J. had found her career, was successful, and was happy. The children were in good order and old enough to understand. My options were either to destroy myself, wither away in Paris, or break away and redefine my life. I chose life. My whole world was made of moving parts, and I was redefining its lines daily. Those lines were constantly changing.

I quickly realized that my life was not normal. I had spent most of my life in the gay community. Fashion was queer, and I loved it. I was not searching for an identity; I just had to somehow find a life that allowed me to be who I am. I felt like I was a part of the fashion family, but the world around me did not allow me to be. Everybody tried to label you and tell you what to do. I was searching high and low to find a place that would be happy to have me. It was like forcing a square peg through a round hole.

To make it very clear, this was not a happy time. I was deeply depressed and lonely. I did not seek help; instead, I painted. For many hours, I poured my fears and darkness into my art. It helped me stabilize and get better, but it was a long process, and it took years to overcome depression and anxiety attacks. Talking to my friends Robert and Hans-Georg and pouring out all my inner poison helped too.

I had to create my new reality for myself. Where should I live? What to do next? Fashion design was not enough; I needed more. I rented an atelier and intensified my hours spent painting. My art collection was gone; I had left it in the house with J., but I loved to paint, so I started to create. I remembered my initial training: before I became a fashion designer, I was and am an artist. I poured all my darkness into my work. Black paint became my color. I had no job, no house, and dwindling resources. Painting was my calling, which had re-found and saved me. Fashion was a passion, but art was a deep, fundamental calling resurfacing within me. A "calling" that I could not ignore any longer. I started writing too, wrestling with my old enemy, "words."

Design and art are both about creativity. For me, creativity was not solely creating a garment, dress, or art piece. Creativity was defining my life. It was living. As an artist or fashion designer, you always must ask yourself, how will we live? Cities? Villages? Tents?

On the moon?... For what events or occasions will we dress? Office? Gym? Dinner? Bed?... **What do we eat? Read? What is success? What are the must-haves and nice-to-haves in life? In my life? All** those elements of designing or creating art always reflect on your own life. We must look at ourselves first before we can create meaning for others. Designing our lives is not an abstract notion; it is part of everybody's daily existence.

We must come up with solutions and think outside the box. This makes living life creative; we are the architects of our own priorities and morals. Redefine values for ourselves and do not follow conventional solutions defined by others.

And so, I started living and continued breaking the rules once more.

End of Part 1

To be continued...

Part II:

Love, lies, being cheated, starting new again, the Countess, Lucy is born, Savannah, Art, Covid, fashion, writing, tears, reinventing oneself, more success and more perseverance…the journey continues.

With a smile and a creative heart!

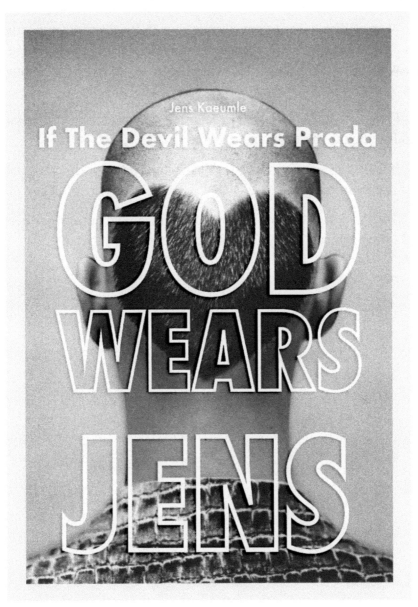

Acknowledgements

Thanks to my family, my parents, my siblings Marc and Anja, and my children Betty, Stanley, and Lucy. Anna and Sophie, too. To Jane Whitfield for all the years together. To Robert Betz, Hans Georg Grossmann, and Andreas Schofer for always being there for me. Thanks also to Bernd Schneider, who is no longer with us and his family.

Special thanks to Ashley Romasko and Briana Hunter for their insights and support. Mike Anderson and Chris Millis for listening to me when I needed it most. Marie Aja-Herrera for her British humor. Mary Norton for saving me.

I am particularly indebted to Jennifer Knapp for her wise support and listening to me without complaining.

Bob and Lauren Tomhave for reading and editing with good pasta and a glass of red wine.

Big thanks to all I could not mention personally but are my friends and have been part of my life. Especially the ones I loved.

About the Author:

Jens Kaeumle graduated from the Royal College of Art in London. He is the winner of the Royal Society of Art "Daphne Brooker" award, which allowed him to associate with Armani, Valentino, and Dolce & Gabbana.

His passion for art and fashion design allowed him to work for Moschino, Emanuel Ungaro together with Giambattista Vali, Levi's, a Louis Vuitton-linked capsule collection with Bathing Ape, creative direction for Tommy Hilfiger Europe and Hackett London.

Having traveled for 25 years between Paris, Milan, Amsterdam, London, New York, and Hong Kong, Kaeumle now lives and works between Savannah, Georgia, Stuttgart, Germany, and Paris, France. Jens Kaeumle is currently a professor at SCAD, the Savannah College of Art and Design.

Milton Keynes UK
Ingram Content Group UK Ltd.
UKHW020644041223
433752UK00018B/1227